COLLISION

ALSO BY KENNETH C. CROWE

America for Sale

COLLISION

How the Rank and File
Took Back the Teamsters

KENNETH C. CROWE

Charles Scribner's Sons
NEW YORK

Maxwell Macmillan Canada
TORONTO

Maxwell Macmillan International
NEW YORK   OXFORD   SINGAPORE   SYDNEY

Charles Scribner's Sons   Maxwell Macmillan Canada, Inc.
Macmillan Publishing Company   1200 Eglinton Avenue East
866 Third Avenue   Suite 200
New York, NY 10022   Don Mills, Ontario M3C 3N1

Macmillan Publishing Company is part of the
Maxwell Communication Group of Companies.

Library of Congress Cataloging-in-Publication Data
Crowe, Kenneth C.
    Collision : how the rank and file took back the teamsters /
Kenneth C. Crowe.
        p.   cm.
    Includes bibliographical references and index.
    ISBN 0-684-19373-6
    1. International Brotherhood of Teamsters, Chauffeurs,
Stablemen, and Helpers of America—Elections.   2. Trade-
unions—United States—Elections—Case studies.   I. Title.
HD6515.T3C76   1993
331.88′11388324′0973—dc20   92-27881
                                                      CIP

Macmillan books are available at special discounts for bulk purchases for sales promotions, premiums, fund-raising, or educational use. For details, contact:

Special Sales Director
Macmillan Publishing Company
866 Third Avenue
New York, NY 10022

10   9   8   7   6   5   4   3   2   1

Printed in the United States of America

To
my three sons, Ken, Roy, and Dan,
and my brother, Bill,

and

to
the courageous leaders of
Teamster Local 282's FORE
(Fear of Reprisal Ends),
working-class heros, all:
John Kuebler (dec.), Ted Katsaros, Larry Kudla,
Charlie Curd, Walter (Tex) Kudla,
Bobby Trott, Richie Van Romer, Lee Olsen,
Mario Marino, John Capolino,
John Nowak, and Joe Liss.

This book
is inscribed with esteem and affection.

Not since the Thirties, when the CIO was born, has there been an event of such profound significance for U.S. labor as your election to the presidency of the Teamsters through rank and file membership mobilization.

—Victor Reuther, cofounder, United Auto Workers, in congratulatory message to Ron Carey

Contents

Contents

Acknowledgments

This book is a by-product of my sixteen years of labor coverage at *Newsday*, which provided me with firsthand exposure to the heroes and scoundrels of the International Brotherhood of Teamsters (IBT). I discovered in my reporting that the IBT remained the most vibrant and militant union in the labor movement despite the corrupt business unionists and mobsters that fed on it. It was a privilege to write an account of the triumph of the union's decent elements and the reform movement, Teamsters for a Democratic Union (TDU). As I enjoy telling acquaintances and associates, this is the first book ever written about the Teamsters with a happy ending.

Of course, many people generously contributed their time, information, and insights in helping to make this project a reality. I wish to thank Rae Lord Crowe, my wife, for her patience, understanding, and contributions as a reader and editor; Roslyn Targ, my agent, for her invaluable services; Natalie Chapman, my editor at Scribners, whose skills made this a much better book.

This work has two godfathers: Tony Marro, the editor of *Newsday* and my friend; and David Laventhol, president of the Times Mirror Company and publisher of the *Los Angeles Times*. In 1976 Laventhol, then the editor of *Newsday*, gave me the opportunity to cover labor. Marro fostered my role as a labor reporter, providing the necessary backing to permit me to attend the IBT conventions starting in 1981. I thank them for guiding me on this path.

In more recent years, other *Newsday* editors supported me in my coverage of the Teamsters and the IBT RICO case: Deborah Whitefield, Dan Beucke, and Ron Roel. To the three of them, I am grateful.

I appreciate the cooperation of the three IBT presidential candidates, Ron Carey, R. V. Durham, and Walter Shea, and their associates, in particular, Eddie Burke and Chris Scott.

I want to acknowledge, too, the gracious assistance of many others in the past and recently, some from the old guard, some dissidents, journalists, lawyers, investigators, and staffers: Bill Genoese, Ed Ferguson, Marla Alhadeff, Randy Mastro, Charles Carberry, Michael Holland, Bob Windrem, Arthur Fox, the late Burt Hall, Mike Moroney, Ken Paff, Susan Jennik, Herman Benson, Robert Sasso, Barry Feinstein, Steven Brill, Joseph Trerotola (dec.), Greg Tarpinian, Jeff Schaffler, Dan Kane, John Mahoney, Jr., John Morris, Bill Nuchow, James Grady, Walter Sheridan, Richard Gilberg, Susan Davis, Rick Blaylock, Steve Early, Steve Kindred, Dan Ligurotis, James D. Harmon, Jr., Stephen M. Ryan, John Sikorski, Duke Zeller, Matt Witt, David Mitchell, Rory McGinty, Peter Giangreco, Jim Smith, Donald Sweitzer, Phil Primack, and Sandra Livingston.

Collision is a continuum of the works of other writers: Steven Brill, author of *The Teamsters*; Dan Moldea, author of *The Hoffa Wars*; Walter Sheridan, author of *The Fall and Rise of Jimmy Hoffa*; and James Neff, author of *Mobbed Up*.

COLLISION

Prologue

Eddie thought he saw someone from the Washington office. From the union. It was just a quick glance in the cabin behind him as he rose from his cramped seat on the Trump Shuttle. He felt a stab of guilt. He hadn't told Rich Trumka, the president of the United Mine Workers, what he was about. No reason to. He hadn't made a commitment yet. This was just an exploratory trip.

But he felt uncomfortable. If that were someone from the Mine Workers, they'd be wondering, What the hell is Eddie Burke doing in New York?

It made him feel like a man on a secret mission. Well, it was secret, and it certainly was a mission. One that could change his world, maybe give him a chance to give the labor movement a good shaking. It could use one.

Eddie smiled, thinking about how different he was from the businessmen all around him scurrying for taxis with their leather carryons. He had just come off the ten-month strike against the Pittston Coal Company in the out-of-the-way hills of Virginia, pressed up against the Tennessee border. A place that was nowhere on the American landscape. That was a strike everyone figured the Mine Workers couldn't win, but it was one they couldn't afford to lose. He was the strategist in that fight, pulling the strings, building morale with gimmicks that would become part of labor legend. That had been a high!

Back in January of 1989, Eddie had been named director of

the United Mine Workers of America's Southeast Region. By that May, he was effectively in charge of the Pittston strike, sparked when the company demanded draconian givebacks, including ending payments to the industry-wide health plan that took care of retired miners. To the Pittston executives sitting in their splendid offices in affluent Greenwich, Connecticut, shedding the costly health plan meant a boost to the bottom line. To the Mine Workers it was a betrayal of a decades-old promise that the industry would care for the sickly veterans of the mines in their old age.

This attempt to abandon the retired suffering from the dread black lung disease and other respiratory ailments was an issue that gripped the emotions of unionists and social activists and lifted the Pittston strike out of the ordinary.

The union realized that a traditionally violent miners' strike laced with shootouts, firebombings, and vandalism would be doomed to disaster. The corporate bosses, as usual, had the weight of the law, the courts, the state police, and the National Guard on their side. The union chose the alternative strategies of civil disobedience and an appeal to the religious and labor communities of the United States and the world to come to its rescue.

Eddie was the perfect choice for the ad hoc role of field commander of the new strike tactics. Like all Mine Workers leaders, he came out of a mine. Over the eight months that he led the struggle, which ended with a victory for the Mine Workers in January 1990, Eddie devised innovative strategies that kept the Pittston strike in the forefront of the labor movement's collective mind, prevented the strikers' morale from flagging, and maintained constant pressure on the corporate managers.

The camouflage uniform was one really nice touch. Under Eddie's guidance, the strikers wore identical jungle shirts, jackets, and pants, making it nearly impossible to identify individuals. They did it to sabotage the usual parade of finks and state police saying: "That guy in the red shirt threw the rock. The man with the blue cap and the beard. He was one of 'em." That had happened at the outset of the strike. Miners were picked at random and arrested. Eddie decided to make life a little more complex for the cops and company thugs. All the strikers dressed in jungle camouflage. Half of them just had to dip into the closet to get out their old army gear. The guys who work the mines are the same ones that fight the wars.

Not only did the judges start throwing the eyewitness charges out of court—how do you tell one striking miner from the other when they all look alike?—but the camouflage gear became the symbol of the strike. Everyone in labor has a special place in his or her heart for the Mine Workers. Now union sympathizers could spot the uniformed Pittston strikers when they showed up at labor marches and rallies and demonstrations around the country. And Eddie made sure that the strikers were sent as emissaries all over the United States to build support for the Pittston struggle.

The strikers became what they felt like: an army battling the company.

On September 17, 1989, the day that Ron Carey announced at Washington Irving High School in New York City that he was running for the presidency of the International Brotherhood of Teamsters (IBT), Eddie Burke led a task force of ninety-eight Mine Workers and a minister, Jim Sessions, into Moss Number Three, Pittston's main coal-processing plant, for the labor movement's first sit-down strike in half a century.

Eddie planned the occupation with the attention to detail and secrecy of a military operation. Pittston had been killing the union in the courts, where judges were piling millions of dollars in fines on the Mine Workers. The Virginia State Police were doing their bit for the company, too, arresting strikers and their supporters by the hundreds. They even arrested a nun, Sister Bernadette Kenny, for driving too slowly on a highway used by the company coal trucks. After seven months on the picket lines, with the company not budging an inch, even militant Mine Workers began to lose their fighting spirit. In search of an event that would stir imaginations and rouse morale, Eddie had an inspiration: occupy a major Pittston plant!

A history buff, Eddie knew that the auto workers' sit-in at General Motors's Flint, Michigan, plant was still remembered with reverence and glee as a shining moment in the blossoming of labor in the 1930s. He rounded up volunteers willing to undertake a secret assignment, with the forewarning only that it was important and could mean serious trouble for them. Probably another arrest. Most of the seven hundred strikers had been arrested at least once; some, two or three times. These weren't make-believe arrests. They got rough handling by the police and the risk of real jail time. But there was no shortage of volunteers.

For a month, only eight people were admitted to the inner sanctum of the planning process. There were a thousand details. Rented trucks had to be arranged. Canteens for water, food, first-aid kits, and walkie-talkies were gathered for the task force.

At 2:00 P.M. on the chosen Sunday, the volunteers, as instructed, showed up at their local union halls. They were loaded into the trucks and quickly driven to the staging area on a road leading to the plant. Speaking through a bullhorn, Eddie told them for the first time that the plan was to march up the road, across a small bridge, and right into the enormous high-rise building that was Moss Number Three. Eddie admitted he didn't know how many state police or company security guards were in the building. They would find out soon enough. No violence, stay calm, stay peaceful, and get ready to be arrested, he said, telling them that their role was to occupy the processing plant and hold it for as long as possible. Should the guards open fire, everyone was to drop to one knee and stay put until ordered to proceed or retreat. "If we get in, one hour is a victory," Eddie told them, giving them the underlying reason for this risky adventure: "This is the way to get the focus back on civil disobedience in this strike."

With the bullhorn still in his hand, Eddie led the half-mile march. Behind him were three teams of thirty-three men each: four union staffers, ninety-four striking coal miners, and the minister. The preacher added a touch of grace and a suggestion of whose side God was on in this struggle.

About ten yards behind Eddie was his sidekick, Rick Blaylock, a bearded, brawny man with a West Virginia twang as rich as Eddie's, leading the first team. Each man carried three canteens of water, a bedroll, a gas mask, clothes, and food for a week. Some were equipped with heavy gloves to toss away any tear-gas canisters fired at them, and Eddie brought along a bunch of quarters to use in the Coke machine inside the six-story Moss Number Three processing plant.

"We're stockholders," Eddie shouted through the bullhorn at two startled security guards standing at the end of the bridge. "We are an unarmed, nonviolent inspection team of stockholders coming to inspect our investment. You will not be harmed."[1]

4

The guards reacted by hopping in a pickup truck and driving away. They weren't ready to take on the hundred men coming at them in military formation. Eddie and his little army rushed across the bridge, quickly covering the remaining yards to the plant. The only occupants were a few supervisors in a fourth-floor control room, who left when the strikers ordered them out.

As the guards hustled to safety, hundreds of men and women, alerted to gather there, began appearing in cars on the road to Moss Number Three. They created a tight jam of parked cars to frustrate any attempt by the state police to move against the occupiers. Cheers exploded from the crowd when one of Eddie's band spray-painted "UMWA Forever" in huge white letters on the top of the building.

Over the following three days thousands of strikers and supporters from around the country filled the approaches to the plant.

Eddie and his sit-down raiders locked the gates behind them, then sat in the building while the growing crowds outside sang and joked and managed to smuggle pizzas in to them. The Mine Workers and their allies considered the occupation a victory in the psychological war that the long strike had become. Eddie had embarrassed the company, showing how vulnerable its defenses were.

A court, as expected, issued an order directing the miners to evacuate the plant.

Eddie agreed with the Mine Workers' hierarchy that it would be wiser to leave the building peacefully, under the proviso that no one would be arrested, rather than face the prospects of a possibly bloody confrontation with the state police. Even so, they added a touch of defiance to their evacuation. They left the plant three hours after the deadline set by a federal judge.

Having accomplished their mission of recharging the batteries of the Pittston strikers, the hundred sit-ins marched out of Moss Number Three shortly after 9:00 P.M. on Wednesday, September 20, to the cheers of the thousands outside. No damage was done to the plant. No one was arrested.

The best was yet to come. When Virginia State Circuit judge Donald McGlothlin, Jr., inflicted staggering fines on the striking miners—more than $64 million—threatening to wipe out the entire treasury of the United Mine Workers of America, Eddie decided to strike back. The judge's father, Virginia state delegate

5

Donald McGlothlin, Sr., had represented Buchanan County in the House of Delegates for twenty years. He was up for reelection that November. The only way to challenge him was through a write-in vote, a method that in most elections amounts to a joke or a protest at most.

Now all of the networking, the support built in the religious communities and among the people of that region of Virginia, paid off. Three weeks before the election, Jackie Stump, president of Mine Workers Union District 28, declared his candidacy for Virginia state delegate, with Eddie Burke as his campaign manager. A blitz of billboards, phone banks, and fliers followed. The wives and children of the strikers knocked on the doors of five thousand homes. On election day, Jackie Stump beat McGlothlin by a 2–1 margin, 7,981 to 3,812.[2]

The Pittston struggle had so electrified the nation's labor activists that they flocked into the region by the thousands either to help with the strike by getting arrested during civil-disobedience demonstrations or just to show their support. Eddie had leased an old campground from a union sympathizer for a dollar to serve as the gathering place where the labor activists could be fed, housed, and organized for use in the strike. He called the place Camp Solidarity.

In New York, Ron Carey heard about the occupation of Moss Three. Wanting to get a firsthand impression of both Eddie and the historic strike he was leading, he traveled to Camp Solidarity.

Carey had never been much of an activist. He was a good local union leader who focused his energies entirely on the needs of his own members—most of them employees of the United Parcel Service (UPS). He had seven thousand men and women in his local working at UPS facilities throughout New York City and Long Island or in department and trucking warehouses. His proudest boast was that he and every one of Local 804's business agents was at a different work site early every morning to check out the members' needs and complaints.

Labor causes so popular among New York City's other union leaders, such as the plight of unionists in El Salvador and Guatemala, didn't attract Carey, although he did show up at demonstrations supporting strikers in the high-profile Eastern Airlines, Greyhound Bus, and NYNEX labor struggles of the late 1980s.

But Carey ventured out of the confines of his own local every three years, when the Teamsters' hierarchy in Washington negotiated new national contracts covering 150,000 UPS workers across the country, including those in Local 804. In a union known for its silent local leaders who wouldn't dare confront the hierarchy, Carey had openly fought the giveback contracts of the 1980s. He took the parent union to court over the issue that only a one-third yes vote was needed to approve the national contracts.

Carey was an unusual Teamster leader in a number of other ways: He ran a straight local despite being in the midst of a city that was a sinkhole of Teamster corruption—with mob connections, kickbacks, big salaries, fancy cars, and relatives all over the payroll commonplace. When Local 804's secretary-treasurer, John F. Long, was indicted by the U.S. Attorney in New York for taking a $2,000 kickback in an investment scheme, Carey pressured him into quitting.* Carey's salary was a modest $45,000, prompting a reporter to compare his income to that of the chef at the Marble Palace, the nickname for Teamster headquarters in Washington, D.C. Chef Alain Boineau was making $52,000.

In *The Teamsters*, author Steven Brill devoted a chapter to describing how well run Local 804 was. He held Carey up as an example to illustrate that there are plenty of decent leaders in a union whose image had been smeared by its high-living hierarchy, with their own jet fleet, their alliances to mobsters, and their penchant for nepotism. Brill had forecast that it would take the emergence of a local leader with Carey's credentials to transform the Teamsters into something new.

That boost from Brill planted the seed that perhaps Carey could be the chosen of the rank and file to clean out the almost mythical stink of the IBT.

The fifty-three-year-old Carey was the first to announce as a candidate for general president of the 1.6-million-member Teamsters Union in the election to be held in December 1991. No one had ever seriously challenged an incumbent Teamster president before.

While the odds against him seemed enormous, the chapter in

---

*Long's conviction was later reversed. Subsequently, he was barred from the IBT.

Brill's book and the national platform the controversial UPS contracts had given him provided Carey with a standing that virtually no other Teamster outside the hierarchy enjoyed. Still, Carey could be compared to a reform mayor who had done a great job running a little city suddenly saying he was in the running for president of the United States on an independent ticket. Carey was an outsider without access to the resources of the Teamsters' political machinery and the manpower and money that implied. He was an outsider with seemingly little chance of even getting his campaign off the ground.

Carey's trip to Camp Solidarity was inspired by a conscious effort to expand his horizons at the urging of his activist lawyers, Susan Davis and Richard N. Gilberg. And there was an underlying practical motive: possibly recruiting Eddie Burke to be his campaign manager.

The Mine Workers were one of the few North American unions whose top officers were elected directly by secret ballots cast by the rank and file. The Mine Workers had been through trying times of their own, with corruption and murder muddying the union's reputation and bringing the Labor Department in to supervise its national elections. Led by Rich Trumka, a dissident faction including members of Miners for Democracy had emerged as a reform administration in control of the union. Trumka and his allies appeared to be the best the American labor movement had to offer.

A spare, not very tall man with piercing eyes, Carey got to shake Eddie Burke's hand at Camp Solidarity, but no attention was really paid to him. Carey watched Burke's interaction with the strikers. He was impressed by the almost family atmosphere—and by the respect Burke commanded from the miners. Carey returned to New York after only a day in Virginia, coming away convinced that Eddie was the man he wanted to run his campaign.

Carey called Eddie a few weeks later. Of course, he was remembered. Anyone running for the presidency of the Teamsters would be. Then Carey went into a puzzling spiel, telling Eddie that he was determined to follow the example of the Mine Workers in making his union responsive to the needs of the membership. He wanted to get rid of the jets and the big salaries and the corruption. He described how deeply moved and impressed he was by what he saw at Camp Solidarity. Then he got to the point: He needed a real union man who understood the rank and

8

file. He wanted Eddie to consider joining him as his campaign manager in what would be the most important election in the Teamsters' history. This was a chance to turn around the biggest union in the country. Think of the impact on the labor movement, the chance to be at the center of labor history!

"Uh-huh," Eddie said. "It sounds exciting." He wondered whether Carey was so hypnotized by his own needs that he didn't realize that Eddie was in the midst of a make-or-break strike for the Mine Workers. He tried to sound gracious: "I hope you can appreciate I can't give any consideration to leaving. My plate's full. I just can't consider anything else at the moment."

"I realize you can't drop what you're doing. We have to get going with the campaign, but we have some time yet. Can I call you again?" Carey asked.

"Sure," said Eddie, "Why don't you call me in the future, buddy."

Eddie hung up the phone and shook his head. He was worried about just getting through the next day of the Pittston strike. "Long-term planning" meant a week or so. Carey's call was good for his ego, but there wasn't any time to think about it now.

Carey made a second trip to Camp Solidarity and called Eddie a couple of times more over the course of the fall of 1989, but the Pittston strike lingered on.

With the arrival of the New Year, Carey began to feel the pressure of precious time draining away. He decided to give Eddie another call.

Around lunchtime on January 4, Carey closed his office door and dialed Eddie Burke's home. Although Carey didn't realize it, Pittston and the Mine Workers had arrived at a tentative contract that New Year's Eve.

One of Eddie's kids fetched him to the phone.

"This is Ron Carey. I'm calling back on that conversation we had in November. I could really use a guy like you, Eddie. It's so important. We have to try to get this union back. Things are looking very good except for the fact we don't have a campaign manager."

"I'm still interested. I think it would be worth talking about," Burke said.

"Hey, when can you come up?" Carey asked. They arranged to meet the following week in New York.

When Carey hung up, instead of elation, his instinctive frugality welled up. "How the hell am I going to pay for this campaign? Now I've got to start thinking about a payroll and traveling expenses."

NO PINKY RINGS

Coming out of the Trump Shuttle terminal at New York's La Guardia Airport, Eddie Burke was overwhelmed for a moment by the rush of taxis and buses against the backdrop of a vast, dreary parking lot. A horn honked, and Ron Carey whipped up to the curb in his four-wheel-drive GMC "Jimmy."

Carey reached out to shake hands. Eddie gripped Carey's hand and turned it over to examine it. Carey knew what he was looking for: a diamond ring, the mark of the mobster or the business unionist. "I don't wear pinkies," Carey said.

"Neither do I," Eddie responded, holding up his own hands. They laughed.

Eddie liked what he saw in Carey's office in a brick building in the grimy, worn-out factory district of the Blissville section of Queens. He smiled when he spotted the poster showing a breaking wave to the right of Carey's desk: "Momentum. Once you are moving in the direction of your goals . . . nothing can stop you."

After a brief tour showing Eddie the pension and welfare office on the second floor and and introducing him to the officers and business agents around the building, Carey took him through the nearby Queens Midtown Tunnel to Manhattan and to the offices of the union's lawyers, Cohen, Weiss and Simon, on West Forty-second Street, next to the Port Authority Bus Terminal, to meet with Susan Davis and Rick Gilberg.

The lawyers gave Eddie the lay of the land. Carey didn't have any money; he was an outsider in Teamster national politics, and he was being backed by the Teamsters for a Democratic Union (TDU), the national dissident organization, which the hierarchy had branded as outsiders meddling in their union for the past fifteen years.

No one in the room had to say it, but Eddie was an outsider, too. He came from another union, but so what? There was a precedent that flowed right out of the labor history books. In the 1930s, when there was a screaming need for it, cross-fertilization of budding unions was common, encouraged and financed by the Mine Workers' charismatic leader John L. Lewis.

Eddie was left alone for a while to read the packet of information about the Justice Department's civil racketeering suit against the Teamsters' hierarchy, along with newspaper clips and the section about Carey from Brill's book. He read the chapter and was impressed. This guy is good, he thought. I've seen assholes of all sorts, but this guy is human. He could see that Carey was a loner in a union of go-alongs, but that was a positive characteristic under the circumstances.

As Eddie sifted through the barrage of information piled on him that afternoon, it occurred to him that he was being given the opportunity to step into a twenty-year time warp: taking on an entrenched leadership so distant from the membership that they didn't understand that private jets and unlimited expense accounts, huge salaries and jobs for their kids, weren't their birthright. After John L. Lewis left office, the Mine Workers' hierarchy had become like the Teamsters', more interested in the good life than the members.

Eddie had volunteered to work in 1969 for Jock Yablonsky in his effort to oust UMWA president Tony Boyle. Yablonsky not only lost the rigged election, but he and his family were murdered by gunmen, later proven to have been hired by Boyle. The public outcry over the killings resulted in another election. This one, in 1972, was supervised by the U.S. Labor Department. Despite his youth, Eddie was given the full-time job in the 1972 election of watching the staff at the union's district office in West Virginia to make sure there was an honest election. Arnold Miller, the reform candidate, won.

This is where I cut my teeth: a supervised election, corruption, Tony Boyle, Eddie thought as he sifted through the material about Carey. Since 1969, Eddie had been on the side of the underdog in three national rank-and-file campaigns, playing an increasingly more important role in each one. If he signed on with Carey, this first direct election of the Teamsters' international officers would be his fourth rank-and-file campaign, and the biggest one yet, involving the American labor movement's most important union.

His instincts shouted, Grab the job. But he knew, too, that he would have to talk to his wife, Patty. They had been sweethearts since junior high and had married in 1969, when he got involved in union politics for the first time. Now with a master's degree, Patty was teaching at the school their two children, Hillary, twelve, and Bradley, nine, attended. His causes as a union activist had put the family through some tight financial times in the past, and he knew that Carey wouldn't have much money to pay him. He would go through the formality of discussing it with Patty, but he knew what his answer would be.

"Goddamn it, I'm gonna do it," Eddie said to himself. "It sure would be exciting to see some new, high-test gas in the Teamsters Union."

1

The Origin of the Teamster RICO Case

The assignment to bring a civil racketeering case against the International Brotherhood of Teamsters (IBT) was dropped on Assistant U.S. Attorney Randy Mastro in January 1986 in the midst of what he expected to be a routine meeting with his boss, Rudy Giuliani, the U.S. Attorney for the Southern District of New York.

Mastro had arrived in Giuliani's office expecting to give a progress report on other civil RICO cases he was pursuing involving mobsters with hidden interests in restaurants in Little Italy in Lower Manhattan and in the Concrete and Cement Workers District Council in New York City. RICO is the popular acronym used for the "Racketeer Influenced Corrupt Organizations" sections of the Organized Crime Control Act of 1970.

Under a civil RICO, if it can be proved that a business or union has been used as a tool in violating the law just twice within a ten-year period, the penalties can be withering. The business could be confiscated. The union's officers could be ousted, and a court-appointed trustee could be named to run the organization. In a criminal RICO, the sentences are just as stringent: up to twenty years in prison.

The twenty-nine-year-old Mastro, who had joined Giuliani's staff in March 1985, had been ordered to focus his attention on civil RICOs just the month before. With the holidays chopping time out of his calendar, none of Mastro's cases was as yet fully developed.

Giuliani, in shirtsleeves, listened attentively while the high-strung Mastro nervously delivered his report. Giuliani's response stunned Mastro. He told the young assistant he wanted him to keep moving on all the cases, but he was adding another assignment: He wanted him to explore the potential for a civil RICO against the International Brotherhood of Teamsters (IBT), the nation's largest private-sector union, with 1.7 million members and the worst reputation in the American labor movement. The name Teamsters was synonymous in the public's mind with violence, thugs, payoffs, and organized crime.

Giuliani told Mastro that the President's Commission on Organized Crime was about to issue a report called *The Edge: Organized Crime, Business and Labor Unions* in which the Teamsters were described as the union most controlled by the mob. Giuliani had gotten an advance copy several weeks before, along with a visit from U.S. Labor Department investigators urging him to launch a RICO case against the Teamsters. He suggested Mastro begin his undertaking by reading the report.

Giuliani's assignment to Mastro didn't flow just from the commission's report. Giuliani was in the process of prosecuting criminal cases against the same Cosa Nostra bosses who used the Teamsters in pursuing their rackets in the trucking and construction industries of New York City. Giuliani made the point that the criminal convictions could be used as irrefutable evidence of the link between organized crime and the union in the civil RICO case.

Underlying Giuliani's decision, too, was the subtle, unspoken pressure of competition. He had to expect Dave Margolis, head of the Justice Department's Organized Crime and Racketeering Section in Washington, to move in the same direction. Giuliani's advantage was the New York work ethic, which he had instilled. He could expect Mastro to be at his desk until 11:00 P.M. every night if the case demanded it. Washington was a four o'clock town.

There would be an issue of jurisdiction. Margolis could claim that the IBT was headquartered in Washington. Giuliani's argument would be that New York City was the home base of organized crime's ruling council, composed of bosses of the city's five Cosa Nostra organized crime families.

Since becoming the U.S. Attorney for the Manhattan-based Southern District in 1983, Rudy Giuliani had emerged as a prosecutor of unprecedented scope, leading his staff on dramatic sorties against Wall Street inside traders and the mobsters who inhabited the city.

Giuliani laid out for Mastro the two linchpins of the case: Angelo Lonardo, the ex-underboss of the Cleveland branch of La Cosa Nostra, and Roy L. Williams, the ex–general president of the IBT. Lonardo and Williams had both flipped after being convicted of criminal charges. They agreed to trade information against their associates for lighter prison sentences.

Lonardo and Williams's new roles as government witnesses had surfaced as they testified in court cases and at congressional hearings. The pair would provide testimony of insiders: Lonardo—from the perspective of a crime boss—on how the mob picked Teamster presidents; Williams—as a former general president of the Teamsters—on how he and the union were dominated by organized crime.

Williams was under a ten-year sentence for conspiring to bribe U.S. senator Howard W. Cannon (D-Nev.) to derail the deregulation of the trucking industry, a key to Teamster power.

Lonardo had been sentenced to life in prison without parole on a drug charge in April 1983. He was seventy-three years old, ill, depressed, and facing the unhappy prospect of spending the remainder of his old age behind bars. Lonardo called the FBI from prison, saying he was ready to deal, becoming in the process the highest-ranking Cosa Nostra figure to break the mob's code of silence.

In his debriefing, Lonardo had described how organized crime families around the country colluded to pick the last two Teamster presidents, Williams and Jackie Presser. Pieces of the tale told by Lonardo had been picked up by an FBI-planted bug in Chicago in 1979, and here he was providing the testimony needed to corroborate that evidence.

Aside from backing up Lonardo's story, Williams was available to admit he not only was controlled by Nick Civella, the boss of the Kansas City branch of La Cosa Nostra, but had been sharing the mob's skim from Las Vegas casinos for years. His entitlement to that money came from helping to arrange loans from the Teamsters' Central States Pension Fund to mob-connected businessmen so that they could acquire control of those casinos.

In October 1985, Williams had emerged as a turncoat in the U.S. District Court in Kansas City at the racketeering trial accusing mobsters from Kansas City, Chicago, Milwaukee, and Cleveland of illegally skimming cash from the casinos. Williams testified that he got $1,500 a month from the skim for arranging for $84 million in loans to the Argent Corporation in 1974 to buy four casinos. In the coming weeks, Lonardo would be laying out his story of lobbying the organized crime bosses in New York City, Chicago, and Cleveland to line up the votes they controlled on the IBT's General Executive Board (GEB) to help win the presidency for Williams in 1981 and Presser in 1983.

Giuliani planned to use Williams and Lonardo as a double whammy against organized crime, first as part of his evidence in a criminal RICO case aimed at destroying the hierarchy of the New York City–based Genovese organized crime family and then in the civil RICO he was assigning to Mastro.

Mastro walked out of the U.S. Attorney's office, trying to suppress the excitement that surged through him. Giuliani's direction to Mastro to explore the underpinnings of a case against the Teamsters was in reality a directive to produce the RICO suit. Mastro knew he had been given the momentous assignment of finally breaking the mob's grip on the Teamsters, which promised to be the broadest and the most important union civil RICO ever brought. Reputations are built on cases like this, a realization that put an added spring into Mastro's walk.

A RICO BLUEPRINT

Mastro immediately plunged into the task of putting together the RICO case. He realized how little he knew about the Teamsters other than its abominable reputation. He knew he had to go through the lawyerly plodding of gathering the evidence to prove what everyone assumed about the Teamsters Union. He had a lot of work to do to determine if the facts would support a RICO case.

The resources were readily at hand.

Mastro started by calling in New York FBI agent Stanley Nye, who was considered the resident expert on the Teamsters, with a broad background in labor racketeering. Nye could begin the process of ferreting out the evidence to put flesh on the skeleton of charges laid out by the president's commission by collecting files from prosecutors' offices across the country to substantiate evidence of corruption at the highest levels of the Teamsters.

There was a huge pile of evidence available about corruption over the three decades, stretching back to the 1957 appearance by then IBT president Dave Beck before the McClellan Committee, as the Senate Permanent Subcommittee on Investigations was called in that era. Beck had taken the Fifth Amendment a hundred times rather than answer the committee's questions.

But Mastro didn't have to dip into ancient history to build his case. He found that in the ten years from 1976 to 1986, more than two hundred Teamsters had been prosecuted. And no one in the hierarchy of the union had ever done anything about it. One of the central theories of the RICO case Mastro was developing began to emerge: the notion that labor leaders can be held accountable not only for what they do but what they failed to do. Union leaders are considered fiduciaries under federal law, meaning that they have an obligation to protect the membership from organized crime, corruption, and the misuse of union funds. Failing to do so is called extorting union members' rights. That concept had been used successfully in the pioneering 1982 civil RICO case filed against Teamsters Local 560, the Union City, New Jersey, local dominated by Anthony (Tony Pro) Provenzano and his family for decades.

The typically arrogant behavior of Teamster leaders was illustrated by Jimmy Hoffa when he named Tony Pro an International vice president—making him a member of the union's ruling hierarchy—in 1960 while Pro was under indictment for shaking down trucking companies.[3] Pro, who was a capo in the Genovese organized crime family and became a prime suspect in the disappearance of former Teamster president Jimmy Hoffa in 1975, remained an International vice president until he was sentenced to prison in 1966.

Mastro found one instance after another of bizarre conduct on the part of International officials in the face of proven corruption. Such as the GEB's decision to pay Roy Williams's $1 million attorney's fees after he was convicted.

The President's Commission on Organized Crime's report provided Mastro an excellent summary of the evils afflicting the Teamsters and the shorthand solution of what to do about them: Apply the RICO remedy. That is what he was planning to do.

The report said, "The leaders of the nation's largest union, the International Brotherhood of Teamsters (IBT), have been firmly under the influence of organized crime since the 1950's."

Mastro read the depressing history of corruption in the Teamsters laid out in the report, starting with Beck's personal crookedness and illustrating the growing power of organized crime within the union through the presidencies of Jimmy Hoffa, Frank E. Fitzsimmons, Roy Williams, and Jackie Presser.

In addition to telling the usual story of Beck's going to prison for income-tax evasion, Hoffa for jury tampering, and Williams for attempting to bribe a U.S. senator, the commission revealed the plight of the Teamster presidents who dealt with the mob: They lived in fear—with good reason.

Hoffa, who was the last Teamster president who could claim an affinity with the union's rank and file, disappeared in 1975 and presumably was murdered by elements of the Genovese organized crime family.

Long before the Hoffa lesson, Roy Williams, in appearance the epitome of the tough, gruff, monosyllabic truck driver–union leader, was cowed by Nick Civella, boss of the Kansas City mob. Early in their relationship, Civella sent Williams a message he never forgot. Two hoods picked up Williams one night in the late 1950s. They told him: "If you don't cooperate [with Civella], we are going to kill your children and your wife and you. You'll be the last to go. Do you understand?" Williams understood.[4]

Williams's service to the mob led him right into the presidency of the Teamsters. Lonardo played the role of lobbyist, lining up the Cosa Nostra bosses' backing for him. When Williams quit the presidency in 1983 in a deal to avoid prison while the appeal of his conviction was pending, Lonardo went on the road again on behalf of Jackie Presser. The GEB followed the expected scenario—electing Jackie Presser to succeed Williams.

The president's commission didn't touch on the persistent, but as yet unconfirmed, stories of Presser's role as an FBI informant. But it did describe how Jackie apparently became a millionaire labor leader and encouraged his underlings to crack the heads of union dissidents.

In 1974, Presser invested $134,000[5] in the Front Row Theatre, a theater-in-the-round in Cleveland. Two months later, Presser began a one-year tenure as a trustee of the Central States Pension Fund, filling in for his father, Bill Presser, who was serving a one-year prison sentence. Before the year was up, the other investors had bought Jackie out. "A review of the records obtained by the Commission . . . raises questions whether the Front

Row Theatre was used as a vehicle to provide approximately one million dollars to Presser for unspecified favors," the report said. Presser took the Fifth when the Commission staff questioned him about the deal.

Presser had a particular hatred for Teamsters for a Democratic Union (TDU), the national rank-and-file dissident organization, whose proclaimed goal was to reform the union. Presser was behind the creation of BLAST—the Brotherhood of Loyal Americans and Strong Teamsters—whose mission was to bloody TDU. On October 15, 1983, a convoy of cars and at least nine chartered buses carried BLAST members from Cleveland, Youngstown, Columbus, Dayton, and Toledo, Ohio, and from Jackson, Flint, and Detroit, Michigan, to the Hilton Hotel in Romulus, Michigan where TDU was holding its annual convention.

The BLAST members invaded the TDU meeting, knocking aside a local policeman after ripping off his keys and hat. They seized the microphone, tore down banners, and chased the TDUers from the hall. Local, county, and state police arrived in force before any further damage could be done.

The commission focused on one big dirty deal that in itself revealed the extent of the betrayal of the membership: the labor-leasing scheme of Eugene Boffa, Sr.

Beginning in the late 1960s, Boffa created labor-leasing companies in Canada, Puerto Rico, and thirty states, including California, Illinois, Missouri, New Jersey, New York, Pennsylvania, and Texas. The plan was simple: A company with Teamster-member drivers laid off all the employees, who were rehired by one of Boffa's companies to do the same work for their old employer under a leasing arrangement. Invariably, the workers were paid less, their fringe benefits were cut, and their working conditions were changed to trim costs. Boffa and the employer shared the savings. Another fringe benefit for the employer was that loudmouths and dissidents were eliminated.

"As Robert Rispo, an enforcer for Boffa, described it, the drivers had no choice but to accept 90 percent or 80 percent of their former salary because 'half a job is better than no job.' Any worker who protested too much was not rehired, and payoffs to union officials left the workers without an avenue for redress of grievances," according to the commission report.

What really made the scheme work was that Boffa had the

backing of mob boss Russell Buffalino of Wilkes-Barre, Pennsylvania, along with then Teamster international vice president Jackie Presser and Salvatore (Sammy Pro) Provenzano—Tony Pro's brother—and Sam Anacona, who as far back as 1961 had been identified by the Justice Department as Kansas City mob boss Nick Civella's representative at the local Teamster headquarters. In addition to cracking heads and helping Boffa run his labor-leasing companies, Rispo did odd jobs, like delivering a payoff to Jackie Presser.

The disappearance of Jimmy Hoffa did in Boffa. FBI agents checking the license plates of cars driven by several mob members and Teamster officials traced them back to a leasing company owned by Boffa. "Subsequent investigation uncovered Boffa's empire of companies," the commission report said. Boffa was sentenced to twenty years in prison, but his leasing companies continued to operate.

Teamster insiders developed the theory in hindsight that the President's Commission on Organized Crime was established in 1983 to create a base of information and evidence that could be pulled off the shelf at a future date for the RICO attack. They cynically contended that union busting was the underlying motive of the president's commission and the RICO that grew out of it.

Before becoming executive director and chief counsel of the president's commission, James D. Harmon, Jr., had been a prosecutor with the Brooklyn Organized Crime Strike Force and an advocate of using the RICO statute against mobsters. Harmon said, "The IBT was not targeted or earmarked. The evidence was just overwhelming. The rank and file of the Teamsters pretty much knew what the president's commission knew. Why didn't the rank and file do something? Our assumption was the reason they didn't was the structure of the union itself." Harmon said, "We did intend for this report to be a blueprint, to be like a cookbook."

A SURPRISE DECISION

With the president's commission report as a guide, Mastro put together a draft complaint to show how a civil RICO against the Teamsters would look. In May 1986, Mastro delivered a copy to

Rudy Giuliani. Giuliani liked what he read and forwarded it to Washington for the required review by the Organized Crime and Racketeering Section of the Justice Department.

The response from Washington could almost have been expected. While Mastro was piecing together his early version of the complaint, Dave Margolis, the head of the Organized Crime and Racketeering Section, spurred by the commission's report, had created a team in Washington for the same purpose.

Washington-based Justice Department lawyers Randy Kehrli, Peter Sprung, and Diane DeForrest were in the midst of putting together their version of a Teamster RICO complaint. In addition, an FBI task force, the "Liberatus Squad," had been created in Washington to help them.

The anticipated battle for jurisdiction of this historic case began with the arrival of Mastro's draft complaint.

Washington had jurisdiction, Margolis argued to his Justice Department superiors, because the Teamsters were headquartered there, because this was a case of national significance—and besides, there was the issue of sweat equity. Kehrli and his team had been working on the project for several months.

Giuliani countered with arguments of his own. The centerpiece of any RICO suit against the Teamsters would be Lonardo's testimony that the mob had played a central role in picking the last two IBT presidents, Roy Williams and Jackie Presser. And the evidence showed that the man to see for the mob's blessing was Anthony (Fat Tony) Salerno, head of the Genovese organized crime family, who had his headquarters in New York City at the Palma Boys Social Club in East Harlem.

Giuliani took Mastro and his arguments to a meeting in Washington with William Weld, the assistant attorney general in charge of the Criminal Division. Weld listened to the pitches from both sides and decided in favor of Margolis and keeping the case in Washington.

Not the type of person to let anything go easily, Giuliani appealed Weld's decision to Deputy Attorney General Arnold Burns, who was both a friend and the highest authority in the Justice Department since Attorney General Edwin Meese III had recused himself from anything to do with the Teamsters. Meese had had a warm relationship with Jackie Presser, who had helped swing the backing of the Teamsters to Ronald Reagan in the 1980 presidential campaign.

In January 1987, all of the players gathered in a conference room to offer their arguments to Burns. Giuliani was riding high. He had achieved a series of stunning victories against New York mob bosses in labor-related racketeering cases: The boss of the Colombo organized crime family recently had been sentenced to prison for his control of New York Teamsters Local 814, and the commission case convictions had just come in with the promise of 100-year sentences for Fat Tony Salerno and his associates.

Burns listened attentively to the reargument as Giuliani stressed his office's accomplishments in trashing the very organized crime bosses whose domination of the Teamsters was the key to the case.

A few days later, Burns issued a surprise decision: The Teamster RICO case would stay in Washington.

2

Warnings Ignored

THE 1981 TEAMSTERS CONVENTION

On the second day of the June 1981 Teamsters Convention in Las Vegas, Diana Kilmury, a heavy-equipment operator from British Columbia, rose to propose the creation of an Ethical Practices Committee to examine the continuing charges of corruption and organized crime influence that had haunted the union for a quarter of a century.

The twenty-two hundred delegates exploded in rage, screaming, howling, booing this woman who dared to impugn the integrity of their union. There was a particular reason to attack Kilmury. She was a member of Teamsters for a Democratic Union (TDU), the national dissident organization, whose mission was to reform the Teamsters. The reformers represented a threat to the establishment. With few exceptions, the convention delegates were part of that establishment, enjoying the perks that went with it—the cars, expense accounts, free trips, lush retirement funds, and jobs for relatives.

If fear was churning her insides, Kilmury didn't show it. She stood apparently unshaken by the hate-filled performance of the delegates. A thirty-four-year-old divorcée who was raising three children by working on construction sites in the far reaches of Canada, a job that took her away from home for five and six months at a time, Kilmury demonstrated a moral and physical courage at the mike that day that few of the delegates could ever hope to match.

Teamster general president Roy Williams, who was chairing the convention, banged his gavel on the podium. "Let's have quiet. Let's listen to her," Williams said firmly. The audience drifted into silence.

Kilmury continued: "When I sit there in Canada and pick up a newspaper indicting yet another Teamster official, what am I supposed to believe? Am I supposed to believe that the two thousand people here are the only good people in the world and that everybody who works for the government is full of BS? That isn't logical. That is not even remotely believable. . . . If you're too damned scared to have an ethical practices committee, you must be up to something."

Kilmury's motion went down to defeat.

The International Brotherhood of Teamsters (IBT) holds a convention every five years to make adjustments to the union constitution and to elect the General Executive Board (GEB): a general president, a general secretary-treasurer, and sixteen International vice presidents.

In theory, the twenty-two hundred delegates at the 1981 convention were going through the democratic processes of adopting constitutional amendments and electing the union's hierarchy. In reality, the nation's organized crime bosses gave their approval and help in selecting Williams for the presidency. But that was a secret only a handful of insiders and FBI agents knew at this time.

The dissidents, with their futile resolutions, irritated the mass of the delegates, who wanted to get the business of the day over with as quickly as possible so they could get on to the gambling, golf, and girls that Las Vegas offered in such abundance. The general attitude was summed up by Patsy Crapanzano, vice president of New York City Teamsters Joint Council 16, head of New York Teamsters Local 27, and a soldier in the Gambino organized crime family, who tried to hurry things along by telling the delegates: "I came here to vote, and I don't want to know what I'm voting about."

Whatever the Teamsters' hierarchy put on the menu of amendments and resolutions was good enough for Crapanzano, who, along with Roy Williams, the squatly built sixty-six-year-old from Missouri who was chairing the gathering, would have provided rich material for an independent ethics committee.

The delegates, who had the power but not the will to shape the direction the Teamsters Union was taking, ignored three clear and diverse warnings of how sordid the leadership had become.

A month before the convention, on May 6, 1981, Teamsters general president Frank Fitzsimmons had died of lung cancer. In a blatant attempt to deter Williams from succeeding Fitzsimmons, the Senate Permanent Subcommittee on Investigations issued a report describing Williams as an "organized crime mole operating at senior levels of the Teamsters Union." The report contended that government investigators had discovered Williams was a protégé of Kansas City mob boss Nick Civella.

On May 15, 1981, the day after the report was issued, the seventeen members of the GEB unanimously elected Williams president of the IBT. That meant he would go into the convention as the incumbent president, which in effect assured election by the delegates to a full five-year term.

But the pressure was still on. Just a week later, on May 22, 1981, the Justice Department indicted Williams, along with Chicago mobster Joseph (Joey the Clown) Lombardo and several others, on federal charges of conspiring to bribe U.S. senator Howard W. Cannon, a Nevada Democrat, to derail a trucking deregulation bill. Although the Justice Department denied it, the timing of the indictment was a thinly veiled message to the delegates who would be voting within two weeks for the top eighteen officers of the Teamsters at the Las Vegas convention.

And then came a statement from a respected labor leader that should have been a clarion call of alarm to the decent unionists among the delegates. Less than a week before the convention, United Auto Workers (UAW) president Douglas Fraser broke one of organized labor's taboos by meddling in the affairs of another union. Fraser called for Williams to drop out as the Teamsters' general president until he was cleared of the federal indictment.

The White House, grateful for the IBT's role as the only major union to back Ronald Reagan in 1980, provided proof that no matter what the Senate, the Justice Department, or Fraser said, Williams was not a pariah in Washington.

President Ronald Reagan sent a videotaped message of thanks to his friends in the Teamsters to greet delegates on the opening day of the Teamsters Convention on June 1, 1981. "As a former union president, nothing makes me prouder than to work together with my union brothers toward a shared goal. I hope to be in team with the Teamsters," Reagan's video image said to the lusty cheers of the twenty-two hundred delegates.

Feeding the siege mentality of most Teamsters Union officials, Williams followed Reagan's message by briefly confronting the massive assault on his integrity by the Justice Department and the Senate subcommittee. "As you are all probably aware, the government tried to deal itself a hand in our proceedings," he told the delegates. He dismissed the subcommittee report accusing him of being dominated by organized crime as "so wrong and so false that I don't intend to dignify it with a response at this time." He said the charge accusing him of conspiring to bribe Cannon was "a damned lie." "No indictment will stop me!" Williams shouted.[6]

Instead of being dismayed by Williams's indictment, delegates expressed admiration and disbelief to any reporter who asked. "They're after us, and they'll always be after us. Anybody in the world could be elected Teamster president and he'd be indicted the next day," said an official from a Pittsburgh local.[7]

TDU spokesman Ken Paff offered a different explanation. Paff said that the combined fear of crossing the hierarchy and hope of winning patronage plums kept the delegates in line and silent in the face of the disgrace that the union had become. He said, "The delegates at the convention are dependent on the International leadership for so many things that they can hardly be accountable to the concerns of the rank and file. This convention is rigged to keep rank-and-file influence out and preserve the power of the Teamster hierarchy."

On the second day of the convention, the delegates made quick work of a menu of reforms offered by TDU. After dispensing with Diana Kilmury's proposal to create an ethical practices committee, they shouted down amendments to raise strike pay to $70 for the first four weeks and $90 thereafter; to ban multiple salaries; to cap the general president's pay at $100,000 and limit other international officers' salaries to $75,000; and to implement the direct election of the International officers by the rank and file.

The delegates roared their ayes just as loudly for the Williams administration's package of amendments raising the general president's salary from $156,000 to $225,000 a year; giving international officers the most generous cost-of-living-adjustment clause in uniondom: 100 percent of the inflation rate; and increasing strike pay a modest $10 a week to $45 a week for the first month and $55 a week thereafter. As Delegate John Cook from Teamsters Local 952 in Orange County, California, told the convention: "You give them too much and they won't want to come off strike."

Williams's nomination for the presidency was made by Jackie Presser, whose gargantuan appetite for power was hidden for the moment in his tortuous rhetoric. "And like a very courageous leader who has stood at the helm of this union, he has withstood in a calm, honest, and irreproachable manner attacks from ill-informed, dishonest, headline-seeking elements who are trying to undermine the greatness of this union," Presser said to the cheering delegates.

Peter Camarata, a thirty-four-year-old, $16,000-a-year dockworker from Jimmy Hoffa's home local in Detroit, was put up for the presidency by the TDU.

As required by the Teamsters' constitution, a roll-call vote began. After an hour, only 287 delegates had voted, indicating that a full roll-call vote could take up to eight hours. Having received only one of the 287 votes, Camarata conceded.

But Williams's supporters weren't good winners. They wanted to rub it in. "These turkeys started this thing. Let's jam it down their throats if it takes all night," shouted a delegate from California.

John Long, secretary-treasurer of Ron Carey's Local 804 in New York, offered a motion, which was rejected, to continue the roll call. Long's motion appeared to be an act of obeisance, an offering to Williams to make up in a small way for the insult from Carey that had appeared in the press. Carey had told a reporter he wouldn't attend the convention. "I'm not really interested. I think it is all preplanned, preset. The results are pretty obvious." He added wistfully, "I sure would love to have the opportunity to make some changes."

Williams came up with a solution of his own. He asked anyone who wanted to go on record as casting a ballot for Camarata to stand. Only ten delegates rose in an embarrassing moment for

TDU, which had claimed forty supporters among the delegates. The final tally was 2,210 for Williams, 10 for Camarata, and 1 abstention.

Camarata looked at the bright side of his loss. He had racked up ten times as many votes as five years before and had managed to move through the convention week physically unscathed. At the 1976 convention, Camarata had run against Frank Fitzsimmons, losing 2,300 to 1—he cast the single vote for himself. And at the 1976 convention, Camarata was punched and kicked at a union party by some Teamster bullyboys.

In 1981, the attacks were more subtle. "We're continually called socialists, Communists, and told we're taking money from the Rockefellers and the Ayatollah Khomeini," Camarata told reporters. Jackie Presser, who relished red-baiting TDUers, usually referred to him as "Commie Rata."

On the final day of the 1981 convention, eighty-seven-year-old Dave Beck, the first of the Teamster presidents to go to prison, spoke a few inspiring words. Beck, who served his time for grand larceny and tax evasion in the 1950s, brought the delegates to their feet by mentioning the magic name of Jimmy Hoffa, describing the missing and presumably murdered ex-president as "one of the great organizers in labor movement history."

An exhausted Williams ended the convention suffering from a laryngitis that turned his booming voice into a whisper. "I'll never forget where I came from. I'll always treat you like I like to be treated myself," he managed to say.

The following week, Williams had a busy schedule: an invitation to the White House to discuss Reagan's tax policies on June 10 and his arraignment on the federal indictment on June 12 in Chicago.

LUCKY JACKIE PRESSER

The summer of 1981 wasn't easy for Jackie Presser. In July his father, Bill Presser, died. Jackie owed his rise in the Teamsters to Bill Presser, who had the right connections in the mob and in the Teamsters.

Bill Presser created Cleveland Teamsters Local 507 for Jackie, then through the years arranged for him to succeed him as head of Cleveland Teamsters Joint Council 41 and the Ohio Conference of Teamsters and as an International vice president.

At the end of August, the *Cleveland Plain Dealer* and *Time* magazine hit Jackie Presser with two somewhat similar exposés that should have immediately destroyed his standing with his peers in the Teamsters and the organized crime figures lurking in his background but strangely didn't.

The publications reported that Jackie Presser had been an informant for both the IRS and the FBI since the early 1970s, providing dirt on Jimmy Hoffa and his allies. The *Plain Dealer* articles also charged that Jackie Presser had taken $300,000 in kickbacks from Hoover-Gorin and Associates, a Las Vegas public relations firm to which the Teamsters Union paid millions of dollars from 1972 to 1978 in the futile pursuit of a better image.

Roy Williams, understandably irked, confronted Jackie and demanded an explanation. "I'm a snitch. So what?" Presser said boldly.[8] Williams didn't press him for details. Instead, Williams reneged on his promise to appoint Jackie director of the Teamsters Central States Conference. That was a post that carried enormous power, more money, and a jet plane to boot.

Presser's greatest fear had to be the underworld's reaction. He managed to convince Milton J. (Maishe) Rockman, his primary link to the mob, of his loyalty. Rockman traveled with Angelo Lonardo, underboss of the Cleveland organized crime family, to New York for a meeting with Fat Tony Salerno, overlord of the Genovese crime family, to assure him Presser was okay. Since Cleveland fell under the suzerainty of the Genovese family, Salerno was a key to Presser's survival. Rockman and Salerno's judgment was colored by the knowledge that if Williams were convicted, Jackie Presser would be a likely candidate to succeed him as president. And they knew that control of the Teamsters' general president was like owning a credit card worth millions of dollars.

Rockman had another favor to ask Salerno. Since the story about Jackie wasn't true, he wondered whether Salerno could pull some strings to get a retraction? The aging crime boss, sipping his espresso, thought about it for a few minutes, then said he would talk to his lawyer, Roy Cohn. Testimony at one of Salerno's racketeering trials revealed that Cohn agreed to talk to his close friend and client Samuel I. Newhouse, Jr., owner of the *Plain Dealer*, about the possibility of a retraction.

On Sunday, October 10, 1982, Presser got his retraction in the *Cleveland Plain Dealer*. A front-page story said that the Department of Justice had closed the investigation without taking any action. John Climaco, Presser's attorney, said in the story, "The closing of this investigation vindicates Jackie Presser, who from the beginning denied that there was any truth in these allegations. The IRS as well as the Justice Department have advised me that Jackie and William Presser have never acted as informants."

While that retraction might have been reassuring to organized crime, *Plain Dealer* editors and reporters were so infuriated by what they perceived to be a betrayal of journalistic standards under pressure from powerful forces that in an extraordinary gesture of disapproval they picketed their own newspaper that same Sunday.

WILLIAMS TUMBLED FROM POWER

Roy Williams's lifelong winning streak ran out on December 15, 1982, with his conviction in Chicago federal court along with Allen Dorfman, the mob-connected insurance man, and three other defendants on the charge of conspiring to bribe Senator Cannon. Shattered by stress and an intensifying chronic emphysema, Williams was at sixty-eight a frail copy of the man who had become International president of the Teamsters just eighteen months earlier. He was now breathing with the aid of an oxygen bottle and confined to a wheelchair.

Williams had become the third Teamster general president in a quarter century to be convicted of a serious crime in a federal court.

Williams withdrew to the isolation of his horse ranch to mull over the years of prison that lay ahead of him. He didn't want to go to jail and urged his lawyers to devise a strategy that would delay the closing of prison gates behind him.

The Chicago mob was concerned, too. But organized crime's focus was on Williams's codefendant, Allen Dorfman, who faced the likelihood of a long prison sentence and the possibility that he might trade his inside knowledge of the mob's financial schemes for a lighter sentence. On January 20, 1983, Dorfman was murdered by gunmen in a parking lot in the suburbs of Chicago.

30

A few weeks later, U.S. District Court judge Prentice H. Marshall stunned Williams by sentencing him to fifty-five years in prison. The apparent severity of the sentence was softened by the judge's reason. Instead of continuing free on bail, Williams would now be forced to undergo medical observation for ninety days at a prison hospital to determine just how serious his physical condition was. The judge told Williams he planned to reduce the sentence substantially after the examination.

Angelo Lonardo, underboss of the Cleveland crime family, again traveled to New York, this time to lobby on behalf of Presser for mob-controlled votes on the GEB. Fat Tony Salerno, boss of the Genovese crime family, told him he would reach out to Teamsters International vice president Sammy Provenzano in New Jersey for his backing. Sammy Pro was the brother of Anthony (Tony Pro) Provenzano, a Genovese crime Family capo and a onetime Teamster International vice president, who was a suspect in the disappearance of Jimmy Hoffa.

On the day Williams was supposed to enter the prison hospital, his attorney, Raymond Larroca, appeared before Judge Marshall in an emergency session. Larroca told the judge that Williams was in the Park Lane Medical Center in Kansas City recovering from acute respiratory distress. Then he offered a trade: Williams would resign as president of the Teamsters in return for being allowed to remain free on bail pending the outcome of his appeals.

Judge Marshall accepted the deal. Williams's resignation would be effective April 20, 1983.

The next day, the Teamsters' GEB convened for a regularly scheduled quarterly meeting at the plush La Posada resort in Scottsdale, Arizona. With Presser as the only nominee, the seventeen-member board took just ten minutes to elect him to fill the remaining three years of Williams's unexpired term as the $225,000-a-year president.

While Jackie Presser was being elected in Scottsdale, a federal grand jury in Newark, New Jersey, was returning an indictment against one of his electors, International vice president Sammy Provenzano, on charges of embezzling $200,000 from a union welfare fund.

Presser stepped outside the meeting room for a brief press conference. In response to a question, he told the reporters he knew of no organized crime influences on the IBT.

ANGELO LONARDO FLIPS

In that same month, on April 7, 1983, Angelo Lonardo, the Cleveland crime family underboss, whose lobbying fostered Jackie Presser's ascension to the presidency of the Teamsters, suffered a terrible blow. A federal judge sentenced seventy-two-year-old Lonardo to life plus 103 years in prison for dealing in drugs.

After his appeals were exhausted, Lonardo quickly decided that he couldn't endure the pain of spending the rest of his life behind bars. He contacted the FBI, becoming the highest-ranking Mafia member willing to betray his pledge of silence to his mob compadres in return for a deal on his prison sentence.

On October 27 and 28, 1983, four FBI agents grilled Lonardo for hours, drawing from him the story of the role played by the nation's organized crime bosses in helping to win the presidency of the Teamsters first for Roy Williams and then for Jackie Presser.

The fifty-eight-page FBI summary of Lonardo's confession included detailed accounts of the two lobbying trips that he and Maishe Rockman made to the crime bosses in Chicago and New York, who jointly reign over La Cosa Nostra organizations throughout the United States. In each case, the new president was elected by seventeen men sitting in a room, meaning that only nine votes were needed to place a candidate in a position to dominate the huge, powerful union, with its enormous patronage and influence over the transportation industries—both trucking and airborne.

Lonardo explained that enough Teamster vice presidents owed their union offices to the mob that the vote for president could be swung to the chosen of the crime bosses.

The flipping of Lonardo from a mob underboss to a government-protected witness would provide a key ingredient in the government's civil RICO case against the IBT when it was unveiled in 1988. But for almost three years, Lonardo's crossover was a carefully kept secret.

JACKIE TAKES THE FIFTH

Throughout his first two years in office, Jackie Presser was haunted by Labor Department investigators and federal prosecutors pursuing allegations that he condoned the practice of carrying several "ghost employees" on the payroll of Cleveland Local 507. Federal law makes paying people for not working—the so-called ghosts—a crime.

Two men, one a Presser relative and the other the son of an organized crime figure, had been sentenced to prison for holding no-show jobs at Local 507. Despite those convictions and the urging of federal prosecutors in Cleveland that Presser be indicted on charges of fraud and conspiracy, the Justice Department formally terminated the Presser "ghost employees" investigation in the summer of 1985.

Speculation was that Presser had ridden through this storm either because of his political connections in the White House or because of his role as an FBI informant.

"Thank God it's over. I'm happy with the outcome" is all that Presser had to say on the subject, but two Senate committees, the Permanent Subcommittee on Investigations and the Senate Judiciary Committee, said they wanted to examine the conficting roles of the FBI and the Labor Department in the Presser case. The two agencies had clashed with FBI agents trying to protect Presser and Labor Department organized crime investigators urging his indictment. Sen. Sam Nunn, a Georgia Democrat, questioned the government's ability to combat labor racketeering in light of the outcome.

But Presser wasn't off the hook yet.

Stephen M. Ryan, the twenty-nine-year-old deputy counsel of the President's Commission on Organized Crime, seized the end of the ghost case as an opportunity to try to force Presser to testify before the commission.

Ryan asked the Justice Department to issue an order giving Presser immunity, which would have forced him to testify or go to jail for eighteen months. Presser, however, was still being protected by his FBI allies. Without offering an explanation, Assistant Attorney General Stephen Trott denied Ryan's request for an immunity order.

Nevertheless, Ryan subpoenaed Presser. On August 13, 1985, Presser returned to be questioned by Ryan in a private session. The young deputy counsel opened the deposition by pointing out that the previous April, Presser had invoked the Fifth Amendment, the constitutional protection against self-incrimination, because of the ongoing "ghost employees" investigation.

Since that investigation was now over, Ryan contended, there was no reason for Presser to hide behind the Fifth Amendment.

That argument didn't move Presser. The only information Presser provided was his name. He took the Fifth in response to every subsequent question, starting with what his union titles were and continuing through his knowledge of the organized crime ties of David Beck, Jimmy Hoffa, and Roy Williams.

Then Ryan asked the piercing question that would be central to future Justice Department civil racketeering cases against the Teamster hierarchy: "Mr. Presser, who really runs your union?"

Jackie Presser took the Fifth.

The questions that followed alerted Presser that he wasn't the only high-level informant with an inside knowledge of Teamster politics talking to federal investigators.

Ryan asked: "Prior to your obtaining the presidency of the International Brotherhood of Teamsters, did you, or someone acting on your behalf, have to seek the support of Mr. Tony Salerno, the head of the Genovese family in New York?

Presser again took the Fifth.

"Does Mr. Salerno play a part in choosing the presidents of the International Brotherhood of Teamsters?"

Presser again took the Fifth.

"Is it true, sir, organized crime influence reaches into the [General Executive Board] and to certain of the individuals who are vice presidents of the International Brotherhood of Teamsters?"

Presser again took the Fifth. He did so in response to 251 questions, including how he became a millionaire.

Ryan enjoyed a greater success with Presser's predecessor, Roy Williams.

For almost a year Ryan had been sweet-talking and pressuring Williams through his lawyers in an attempt to get him to cooperate with the commission. In the midst of the commission's Chicago hearings in April 1983, Ryan finally got his opportunity to meet Williams in person. He got a telephone message that Williams would see him that night at a Holiday Inn in Rosemont, a Chicago suburb with a reputation as a mob area and a dumping ground for bodies. Arriving at 11:00 P.M., Ryan waited as instructed, in the lobby. As he sat there at the appointed hour, he suddenly realized that he had ventured into this situation without backup, without any agents to come to the rescue if things got nasty.

A huge man, looking like the prototypical leg breaker, came up to him. "Are you Ryan?" he asked in a voice that resonated with muscle. "Go sit over by that plant," he said, pointing.

Instead, Ryan sat on the opposite side of the lobby, watching to see if some gunman would walk in, in search of a target by the plant. Nothing that wild was to happen. Another emissary appeared to lead him to Williams's room.

Williams evoked some sympathy from Ryan, who viewed him less as an evil character who had betrayed his calling than as a man caught by forces beyond his control. Still caring for the members, still essentially a truck driver, Williams did the bidding of Kansas City mob boss Nick Civella to survive. "Roy Williams lived with a degree of a guilty conscience. He hated a part of himself for it," Ryan later recalled.

That night, they talked for an hour and a half, Ryan pressing the point that there was a legacy of an organized crime presence in the Teamsters that had to be rooted out. Williams responded with a "harrumph, harrumph" grunt, unwilling to confront the issue. Before they parted, Ryan told Williams that he was pursuing an immunity order that would give him the choice of cooperating or serving eighteen months in jail. Knowing that Williams dreaded the prospect of going to prison, Ryan emphasized that his failure to cooperate would mean serving the eighteen months before any of the time on his ten-year prison sentence would begin ticking off the clock. Besides, Williams's cooperation undoubtedly would mean cutting a large chunk of time off the ten-year sentence.

Ryan left Williams weighing his loyalty to his comrades in the hierarchy of the Teamsters and his self-esteem against the certainty of dying in a prison hospital unless he agreed to talk.

In August 1983, Ryan debriefed Williams. The debriefing, a word with a CIA ring, was an informal conversation without tape recorders or stenographers. Ryan used it to bring Williams further along toward his first public admission that organized crime had dominated him and the Teamsters for decades.

On September 13, 1983, Ryan arrived at Roy Williams's modest farm in Johnson County, Missouri, shortly after noon, accompanied by Mike DeFeo, head of the Kansas City Organized Crime Strike Force. He carried with him an order, approved by Stephen Trott, the assistant attorney general, that compelled Williams's testimony in return for a limited grant of immunity. Whatever the ex–general president of the Teamsters said would not be used against him.

Ryan had scored a coup. Moving Williams across the psychological divide into the role of a cooperating witness would provide the government with an insider from the Teamster hierarchy who would swear to the mob's domination of the union. Williams's cooperation would also serve as another crucial facet of the 1988 Teamster RICO.

Ryan began: "Mr. Williams, would it be correct to say that you have not wanted to give this deposition because you are afraid of what people in the organization known alternatively as La Cosa Nostra or the mob or organized crime, what they might do to you as a result of your testifying either before a presidential commission or court of the United States?"

Williams, looking old and exhausted and having difficulty breathing, responded: "I have certain fears. Yes."

For the next ninety minutes, until he was too worn out to continue, Williams poured out a brief outline of his life: starting to work as a truck driver in late 1934, spending thirty months fighting in Europe in World War II—at which point Ryan interjected to ask about his Silver Star won under battle conditions. "I had five Bronze Stars and a Silver Star," Williams said.

Ryan asked what could be construed as leading questions of a man who until that moment had consistently denied any ties to organized crime. For the most part, Williams, now at the end of a Teamster career spanning more than forty years, answered, "Yes, sir" to each of the questions put to him by the young lawyer.

"Was Nick Civella your main link to any organization known as La Cosa Nostra, the Mafia, or the mob in this country?"

"Yes, he was," Williams replied in the breakthrough statement. It was the first formal admission, by a member of the hierarchy, of organized crime's presence in the Teamsters. "The deposition didn't represent the plumbing of his knowledge," Ryan said later, "but the first peeling of the onion."

Williams admitted that Civella promoted his career within the Teamsters in exchange for which Williams found jobs for the crime boss's relatives and associates—and later helped to arrange the multi-million-dollar loans from the Teamsters' Central States Pension Fund that Civella sought for his fronts in the Las Vegas gambling casinos.

He described Jimmy Hoffa's close alliance with Civella and the fear of assassination that haunted Hoffa even in the early days because of anxiety over perhaps crossing one crime group or another. He said that Frank Fitzsimmons, who succeeded Hoffa, experienced the same dread of being murdered by mob hit men.

"Every big [Teamsters] local union I think had some connection with organized crime," Williams said.

In response to a question on whether a general president of Teamsters could clear the mob out of the union, Williams said: "Not without having a bigger organization than they got. They was here a long time before any of us ever got here, and they have got pretty powerful. And you fellows haven't been able to do nothing with them, either."

The old truck driver's perceptive answer fit in with the recommendations issued by the President's Commission on Organized Crime four months later. The report urged the use of the civil RICO suits instead of continuing to spin the wheels of law enforcement with body counts: the long list of indictments and convictions of one Teamster leader after another, who might go to prison and might be removed from the union, only to be replaced by a son or nephew or crime-family relative, equally corrupt.

JACKIE PRESSER TRIUMPHANT: THE 1986 TEAMSTERS CONVENTION

The 1986 Teamsters Convention opened in the Las Vegas Convention Center on a searingly hot day in May, with Vice President George Bush warmly greeting the nineteen hundred delegates in a video message.

"You can take pride in the fact that during the past decade, while other unions have been experiencing declining membership due to basic changes in our economy, your union continues to grow, enhancing its diversity by organizing new members in just about every craft imaginable," Bush's video image said to his appreciative audience. Unfortunately, the vice president's statement wasn't true. Since the 1981 convention, Teamster membership rolls had sagged 300,000 to 1.6 million, down from 1.9 million in 1981.

But in the effervescent atmosphere in which politicians of all ideological hues were paying tribute to the great Teamsters

Union via video—Thomas P. (Tip) O'Neill, Democratic Speaker of the House, Jim Wright, House Democratic majority leader; Robert Dole, Republican Senate majority leader; and Paul G. Kirk, Jr., chairman of the Democratic National Committee—the fudging of a few numbers in a friendly speech didn't matter. Republican National Committee chairman Frank Fahrenkopf, who showed up in person to deliver his tribute, offered a broad hint of whose side he was on in the troubles that tortured the Teamster hierarchy: "We all, I think, Republicans and Teamsters, live in the real world, a world of patriotism and family values. And we believe that hard work should be honored and rewarded, not punished," he said to applause.

The bipartisan support of the nation's leading political figures was important to Teamster general president Jackie Presser and the delegates who filled the convention hall as proof once again that the Teamsters weren't pariahs.

Presser and all seventeen of the International officers who composed the Teamsters' GEB were running for reelection to new five-year terms at this convention. Despite the serious attacks on the character of Presser and the entire International leadership through the months and days leading up to the convention, no one with any knowledge of the IBT had any doubts that the entire slate of incumbents would be elected.

In the face of so many indicators from so many substantial sources that Jackie Presser was an informant, a tool of the mob, and an unscrupulous predator, why did the delegates fail to seize the moment of the convention to reject him? Most likely it was just plain timidity. To stand up in the Teamsters Union invited reproach. To speak out invited retaliation.

Obviously, the Teamsters were incapable of reforming themselves, and the union's power was so enormous that the nation's top elected officials were as willing as the delegates to ignore the evidence of corruption.

The year 1986 had opened with Judge Irving R. Kaufman, chairman of the President's Commission on Organized Crime, presenting Pres. Ronald Reagan with the first copy of the commission's report in which the Teamsters were excoriated as the most mob controlled union in the United States and Presser was depicted as owing his elevation to the presidency to the help of organized crime.

On May 9, 1986, ten days before the convention, the Senate

Permanent Subcommittee on Investigations issued a report that included the first official confirmation that Jackie Presser was an FBI informant. And the Justice Department bureaucracy, discovering that FBI agents lied to help Presser escape indictment in the "ghost employees" case, approved the filing of criminal charges against him. On May 16, three days before the opening of the convention, a federal grand jury in Cleveland indicted Presser, International vice president Harold Friedman, and business agent Anthony Hughes on embezzlement and racketeering charges involving the payment of $700,000 to ghost employees of Cleveland Teamsters Local 507.

Teamsters for a Democratic Union (TDU), as in the past, was challenging the way delegates were selected for the 1986 convention, but TDU's position was for the first time being validated by outsiders. While the Labor Department consistently ignored TDU, the commission's report said that Department of Labor documents showed that the Teamsters' method of automatically giving the first seven delegate slots in each local to the local's officers was illegal. "The Commission recommends that union members have the right to vote for delegates to their union's convention," the report said.

Aside from the Teamsters, only one other national union, the Amalgamated Transit Union, failed to elect top officers by either a rank-and-file election or elected delegates. The president's commission concluded that the Teamster system helped organized crime keep its choke hold on the union, while Labor Department officials believed it gave the incumbent hierarchy too much control over the convention, all but eliminating real democracy.

In a parallel attack, TDU had gathered the signatures of 100,000 rank and filers on petitions urging the adoption of the direct election of the union's top officers by the membership in secret-ballot elections. On the opening day of the convention, delegates found letters on their chairs signed by a hundred local officers, business agents, and elected convention delegates urging a change in the union constitution to provide for direct elections.

Against that background, the delegates, ostensibly as enthusiastic as ever about Presser, filled the arena. The few who would talk to reporters said they didn't believe the charges against their leader. The government was out to get Jackie. It was as simple as that. The videos from Vice President Bush and the other politicians praising them and their union reinforced their self-confidence.

U.S. secretary of labor William Brock came to deliver an unexpected speech at the opening of the convention, one that would stun the delegates. Brock began by questioning whether criticism of the Teamsters was justified.

The delegates gave Brock a standing ovation when he told them he rejected the advice of those who urged him not to attend the convention.

The applause stopped interrupting him as he got into the guts of what he had to say. "Today is a day for honest communications between us about some problems in this union." Brock told a silent audience—no one was chatting in the background, as conventioneers usually do during speeches by the invited guests—that the Teamsters were suffering the same problems as the Republicans in Watergate, and they couldn't ignore it.

> But two million people who decide they want to can change things. The challenge is real, and so is the opportunity. You're not powerless. You've got the tools and the people.
>
> Are there institutional processes which make it easy for the some who want to exploit members to do so? If there are, change them. Are there locals where people are doing just that, where crime interests reign? Are members' interests ignored or trampled? If there are such locals, put them in trusteeship. Are there areas where good people have been silent too long, where it's just plain time to clean house? If so, do it.
>
> As secretary of labor, it isn't easy to hear about mobbed-up locals or pension-fund abuse, misuse of members' blood and sweat in any organization. It's impossible for me to ignore that. It is necessary for you to address it. . . . Sure as dawn follows dark, perception will follow that reality.

The audience was absolutely silent. The delegates were uncertain how to respond to the secretary of labor, who had offered his criticism in the stance of a friend. When TDUer Diana Kilmury delivered essentially the same message five years before, the delegates howled her down. After what seemed an ominously long time, Jackie Presser began clapping, and simultaneously applause burst from the crowd. They rose to their feet.

Presser stepped up to stand beside Brock. "Can't ask for much more than that," Presser said in a flat tone.

Brock left the stage, immediately slipping away before the press could reach him. He later denied that he knew that the RICO case was in the process of being put together. But he sensed that the avalanche of revelations couldn't continue without dire results for the Teamsters.

An hour later, Presser delivered his state of the union address, in which he aimed directly for the jugulars of his enemies. In a commanding voice, he suggested that he was the sacrificial lamb representing everyone in the huge room: "Our great union is again under attack. As you know, the government has indicted me on the issue of the stewardship of Local Union 507.

"We will have our day in court, and when that time does come, I can assure you, we will be vindicated. The charges are totally without merit. They are political and false. They do not contain any allegations of personal gain nor profit."

He argued that underlying the indictment were those who wanted to destroy the free labor movement. "That is why select members of the media and a Senate committee pressured the Department of Justice to make a political decision to indict me after career law enforcement professionals on the basis of the facts, on the basis of the law, and on the basis of the quality of the evidence against me, and on the basis of the interests of justice twice rejected a Cleveland strike force's recommendation to indict me."

No allusion was made to his role as an FBI informant or to the Teamsters' endorsement of the antiunion Reagan administration in two presidential elections. Nor did Presser or anyone else during the week-long convention mention Roy Williams, who had angrily proclaimed his own innocence until his conviction and his admission that he was a puppet on the mob's string.

A little later in the program, New York Teamster leader Barry Feinstein, a towering man with a booming voice, made a motion of support for Jackie Presser and read the names of sixty-seven endorsers, the key officials of every joint council in the United States and Canada and the heads of all the Teamster trade divisions. "We are sick at heart, but we are firm in our resolve. We will not be controlled by the press. We will not be dictated to by the government. . . . We move, Mr. Chairman, that the delegates in the convention assembled affirm their support for our president in his battle against government tyranny." The delegates jumped to their feet, cheering and clapping.

That night at Caesars Palace, the Eastern Conference hosted its traditional convention party on so lavish a scale that even the Teamster hierarchy was impressed. Eastern Conference director Joseph (Joe T) Trerotola dug into the members' pockets to spend $647,960[9] on piles of shrimp, roasts, cold cuts, caviar, cheeses, wines, liquor, and soft drinks for several thousand guests filling two huge ballrooms.

To a fanfare, Joe T was carried into the party on a sedan chair borne by four burly bodybuilders in the dress of Roman legionnaires. Next came a grinning, waving, bloated Jackie Presser seated on an ornate red chariot pulled and pushed by another four hugely muscled men costumed in togas and gold helmets with red plumes. The stunt was cheered by the festive crowd. The delegates shouted, "Hail, Jackie," as the chariot circled the room.[10]

The next day, C. Sam Theodus provoked a prolonged debate by making a motion to replace the existing system of delegates voting openly to elect officers with a rank-and-file secret-ballot system. Theodus, the self-declared candidate opposing Presser for the presidency, was endorsed by TDU. But Theodus could not be smeared, as TDUers often were, as some sort of left-wing hippie. He was a real Teamster who had worked in a warehouse doing heavy lifting for ten years, followed by another ten years as a truck driver. In 1972, he had begun the step-by-step climb from shop steward to business agent and then, in 1981, to president of the largest local in Cleveland, Local 407, whose five thousand members were used to democracy and decent leadership.

In contrast to the grossness of Presser, Theodus was the model of what a union leader should be in appearance and life-style. At fifty-five, still a handsome man, he had 210 pounds spread across a solid six-foot two-inch frame that he kept in shape by jogging and working out in a gym. None of his nine grown children was on a Teamster union payroll. At the time of the 1986 convention, Theodus was paid $45,000 a year plus a union car and $25 a week for expenses. His salary, and those of other Local 407 officers, was based on the wages and overtime paid to truck drivers under the Teamsters' National Master Freight Agreement. Presser at the time was making $755,000 a year in salaries and expenses from his multiple Teamster posts, including the presidency.

Unlike the mass of the nation's elected Teamster officials, Theodus had a clear vision of his union's problems. When he announced his candidacy shortly before the convention, he said: "We have a history of being controlled by outside sources, allegedly the Mafia. People are making statements the mob put Jackie in, the mob put Williams in, and the mob put Hoffa in. The only way the Teamsters are going to rid themselves of that stigma is to put control of the Teamsters in the hands of the membership through the right to elect all of their officials."

Theodus had no illusions that he would present a serious threat to Presser's reelection. He made the point that the Teamsters' election process discouraged those who wanted to see the union reformed from opposing the incumbents. "The system doesn't allow them to. Who is going to the convention to stand up in front of the guy who controls the union and say they are voting for somebody else?"

Not many.

Theodus's motion provoked a prolonged debate. Presser loyalists rushed to the microphones on the convention floor to demean the idea of a rank-and-file vote as subversive, socialistic, and un-American.

Theodus's proposal was rejected overwhelmingly, as were all of the offerings from TDU-aligned delegates. Voted down were motions to double strike benefits to $110 a week, to cap officers' salaries at $100,000 and the general president's at $125,000, to go on record against two-tier contracts—under which new hires get paid less than veteran employees doing the same work—and to return to a policy allowing the rejection of contracts by a simple majority rather than a two-thirds' vote.

"The sorry fact is Jackie Presser could get those delegates to vote to put the headquarters on Mars," TDU leader Ken Paff said bitterly afterward.

With the TDU motions out of the way, the ancient symbol of Teamster corruption, Dave Beck, was trotted out for his quinquennial convention speech. The ninety-four-year-old Beck mentioned in passing that the last really contested race for the presidency was in 1912, when Dan Tobin ousted incumbent Cornelius Shea, defeating him by twelve votes.

But the 1986 election wouldn't repeat history.

The election was held on the third day of the convention. The nominating speech for Theodus was interrupted six times by boos.

Then the balloting began, with delegate after delegate voting for Presser. After an hour and twenty minutes of the roll-call vote produced only twelve votes for him, Theodus rose to say he was "willing" to concede. There was a chorus of nos.

Joe T, who was presiding, told the delegates: "Brother Theodus could concede if he wants to, but we are going to continue with the roll call."

Theodus again affirmed he was "willing" to concede. That wasn't good enough for Joe T. "Not that you are *willing* to concede. Are you *going* to concede now?"

"I concede," Theodus said.

Joe T wasn't letting Theodus and his TDU allies escape their affront to Jackie Presser. "Let the record show that at two-thirty P.M., Sam Theodus conceded. However, it is the ruling of the chair that the roll call will continue. Please proceed."

Ron Carey, who had come to this convention, wasn't in his seat when the roll call reached Local 804. He was recorded as absent. The long roll call went on.

Presser's name was repeated like a mantra of loyalty. Even some TDU-oriented delegates crossed over to his side after a cautious reassessment of the impact of voting against him.

At the end of the four-hour ordeal, the final tally was Presser, 1,729; Theodus, 24.

A gleeful Presser revealed the purpose of continuing the vote after Theodus was forced into the humbling concession. It was all about TDU. "In accepting the general presidency of this union, it's my pleasure to say to you and to the American public that have been conned for so many years with respect to the might and the strength of that outside organization that continually has attacked us. Let the record show that there wasn't even twenty-five of them present to vote in this convention."

On the fifth and closing day of the convention, Jackie Presser told the cheering delegates, "To those who don't know it, I am going to say it. We attended the funeral of TDU this week."

Diana Kilmury, as always, managed to bring the delegates to their feet howling, booing, and screaming when she stepped to a microphone on the convention floor and said she had just put on a badge. She told her hostile audience: "It's a picture of a dandelion, the bad weed, but underneath it says, 'We never die.' And, Mr. Presser, we never will die. Your funeral is premature."

3

The Creation of TDU

Steve Kindred climbed onto a Greyhound bus in the Cleveland depot on a dreary April morning in 1975 with five pounds of Spanish peanuts, three pounds of raisins, and a list of Teamster activists in his pack. He had a ticket in his pocket entitling him to travel wherever Greyhound went for the next twenty-one days for the bargain price of $89.

Kindred was on an excursion to recruit warehouse workers and over-the-road drivers, covered by the National Master Freight Agreement, for an ad hoc organization being formed to give the rank and file a voice in formulating demands in the next nationwide contract. The 1973 agreement had been a second-rate contract.

The thirty-one-year-old Kindred, a product of the 1960s student antiwar movement in Chicago, had become a Teamster member, in the process combining his need to make a living and his idealist drive to transform American society into something better for the working class.

The history of the Teamsters is speckled with rank-and-file dissident organizations focused on a local union, sometimes a region. Usually, their life cycles were brief. But in 1975, the nucleus of a group came together that would emerge as the national reform movement that would eventually transform the International Brotherhood of Teamsters (IBT).

That March, a dozen members of the independent Chicago Truck Drivers Union and Teamsters from Pittsburgh, Akron,

Cleveland, and Chicago met in the tiny living room of Ken Paff's Cleveland home to discuss what could be done to influence the 1976 master freight negotiations. They talked for four hours, finally agreeing to create a grass-roots organization and to hold a conference that August in Chicago as the staging ground for a national campaign. Having reached that decision, they set out to develop an audience and a membership.

Kindred was available. He was an effective organizer, good with people. They would send him on the road to rouse potential rank-and-file leaders across the country. Kindred obtained the names of thirty organizers for PROD—the acronym for the Professional Drivers Council for Safety and Health. PROD was created by Ralph Nader in 1971 to focus on trucking safety—since obviously the Teamsters Union wasn't. The names of other activists surfaced in the truckers' grapevine and from various publications.

The hat was passed at the gathering in Paff's house and $100 was collected. Not much, but enough for the Greyhound ticket. Kindred used the list of activists to set up as many appointments as he could. Then he set out.

Kindred's first stop was Columbus, just a couple of hours from Cleveland. He had telephoned ahead arranging to meet a warehouse worker, a PROD member, at the bus station. In a routine that was to be repeated time and again as he wandered through the Midwest into the South and Southwest, out to California and back across the country to Cleveland again, moving through the bus depots of twenty-two cities in the process, Kindred sat down to wait for his appointment. He passed the time reading, making a few notes in his journal, munching on peanuts and raisins, and drinking coffee. He had a couple of hours to wait.

The warehouse worker suggested a sandwich when he arrived, an offer seized upon by Kindred, anticipating correctly that his Columbus host would pick up the tab. As a PROD member, the warehouse worker was well aware that dissident organizers like Kindred traveled with light wallets.

The thirty-one-year-old Kindred betrayed his college education and background as a Methodist preacher's son in his speech and his aura of gentleness, but having been a taxi driver and a truck driver in Chicago and Cleveland, he had earned the right to be discussing their union in a seedy lunchroom in Columbus, Ohio.

Kindred laid out his background, knowing that the red-baiters in the Teamster establishment would be doing it, anyhow. He told his new acquaintance that he was a member of a small group called the International Socialists, a tag that could frighten, enrage, or be passed off as understandable. Kindred reminded his host that in 1970, Bill Presser and Frank Fitzsimmons had called the wildcat strikers in Cleveland Communists when they marched in defiance of Presser's orders to return to work. The wildcat strikes, which spread across the country, had ended after three months with the proposed three-year wage hike of $1.10 an hour boosted to $1.85 over thirty-nine months to bring peace to the trucking industry.[11]

Kindred continued: "I don't have to tell you the 1973 contract was a disaster." He told the warehouse worker that Teamsters from five cities had gotten together to organize a rank-and-file agenda for the upcoming 1976 national trucking negotiations. He asked the warehouse worker for his ideas: what he would want to see in the next master freight agreement. Then Kindred explained that he had been picked for his mission because he was laid off and available. His goal was to recruit as many rank and filers as possible to come to a meeting their group would be holding in Chicago on August 16. The idea was to influence the national negotiations by reaching a consensus on realistic demands, not a wish list. They were calling themselves Teamsters for a Decent Contract (TDC).

After a couple of hours, they shook hands, and Kindred was on his way to his next stop, Dayton. The scenario was repeated— waiting time in the terminal, a meeting in a coffee shop, and onto a bus to the next city. There wasn't time to go to people's houses or money for the luxury of hotels. Kindred brought along a little pillow and a light blanket. He slept on the bus, shaved and washed in public restrooms, and ate most of his meals on the largess of the Teamsters he met along the way, with his peanuts and raisins as fall-back provisions.

He traveled to Cincinnatti, Indianapolis, and Memphis, where his prearranged appointment schedule with activists ran out. Teamsters in Memphis suggested contacts in Little Rock. Little Rock set him up with groups in Oklahoma City and Dallas. Dallas was a no-show. There were three or four of those. He assumed the missed appointments were due to fear, not an unusual state when someone stepped across the line into dissidence in the Teamsters Union.

From Dallas he went to Los Angeles, familiar territory. Kindred spent three days off the bus, staying with friends, enjoying showers and a comfortable bed. He met with Doug Allan, a Local 208 shop steward with a reputation as a zealot; with Sharon Cotrell of Local 692, one of the first women dockworkers in the Teamsters; and with Gordon E. (Curly) Best, the ex-president of Teamsters United Rank and File (TURF). TURF, founded in 1971 in the wake of the wildcat strikes, was the first national rank-and-file reform organization. But by 1974 it had foundered.

Kindred continued his journey north to the San Francisco Bay area, then turned east to Kansas City, to St. Louis, and to Effingham, Illinois, on to Chicago, Indianapolis, and Toledo. Twenty-one days after he left, Kindred arrived back in Cleveland with his notebooks filled with telephone numbers, addresses, ideas, and commitments to report to Paff.[12]

The response to the call for the meeting was enthusiastic enough to give Ken Paff the hope of a solid turnout of Teamster rebels for the meeting. The always active grapevine, nourished by truckers driving from terminal to terminal across the country, also spread news of the gathering in Chicago.

Almost three months later, on August 16, about forty drivers and warehouse workers filled a long, narrow meeting room in Chicago's small, aging Midland Hotel. They came from Rochester, New York, Pittsburgh, Indianapolis, the major terminal in New Castle, Pennsylvania, Cleveland, Little Rock, and Memphis. Fifteen cities in all were represented. Some even came from the West Coast, Los Angeles and Long Beach.

Fear was a real presence. A dozen burly rank and filers, some armed with baseball bats, guarded the entrance to the room. Two weeks before the meeting, Jimmy Hoffa had disappeared. That made everyone apprehensive. If a man of Hoffa's high profile and power could be eliminated, it didn't take much imagination to realize how vulnerable were ordinary truck drivers like them. Just recently Teamsters Union thugs had broken up a rump meeting of shop stewards discussing their disenchantment with a contract in Evansville, Indiana. So there was a real reason for concern.

Cigarette smoke filled the crowded room as the group discussed contract goals. The consensus was that TDC's agenda must remain simple. They agreed on a list of thirteen demands for the 1976 negotiations. Among the TDC proposals were a two-year contract, with hourly wages to be raised two dollars an hour; an unlimited cost-of-living-adjustment ("cola") clause; automatic cola increases in fringe-benefit payments; full fringe benefits for laid-off workers for up to a year; a return to the right of a terminal to strike for twenty-four hours in grievance disputes; air conditioning in all new trucks; and the right to a separate vote on all supplements and riders to national contracts.

Ken Paff chaired the discussion on demands and by the end of the meeting had been elected the budding organization's national coordinator. His responsibilities would include publishing a brochure outlining TDC's contract demands, arranging for petitions under which the signers would pledge to vote no unless the demands were met, and getting bumper stickers made.[13]

Just short of his twenty-ninth birthday, Paff, who had been driving a truck in Cleveland for the past four years as a member of Local 407, was the stern, abrupt, caustic counterpart of the smiling, joking Kindred. Paff, too, had come out of the student movement and was an International Socialist. A graduate of Berkeley with a degree in physics, Paff dropped out of graduate school to become an activist. He taught school for a while and for a year was a computer programmer until he found his way into the Teamsters by learning to drive a tractor trailer. Paff's roots were in the working class. The youngest of seven children, he had been raised by his divorced mother in California.[14]

Paff provided the kind of egoless, highly organized, and determined leadership that the fledgling organization needed. The instructions were to turn out a brochure. He sent Kindred to a surplus-paper house to get a roll of high-quality, heavy stock. By mid-September, twenty thousand brochures were being distributed at truck stops and in company barns around the nation. Paff traveled the country holding press conferences with local rank and filers in trucking centers. The reaction brought a demand for one-hundred-thousand more brochures. Teamsters stood up at local union meetings to pass resolutions backing the TDC demands, and tens of thousands signed the no vote pledge petitions.

Had General President Frank Fitzsimmons and the parasites who surrounded him in the Teamster bureaucracy known about the unpaid efforts of Paff and the spartan conditions Kindred had endured on the campaign trail, they might have been amused. But the more perceptive also might have realized that the monklike devotion of the dissidents and their willingness to sacrifice the pleasures of a life of expense accounts and nice salaries for the cause of worker justice could become a threat to their milking of the union. The Teamster establishment, which for two decades had endured the relentless pursuit of congressional and federal investigators, was about to be set upon by a new pack of baying hounds within the ranks of the union who would be just as tenacious and dangerous.

THE ROOTS OF PROD

The year 1975 was to be a formative one for reform movements in the IBT. Even as Paff, Kindred, and their allies were preparing for their conference in August, PROD was in the process of moving beyond its original agenda of truck safety into the broader realm of attacking the corruption and selfish autocracy of the union's hierarchy.

In 1970, Robert Fellmeth took some time out from his studies at Harvard Law School to go to work for Ralph Nader's Public Interest Research Group in Washington, D.C. He was assigned to examine the Interstate Commerce Commission (ICC).

Fellmeth's research was collected in his book *The Interstate Commerce Omission*. He discovered that safety in the motor-truck industry was a disaster. Trucks were rolling accidents just waiting to happen. The ICC's Bureau of Motor Carrier Safety had been transferred to the Department of Transportation and in the process had lost its teeth. The maximum fine that the bureau could impose for safety violations was fifty dollars.

Fellmeth found that truck drivers were being required to drive ten hours a day, commencing at any point in the night or day. Break time and waiting time didn't count toward those ten hours. Under such conditions, it wasn't surprising to find truckers popping pills to keep awake.

What was the mighty Teamsters Union doing for its members? Nothing.

Fellmeth inserted a questionnaire on truck safety in the industry magazine *Overdrive*. The respondents provided a mailing list for a Nader-sponsored conference on safety that drew three-hundred over-the-road drivers to Washington on October 1, 1971. After hearing their complaints, Nader decided the over-the-road drivers, as the truckers who move freight between cities are called, needed someone to speak for them.

He found Arthur Fox II.

Fox had grown up in a comfortable, liberal family in New Jersey. He graduated from the University of Virginia Law School in 1968 and had gone to work for the National Labor Relations Board (NLRB). But he felt uncomfortable as a government bureaucrat. A product of the sixties, Fox wanted to get involved in doing something that would change the world. A friend who was working for Nader's Public Citizens Litigation Group brought Fox and Ralph Nader together in October 1972.

Nader told Fox he had a grand opportunity available for him that would help make the lives of hundreds of thousands of truck drivers better and safer. He hired Fox as the executive director of PROD, a paper organization with neither members nor a treasury.

Nader agreed to a salary of $8,000 a year for Fox, who had been making $21,000 a year at the NLRB. The hook was that Fox would have to recruit the members, whose dues would pay his salary, along with pursuing the mission of raising the level of safety in the trucking industry.

Fox didn't have an inkling of the enormous task that lay ahead or the deep-seated hostility of the Teamster establishment toward interference by outsiders. In a display of naïveté, Fox told Nader that if he did the job properly, PROD should self-destruct after two years. He assumed that the Teamsters Union would take over PROD.

At thirty, Fox had longish brown hair, in the style of the period, along with an appreciation of opera and a knowledge of gourmet cooking and eating. Yet he had the remarkable ability to look tatooed truckers in the eye and win their trust.[15]

At the outset, he was a one-man organization. He filed rule-making petitions with government agencies on hours of work, truck noise, and the maintenance of vehicles. He wrote Op-Ed pieces. He got statements about the horrors facing truck drivers on the roads entered into the *Congressional Record*.

The rank and filers willing to get involved with Fox needed

his skills as a lawyer as much as his energies as a safety advocate. He found truck drivers afraid to drive dangerous trucks but unable to refuse unless they were willing to risk the loss of their jobs. The union did little or nothing for them.

Fox won the drivers' confidence by taking on the union and the NLRB on behalf of Jim Banyard, a city driver in Cleveland, and Clay Ferguson, an over-the-road driver in North Carolina. Banyard had been fired for refusing to drive an overloaded truck. The union/industry grievance panel upheld his discharge. Ferguson went through a similar experience when he refused to take out a Roadway truck whose fifth wheel was loose. The fifth wheel is the link that connects the trailer to the tractor rig that pulls it. Ferguson, a member of North Carolina Local 391 headed by R. V. Durham, was fired, and again the union/industry grievance panel upheld his discharge. Fox found that the language in Teamster contracts said it was okay to violate the law.

Both drivers filed charges with the NLRB, which refused to issue complaints on the usual grounds that their union had represented them properly.

Fox researched federal labor law, coming up with the sophisticated legal theory that Banyard and Ferguson were standing up not only for their own safety but for all drivers. He took their cases back to the NLRB under a provision that had lain fallow, a definition of concerted activity. Fox sued the NLRB and beat the agency in the courts. Ferguson and Banyard were reinstated with back pay.

Those victories were like recruiting posters for PROD. Teamsters sent in their annual dues of twenty dollars with the expectation that the money would turn out a labor lawyer for them if they needed one.[16]

TEAMSTER DEMOCRACY AND FINANCIAL RESPONSIBILITY

In 1975, two forces ratcheted PROD toward an expanded mission: the hiring of a young law school student, John Sikorski, and the membership.

A Harvard graduate who had just completed his first year at the prestigious New York University Law School, the twenty-two-year-old Sikorski had a Teamster background and a deep-seated distaste for exploitive union bosses. He had decided to take a year off from school to work with Fox.

During summer vacations from Harvard, Sikorski had worked as a member of two different Teamster locals in his hometown, Cleveland. He spent two summers on a moving van and two more as a dockworker for Yellow Freight. During the school year, he unloaded trucks as a member of Teamsters Local 25 of Boston.

The husband of his mother's best friend had been a steelhauler and a member of the Fraternal Association of Steel Haulers (FASH), an organization primarily of owner-operators, formed after a bitter strike in 1967 to improve their representation by the Teamsters. Eventually, FASH split from the Teamsters to form an independent organization. Sikorski was fascinated by FASH. His family friend kept him current by sending him FASH literature when he was away at college.

On campus, Sikorski wore his Teamster jacket, got the Teamster magazine, and hung out with labor economists. Every Thursday afternoon he sat in on the seminars at Harvard's Trade Union Leaders training program.

Sikorski's first assignment as a summer intern from Fox was to work on a project designed to come up with proposals for the 1976 National Master Freight Agreement. Sikorski produced a study that punctured the myth that the Teamsters were the highest-paid blue-collar workers in the nation. The steelworkers, the coal miners, and the autoworkers not only earned higher wages, but received better fringe benefits, too. That was an embarrassing revelation, but it was Sikorski's research in another area that was to have a lasting impact on the Teamsters.

On July 22–24, 1975, *Wall Street Journal* investigative reporter Jonathan Kwitney turned out a three-part series on the rip-off of the Teamsters' Central States Pension Fund by organized crime figures and Teamster insiders. Kwitney had obtained the pension fund's secret ledger of loans, a document that showed that 89 percent of the fund's $917 million in assets was invested or firmly committed to real estate loans as of February 22, 1972. He discovered that about a third of the loans were delinquent and that the borrowers read like the guest list from a mob convention.

Buried at the bottom of the second day's installment of the Kwitney series was a paragraph that leaped out at Sikorski:

. . . Jackie Presser, William's son, who has been appointed fund trustee in his father's place, who now earns about $200,000 a year from various teamster and other union jobs, and who reportedly was once president of a company that borrowed $1.2 million from the fund to open a bowling alley in Cleveland and defaulted on the debt.

Sikorski, who had grown up in Cleveland, had always had a revulsion for the Pressers, father and son, particularly when reading about the deference paid them by politicians despite their mob-tinged backgrounds. He decided he would like to determine if Jackie Presser's multiple salaries were part of a pattern. "Our members were telling us safety is fine but there is a more fundamental problem, the sellouts and the corruption. We realized we had to become more political and get involved in more of these issues," Sikorski explained.

Then something else electrifying happened: Jimmy Hoffa disappeared on July 30—within a week of the final installment of Kwitney's exposé of the misuse of the Central States Pension Fund. No one doubted that the mob, wanting to protect its access to the pension funds' treasure trove, had erased the tough, ebullient Hoffa, whom the membership worshiped. Sikorski was so excited by the rush of events that summer, the significant work he was engaged in, and the bravery of the Teamster dissidents he met that he decided to continue working for PROD for a full year.

Fox told Sikorski to go ahead with his probe into multiple salaries.

Sikorski came up with a list of prominent officials from the Proceedings of the 1971 Teamsters Convention and the crooked ones culled from Bobby Kennedy's book *The Enemy Within*. He then found his way to North 4677, the public disclosure room for union financial reports, in the Department of Labor building in Washington.

The research took him far beyond his original short list. He spent five to six hours a day for seven months scribbling names and numbers onto five-by-eight orange index cards. "I remember getting fascinated when the first ones added up to $100,000," Sikorski said. "But the airplanes really blew me away. I couldn't believe the amount of money being spent on airplanes."

As he became more skilled at delving into Labor Department

records, he ordered the by-laws of the various Teamster entities, the rules by which unions are run. In these, he discovered that so-called leaders had legalized the perks of exhorbitant allowances and expense accounts and fat multiples pensions. The revelations infuriated him.

His experience as a working Teamster and his conversations with older workers who expressed fears over whether they ever would collect pensions drove Sikorski.

"I remember a couple of conversations in the dock room at Yellow about old-timers getting screwed out of pensions. Almost a hush would come over the break room, with the older guys getting very nervous and worried about their pensions. . . . I had unloaded trucks on the four-to-eleven shift in the summer after the sun beat down on them, making them into ovens, and I had worked in winters in the bitter cold in Boston. That pension money was theirs. I remember talking to my mother's friend in the steel haulers about the long hours they put in. When I found out about these high salaries and the Teamster air force, that got me furious," Sikorski said.

Sikorski's effort turned up dozens of Teamsters whose names appeared on the financial reports of several different union payrolls. He documented in detail a dirty little expensive secret: While Presser was among the greediest, multiple salaries and multiple pensions were commonplace among the officials and bureaucrats in the upper reaches of Teamster power. This was a potential bombshell.

Another thing Sikorski found was that almost 40 percent of the Teamster locals weren't bothering to file their annual financial reports—and the Labor Department was doing nothing to enforce the law requiring the reports.

Having amassed all the information, Sikorski faced the problem of figuring out how to use it. Fox came up with the idea of a book with detailed appendices. Sikorski did a draft that Fox then polished. Their report, *Teamster Democracy and Financial Responsibility*, documented not only the salaries and perks of a vast array of Teamster leaders but their organized crime ties and criminal records, including convictions for selling out union contracts to employers for kickbacks and thefts of union funds. Reflecting Sikorski's roots, the Pressers were singled out for particular attention in a chapter on Cleveland.

Fox had the book printed at a union shop in northern Virginia in April 1976, just in time to begin distributing it before the IBT's quinquennial convention that June. He obtained a $3,500 grant from the Field Foundation, enough money to send three copies to every local union.

Along with the books and a brief cover letter, Fox included a list of suggested amendments to the Teamsters' constitution designed to reform the union. The amendments called for an end to multiple salaries, a cap on how much a Teamster official could be paid, the direct election of all officers from the general president on down, and the separate ratification of local or regional supplements to national contracts by the members affected by them.

The press gave *Teamster Democracy and Financial Responsibility* the due that Fox and Sikorski anticipated. "The *L.A. Times* and the *Chicago Tribune* did banner headlines: Teamsters Corruption Unveiled," Fox said. "There wasn't any newspaper that didn't carry that story. On the airplane going out to the convention, I flew from here to Chicago to Las Vegas, and one out of every four people had my book open on his lap."

A BAD YEAR FOR FITZ

To a stirring rendition of *When the Saints Go Marching In*, General President Frank Fitzsimmons led the hierarchy of IBT onto the dais at the Las Vegas Convention Center on the morning of June 14, 1976, to open the union's twenty-first convention.

Fitz, as everyone called the jowly sixty-eight-year-old ex-dock-worker from Detroit, who now chummed around with presidents of the United States, was steaming. He had been through a hard winter and spring. First the dissident TDC had picketed the Marble Palace in January; then they forced him to stage the first nationwide trucking strike. It lasted only three days, but was long enough to win a three-year contract, with a $1.65-an-hour pay hike and a full cost-of-living-adjustment clause. But TDC didn't let go. They ran a wildcat strike in Detroit for another five days, and when it was over, they had won eight convention delegate slots in the election in Fitz's home union, Local 299.[17] Even then the turmoil didn't let up. "NBC Nightly News" ran an unflattering five-part series on the Teamsters, followed in May by front-page stories across the country based on PROD's report *Teamster Democracy and Financial Responsibility.*

On the eve of the convention, thirty-five rank-and-file activists who had assumed leadership roles in TDC met in Cleveland to change the name of their organization to Teamsters for a Democratic Union (TDU) and to expand their mission from getting a better contract into a national reform movement to rid the union of gangsterism and corruption.

As irritating as the media and dissidents could be, Fitz had deeper problems on his mind. Just two weeks before the convention, the Labor Department had served subpoenas on him and several other trustees of the Central States Pension Fund. That was serious stuff.

In his opening remarks to the twenty-three hundred delegates, he delivered his famous lines:

"Yes, we have had setbacks. We'll have them in the future, possibly. But for those who think and those who would say it is time to reform this organization, that it is time that the officers quit selling out the membership of this union, I say, Go to hell!"[18]

The delegates cheered.

Fitz was followed to the microphone by U.S. Secretary of Labor William J. Usery, Jr., who had some friendly words of his own to offer the crowd. "Let me assure you that even though I don't have a Teamsters' card, I belong to this club, because I believe in it. . . . I was delighted when my friend and your president, Frank Fitzsimmons, asked me to take part in the twenty-first convention of the International Brotherhood of Teamsters."[19]

Within a month, Usery would be sitting before the Senate Subcommittee on Labor, which was investigating irregularities in the Central States Pension Fund, trying to explain away his reference to Fitz as a friend and his membership in the Teamsters' club.

In his state of the union address, Fitz did PROD and Arthur Fox the favor of attacking them, putting them on center stage in the press and in the minds of the delegates. "I ask the question of Arthur Fox and his organization of PROD, as I said this morning, Who in the hell appointed them to act as the Teamster conscience? . . . This self-styled savior of the Teamsters, Arthur

Fox Esquire, he is a lawyer, you know, really never worked at a craft which entitled him to a Teamster or any other trade-union membership."

Then Fitz told his audience how he got where he was: "I didn't work my way up through a rump group or dual unionism. I came up through the system, which is our constitution, which is good enough for you and me. And by all that is holy, it's good enough for a watch pocket half full of malcontents. So much for PROD."

He also alerted them indirectly to the latest probes of the Central States Pension Fund. "Now comes that old workhorse, the Central States Pension Plan. It has been whipped with adverse publicity over the past two decades and has been investigated by every Dick Tracy in the land. But it just keeps plodding along, paying one of the highest benefits to retirees of any negotiated pension plan in the land.

"Yet old Central States Pension Plan is accused of poor investments. If you believe the news stories, all the money not lost in poor investments has been looted, and retirees haven't been paid in years."[20]

Little did Fitz realize that within a year the Internal Revenue Service would force him and the entire board of trustees of the Central States Pension Fund to resign and the U.S. Labor Department would bring the court action that placed the multibillion-dollar assets under professional money managers in an effort to prevent the mobsters and insiders from looting so much that there wouldn't be any money left to pay pension benefits.

As much as he would have liked to put PROD behind him, Fitz had to endure a motion by Pete Camarata, a Local 299 shop steward, to put ceilings on the salaries of the general executive board (GEB) limiting the president to $100,000 a year, the secretary-treasurer to $70,000, and the vice presidents to $60,000. Camarata could barely get his motion on the record with all the catcalls and boos. The motion was defeated. Instead, the delegates raised the top officers' salaries 25 percent.

When the time came for electing officers, Fitz and the rest of the GEB, all running unopposed, were elected by acclamation. Then Camarata rose to say he wanted to go on record as the one dissenting vote. The move was rejected by Fitz as being after the fact.

That evening, Camarata went with Steve Kindred and another Teamster dissident to a convention party at the Aladdin Hotel. As he was leaving the building, Camarata was hit from behind, knocked unconscious, and stomped. Kindred suffered two dislocated shoulders in the fracas. Frank Fitzsimmons was standing about fifteen feet away, watching the beating.[21]

TWO NATIONAL REFORM MOVEMENTS

Ken Paff and Steve Kindred's work in TDC and Arthur Fox and John Sikorski's efforts on behalf of PROD laid the foundations for the emergence of two separate—and competing—national reform movements in the fall of 1976: PROD and TDU. While there always had been dissent in the Teamsters at the local level, the new reformers had a broader vision of changing the union through the strategy of forming local chapters working under the umbrella of a national organization with a purposeful philosophy.

Over the 1976 Labor Day weekend, seventy-four PROD leaders from around the country met to formally transform their organization from one pressing for trucking safety into a full-fledged, grass-roots-based reform group aimed at democratizing the Teamsters and eliminating corruption from the giant union. As part of the new look, Sikorski, putting off his return to law school for another year, became PROD's executive director. Fox remained as the organization's legal counsel.

A couple of weeks later, on September 18 and 19, 1976, two hundred rank-and-file Teamsters from forty-four locals around the country gathered at Kent State University for the founding convention of TDU. On the opening day, Jackie Presser, the Teamsters' foremost business unionist and red-baiter, led a demonstration outside the site. Most of Presser's 125 or so demonstrators were Teamster retirees he had brought from a breakfast meeting that morning. Kindred recalled that the demonstration was a flop, because TDUers defused the crowd's hostility by going outside to discuss the extensive corruption and draining of the pension plan, an issue that concerned the retirees. "Jackie didn't like that very much," Kindred said.

Several of TDU's originators came out of the student and activist movements of the 1960s, making them targets for red-baiters trying to undermine the reform movement. While Kindred and Paff had a grounding in socialism, they crafted an organization whose goal of transforming the Teamsters into a decent, progressive union appealed to rank and filers of every political stripe. Confronting the left-wing issue at the time of the Kent State convention, Kindred told a reporter: "I'd be a fool to use TDU for socialist politics, because it would stay very small. I want it to be very big." He said, "I speak for guys in Little Rock, Arkansas, who know what my political views are and wish I didn't have them. Some of us are young radicals; some of us are old conservatives. We get along pretty good because we've got a job to do."

Paff said that the 1960s gave him and his cohorts certain qualities that helped them from the outset and through the intervening years.

> We knew how to put out a newspaper. We had an idealism. When I think about my early contributions to TDU, they seem pretty simple, but they were damned important at the time. The primary one was to tell the truth. If you had a meeting and there were twenty people there, these old-timers would want to say two hundred people. I would say, "You can't do that. It's bullshit." And they would say, "Well, nobody will know we were lying." I would say, "The twenty people would know, and they're our friends. Our own friends won't believe us anymore, and they are the most important twenty people in the whole, wide world." I won that argument.

Fox traced the tenacity of Paff and Kindred, in their quest for a better Teamsters Union, to their fervor. "They are real ideologues. Their religion is worker justice," Fox said.

TDU's publication, *Convoy*, was to become the newspaper of record for the Teamsters, the place where contracts were given a hard analysis and the significant happenings at both the local and international levels were examined, exposed, and reported. *Convoy* was in sharp contrast to the incestuous puffery and bowling pictures of the IBT's official magazine, the *International Teamster*.

61

A HARBINGER OF THE RICO SUIT

In a move that presaged the underlying elements of the Justice Department's civil RICO case, not to be filed for another decade, Arthur Fox brought internal union charges in April 1977 against Frank Fitzsimmons, demanding his removal as general president of the IBT.

Fox accused Fitzsimmons of nine major offenses, including permitting union pension funds to be looted, associating with mob figures, nepotism, and wasting union money. "We said Fitz was guilty of nepotism, multiple salaries—hear no evil, see no evil. Guilty of corruption in every sense of the word."

The union was forced by its constitution to empanel a hearing board, which dismissed the case as unfounded, but Fox accomplished his minimum goal of keeping pressure on Fitzsimmons and the government to do something about the glaring scandal that the union had become.

In 1979, PROD ended three years of competition with TDU for the same pool of members. The two organizations merged under the TDU banner. Sikorski already had left to finish his law degree, while Fox stayed on as TDU's Washington lawyer.

Over the following years TDUers occasionally won control of a local union, but its first major national triumph didn't come until 1983, when Jackie Presser tried to ram through a concessionary extension to the National Master Freight Agreement.

On July 6, 1983, three months after he had been named the IBT's general president, Presser called the union's National Freight Negotiating Committee, composed of local leaders from across the country, to Chicago to present them with a "rider" to the existing national contract. The rider supposedly was designed to save union jobs by slashing as much as 31 percent of the pay and benefits of workers rehired after a layoff. A survey had shown that 100,000 of the 300,000 Teamsters covered by the national freight agreement were on layoff.

In what was like a scene from a top-secret Pentagon briefing, the union leaders were given copies of the "Voluntary Laid-off Employees Relief Rider" to read on the spot. At the end of the meeting, every copy was carefully collected. But not carefully enough. One was stolen, and within a week Ken Paff was reading a copy of it at TDU's headquarters in Detroit.

TDU revealed the details of the agreement and the plans to hold a mail ballot on it in August in an "emergency bulletin," distributed across North America wherever truck drivers gathered. Presser had always branded the dissident group as liars and provocateurs. When the "emergency bulletin" proved to be absolutely accurate, TDU's credibility soared even among its enemies.

TDU's position was that the Presser deal wouldn't save jobs; it would simply result in a two-tier union, with thousands of experienced workers getting paid a lot less than co-workers for doing the same job.

In the midst of the fury over the secret deal, TDU released its annual "$100,000 Club" listing the Teamster leaders and their children who were drawing large incomes from multiple union positions. Jackie Presser, who made $394,895 in 1982, added another $170,000 to his income by becoming general president—an increase of 43 percent to $565,000 a year.

Local union meetings, called to discuss the vote on the rider, turned into rallies against the agreement, with 400 members of Columbus Local 413 and 500 members of Cleveland Local 407 voting unanimously at their gatherings to demand Presser's resignation.

"Even many officers who normally bump their noses when Presser stops short are afraid to endorse this sell-out," TDU said in the September 1983 issue of *Convoy*.

Presser put his prestige on the line in a vigorous campaign to win acceptance of the proposal, which he argued would save and even produce needed union jobs. In the mail ballot, counted on September 16, the members rejected the "rider"—Presser's first sally as a national negotiator—by 94,086 to 13,082.

Paff remarked caustically: "It showed how badly our millionaire president is out of touch with Teamster members."

———

Arthur Fox said in retrospect, "Every revolution has a philosopher and a general. I like to describe myself as the philosopher. I basically wrote the blueprint—that a union has an affirmative duty to clean house."

No one would dispute the fact that Ken Paff was the general of the reform movement, the central strategist in a guerrilla campaign that spanned four Teamster presidencies—Fitzsimmons, Williams, Presser, and McCarthy. During that long struggle, TDU would evolve from being a lone voice of dissent, in the shape of Pete Camarata at the 1976 convention, to a major force in the union's first rank-and-file election for the general president in 1991.

4

The Racketeering Case Surfaces

Early in 1987, Randy Kehrli moved his Teamster RICO team into the offices once occupied by the Watergate investigators in the District of Columbia courthouse. The symbolism of establishing his headquarters in this historic space for the unprecedented racketeering case against the Teamsters wasn't lost on Kehrli.

Once he had assembled his crew—including attorneys Peter Sprung and Diane DeForrest from the Justice Department's Organized Crime and Racketeering Section, investigator Mike Moroney from the Labor Department, and the FBI's Liberatus Squad—Kehrli ordered a mind-boggling array of records.[22] He asked the Labor Department to assemble the financial reports of the International Brotherhood of Teamsters (IBT) dating back to 1972, along with those of 111 Teamster locals, sixteen joint councils, and five area conferences. In addition, he wanted a list of all Teamster officials and organized crime figures who had testified before Congress since 1956.

And that was only the Labor Department. There would be additional requests for massive piles of documents from the FBI files and for criminal and civil court records from cities across the nation.

While it would be expensive and time-consuming, all of the data would be fed into computers in order to get a handle on the enormous mass of names and crimes and financial data.

Kehrli, a thoughtful man who used the brainstorming technique in search of solutions, had become convinced that a rank-

and-file election of the Teamsters' top officers was the answer to ending the mob's grip on the huge union. That was the approach favored by Teamsters for a Democratic Union (TDU).

When the first inkling of the RICO suit surfaced in the fall of 1986, newspaper accounts predicted the Teamster leadership would be replaced by court-appointed trustees. Ken Paff of TDU reacted by writing to Assistant Attorney General Stephen Trott urging the Justice Department to use democracy to reform the Teamsters. Instead of imposing a court-appointed czar to run the union, Paff pleaded for government-supervised rank-and-file elections of IBT officers.

"It is easy to see how rank-and-file elections under government supervision will remove or drastically reduce the influence of organized crime. With 1.6 million voters spread all over the United States and Canada, organized crime simply cannot control the outcome, at least if these voters believe there is a secret ballot," Paff said in his letter.

Pointing to the United Mine Workers as a model, Paff said that the rank and file in that union threw out the "rascals" when given the opportunity of government-supervised elections. "IBT members are no different from other American voters. They do not reelect felons, or potential felons, if they have confidence in the secrecy of the ballot," Paff said, adding that in the past national IBT leaders shrugged off negative stories in the press, since the union's election process effectively insulated them from the ire of the members.

As the months passed, concerns began to emerge in the upper echelons of the Justice Department that the way Kehrli was putting together the Teamster RICO case might take years and cost millions of dollars. The tenacious Rudy Giuliani, who had kept tabs on Kehrli's progress, seized this opportunity. He told his old friend Deputy Attorney General Arnold Burns that the U.S. Attorney's office in New York could handle the Teamsters case faster and less expensively than the Kehrli operation.

In the midst of renewed turf war for the case, on June 10, 1987, *Los Angeles Times* reporters Ronald J. Ostrow and Robert L. Jackson broke the story of the Justice Department's plan to use a massive civil RICO suit to take over the IBT.

The *Times* story emphasized not the democracy solution that Paff was pressing but the point that the entire General Executive Board (GEB) of the IBT including Jackie Presser, would be forced out of office if the Justice Department lawyers had their way. The story erred on only one point: "The suit would be filed by Joseph E. diGenova, the U.S. Attorney for the District of Columbia, sources involved in the case said." That line was fed to Ostrow and Jackson either in the belief that it was true or in an attempt to use the story, which was distributed all over the United States through the *Washington Post/Los Angeles Times* wire service, to pressure Justice Department policymakers too keep the case in Washington.

The revelation that the RICO case was coming soon didn't startle Presser as much as arouse him. He had been expecting it for months and had warned the IBT's legal, legislative, governmental affairs, and communications departments to be ready with a counterattack charging that the government was trying to take over a free trade union as a prelude to destroying organized labor.

The union telegraphed the stance it would take in response to the RICO action, which no one in the Justice Department would officially admit was in the works. The press release, put out under the name of Duke Zeller, the IBT's communications director, said: "Organized crime has never, does not today and never will control the International Union. . . . Takeovers of unions are nothing new—Communists and Fascists have been doing so for decades. However, it is a sad day in the history of the United States and the American labor movement when such tactics are employed."

GIULIANI WINS ANOTHER ONE

On August 19, 1987, Deputy Attorney General Arnold Burns formally shifted the Teamster RICO suit to Giuliani in New York, where the focus would be the removal of the GEB and the imposition of a court-appointed trustee to run the 1.6-million-member union.

The Kehrli team was stunned by the transfer. Kehrli, Sprung, DeForrest, and Mike Moroney went to the bar of the Marriott Hotel on Pennsylvania Avenue to lament and rant over the loss of the biggest case of their lives. After all of their hard work, the New Yorkers were taking the prize because their boss, Dave Margolis, the swaggering, cowboy-boot-wearing chief of the Organized Crime and Racketeering Section, couldn't swing enough political weight to keep Rudy Giuliani at bay. They couldn't criticize Giuliani, who had compiled such a stellar record against organized crime. He was a winner, and he had won another one.

Moroney's gloom lifted quickly when Randy Mastro, recognizing Moroney's expertise, asked him for his suggestions on the direction the case should go. In response, Moroney prepared a memo stressing his position that a government takeover of the Teamsters would be wrong and wouldn't work. "Government, no matter how good its intentions, is not capable of running an international union with over seven hundred affiliates. The awful, recent experience of a trustee's attempts to run Teamsters Local 560 should be sufficient to support this argument," the memo said.

Moroney's memo contained a series of recommendations that would later prove influential. It called for Labor Department–supervised rank-and-file elections of International Teamster officers in accordance with the concept of one member/one vote; a court-appointed monitor to oversee all IBT financial transactions; and a court-appointed special counsel with a staff to investigate organized crime influences and corruption at every level of the union, from the locals to the International in Washington, and to seek the removal of the guilty under the appropriate provisions of the Teamsters' constitution through either the GEB or a federal court. The cleansing process would include all those with serious criminal records as well as members and associates of organized crime. It would eliminate nepotism, multiple paychecks from several different union positions, and severance-pay deals for those terminated because of criminal convictions or defeat in elections.

Mastro's request for recommendations from Moroney inadvertently sparked an internal squabble in the Labor Department's Office of Labor Racketeering (OLR). The glitch occurred when Raymond Maria, the deputy inspector general in charge of the OLR, attempted to block the distribution of the Moroney memo. Maria took the position that Moroney's role should be limited to turning in facts, not issuing what amounted to a policy-position paper. "Under no circumstances should you represent the memorandum is a policy statement of OLR. I further instruct you not to disseminate this memorandum to anyone outside OLR, including Department of Justice attorneys or other law enforcement agencies," Maria said in a memo to Moroney.

Moroney reacted by resigning. His memo found its way to Mastro and its underlying concepts emerged in the final settlement of the Justice Department's RICO suit two years later.

THE IBT TRIES TO HEAD OFF THE RICO

The coffee shop in the Delta Terminal at New York's La Guardia Airport was filled with Teamsters early on the morning of September 15, 1987. Many of them were wearing distinctive blue jackets with Teamsters Union insignias.

Robert Sasso, president of Local 282, whose members deliver concrete and construction supplies for building sites in New York City and Long Island, said what was on everyone's minds at the table where he was sitting: "It's un-American. That's for sure."

This airport scene was being repeated all over the United States, wherever there were Teamsters, and there are Teamsters everywhere. This was the day they were flying into Cincinnati for what the IBT was billing as an unprecedented gathering of the backbone of the union, the leaders from seven hundred Teamster locals. Every Teamster local has an executive board composed of seven persons: the president, the secretary-treasurer, the vice president, the recording secretary, and three trustees. All had been urged to be in the Cincinnati Convention Center for a crucial grass-roots conference in search of answers to the "totalitarian attack on the free trade union movement in America." To ensure a response, the bureaucratic machinery of the giant union had been put into play to contact every local union and to ask whether its executive board members were coming to Cincinnati. Such a question could be taken as an order coming from the Marble Palace.

The September 15 conference had been called as part of the aggressive strategy Jackie Presser's brain trust had plotted as a counterattack since learning about the coming Justice Department civil racketeering suit against the IBT.

John Climaco, the union's general counsel and Presser's personal attorney for many years, used the August 3, 1987, national conference of the Teamster Warehouse Division in San Diego to describe the strategy the union would pursue: an all-out effort to abort the RICO suit.

Climaco told the gathering of four hundred Teamster officials:

> Now, I love to fight, and I'm up to any good legal battle. But I want this battle to end without one lawyer walking into a courtroom. How can you stop your international union from being taken over by the government? You must convince leaders in government and Congress that this must not be allowed to happen in America.
>
> The Department of Justice leak about this proposed lawsuit was intentional. It was intended to place pressure on opinion makers in the administration in an attempt to begin a groundswell movement within the media and the general public to make it politically difficult for anyone to refuse authorization to institute this unprecedented and undemocratic civil RICO action.
>
> But this is not just a Teamster issue. It's a direct attack on the American free trade union movement.

Barry Feinstein, the New York Teamster leader, then fine-tuned the strategy for the audience by describing the special meeting to be convened in Cincinnati the following month. "The grass-roots strength of the union is in your hometown and in your home state. That is where we must go to fight the fight. Rank-and-file members make us strong, and that is where we must turn with this problem."

Two weeks later, the Teamster campaign got a boost from the AFL-CIO's policy-setting Executive Council, which passed a resolution on August 19 urging the government to stick to the prosecution of corrupt individuals and to leave the Teamsters as an institution alone. "There is no valid law enforcement justification for intricate and contrived stratagems whose purpose is to make it easy for the government to take control of unions composed of thousands of honest, hard-working trade unionists. And there can be no doubt that government supervision is synonymous with the destruction of free trade unions, not with their salvation," the resolution said. Thirty years earlier, the AFL-CIO had expelled the Teamsters from the federation because of the aura of corruption under Jimmy Hoffa.

While the Justice Department's court attack on the IBT was

jelling, AFL-CIO president Lane Kirkland and the rest of the federation's hierarchy were well aware that three of their own presumably were on the government's hit list: the International Longshoremen's Association, the Laborers International Union of North America, and the Hotel Employees and Restaurant Employees Union. Along with the Teamsters, those unions had been listed as mob influenced in the 1986 report of the President's Commission on Organized Crime. With rare exceptions, international union leaders refrain from criticizing corruption and violence against members in other international unions; the de facto club doesn't work that way.

Policy statements of the AFL-CIO are not taken lightly in Washington, where the federation's political machinery is well respected and has helped propel representatives and senators of both parties into office.

Presser appointed Barry Feinstein the national coordinator of the campaign to kill the impending RICO suit. Although he came from a city that housed organized crime's ruling national commission, a city where it wasn't unusual to find crime-family soldiers and their relatives openly running Teamster locals, Feinstein had developed an unsullied reputation as an influential factor in New York politics. Feinstein, like his father before him, headed Local 237, which represents twelve thousand public employees in New York City and Long Island.

A towering man and a fierce advocate of whatever cause he is pursuing, Feinstein said in an interview a few days after the AFL-CIO statement was issued, "Can you imagine a trustee appointed by this government, some cop running this union, deciding what we will demand when we sit down at the bargaining table with the trucking industry or UPS? Deciding whether we will or will not organize a major corporation that makes contributions to this White House? We're talking about a 1.7-million-member organization under the control of a czar."

Either blindly loyal or assuming that posture, Feinstein had flared when asked his response to documented charges that Presser was an FBI informant: "Jackie has already said, 'Suck my prick.' ... Leaks in the Justice Department's prostate system amazes me. We don't pay any attention to fairy-tale stories, unsubstantiated stories, leaks, those things intended to exacerbate a situation. We don't pay any attention."

On the morning of September 15, 1987, almost four thousand

Teamsters turned out from union halls across the country and filled the Cincinnati Convention Center to overflowing amid banners emblazoned with the slogan ". . . And Justice for all. Even Teamsters." Barry Feinstein had wanted to hold the gathering in Chicago but cõuldn't line up the facilities needed on such short notice.

National politicians also responded to the Teamster call. Democratic presidential hopeful Jesse Jackson and Republican candidates Alexander Haig and Jack Kemp were on the stage with Jackie Presser, a blue Teamster cap perched on his head to hide his thinning hair, a side effect of the treatments to quell his cancer. Another aspiring presidential candidate, Sen. Paul Simon, the Illinois Democrat, sent a videotaped message of support, as did Presser's friend, Sen. Orrin Hatch, the Utah Republican considered a conservative antiunionist by labor leaders.

The crowd rose to its collective feet, cheering and applauding, in response to a Jackson speech bite created for the occasion: "Bust unions; discredit union leaders; now take over unions. Teamsters: you are the starting point!"

"A union is in jeopardy. The entire labor movement is in jeopardy," Presser said, describing the audience as soldiers in the struggle to back down the government. "I'm strong. I don't have cancer. I'm healing. I lost a lung. I lost a rib. But I'm in for the long haul," Presser said in words of reassurance. Although he managed to get through most of the afternoon without faltering, Presser left early, worn by his illness, leaving Feinstein to deliver the central message of the day. "We must mobilize our membership as never before," Feinstein shouted, "in a hurricane of protest that will shake the very foundations of a Justice Department out of control."

Feinstein sent the Teamsters back to their locals across America with a checklist of goals: to have members send letters to Congress by the thousands, to get signatures for protest petitions from hundreds of thousands, to form women's groups in each local for the fight, and to press their local congressional representatives to go on record against the takeover of the Teamsters. "We need our rank-and-file members to participate in this. We're going to ask all of our 1.7 million members to sign a petition," Feinstein said, emphasizing that the petitions, weighing hundreds of pounds, would be delivered to Ronald Reagan at the

White House so he would have a clear understanding of how everyone in the union felt.

"If we ain't together, we are dead," Feinstein thundered, urging the Teamsters to build a coalition with AFL-CIO unions for a war on the Justice Department. "We want this grass-roots movement across the country," he concluded in parting.

The concept underlying the strategy of using the labor movement's rank and file to cut off the Justice Department action was a valid one. It might have worked had the mass of unionized American workers been aroused enough to respond with a self-generated enthusiasm, filling the streets and frightening the nation's establishment. But that didn't happen. The top-down effort didn't even arouse the lethargic rank and file of the Teamsters, no less the entire labor movement. American workers didn't feel threatened. Neither did the leaders of most unions at the Washington or local levels.

THE IBT RETURNS TO THE AFL-CIO

At the GEB's quarterly meeting in Greenleaf, Florida, that October, Jackie Presser surprised the Teamster hierarchy by suddenly saying he had been negotiating a return to the AFL-CIO.

A bitter debate followed, with William J. McCarthy, then a vice president, leading the opposition to rejoining the House of Labor, as the AFL-CIO is called. McCarthy had no use for the federation. The motion to reaffiliate with the AFL-CIO was passed by a majority vote—with only McCarthy voting against.[23]

The Teamsters ended thirty years of isolation from the AFL-CIO at the end of October. Insiders ascribed the motives for returning to the federation to a desire by Presser to end his career with a positive achievement by reuniting the labor movement; the more cynical claimed he was trying to buy the federation's support for the fight with the government. The reunion meant $6 million a year in new dues for the AFL-CIO treasury.

Presser's homecoming speech at the November 1987 AFL-CIO convention in Miami Beach demonstrated that he was moving into his final days. Wearing his baseball-style Teamsters cap to hide his baldness, Presser delivered a brief, disjointed, confusing talk to the puzzled delegates.

At sixty-one, weighing in excess of three hundred pounds,

Presser not only had endured the unrelenting stress of Labor Department and Justice Department investigations and the anxiety of playing double agent for the FBI and the mob; he also had undergone two major operations within the past three years, a triple heart bypass operation in December 1984 and the removal of a cancerous growth and part of a lung in January 1987.

Duke Zeller, the Teamsters' communications director, told skeptical reporters after Presser's speech at the convention, "He has been cancer-free since that day." He attributed the Teamster president's baldness and obvious nausea to the aftereffects of chemotherapy and radiation treatments.

Whatever the state of Presser's reputation and deteriorating health, his administration tried to maintain the momentum to undermine the threatened RICO suit. Shortly before Christmas, the Teamsters delivered a letter signed by 246 House members, including 168 Democrats and 78 Republicans, to Attorney General Edwin Meese III. The signers urged the Justice Department "to consider carefully the options available to it and to reject those that are inconsistent with the overall national goal of fostering an independent and democratic union movement."

With Meese recusing himself from all Teamster matters because of his past political dealings with Presser and other members of the union's hierarchy, the case was now in the maws of the Justice Department system—and those handling it claimed that none of the pressure being applied by the Teamsters reached them.

MASTRO BRINGS THE CASE

Looking back, Randy Mastro said in a later interview,

> There was never a moment when political considerations were raised. There was never a moment when political considerations entered into the decision making on the case. I prepared the case, and the proposals we made on how to do the case were eventually adopted and endorsed not only by Rudy [Giuliani], but by the highest levels of DOJ.
>
> While there have been suggestions in the past of political pressure playing some role in what happened to the case, I can

tell you from the perspective of the government's lead attorney on the case that they played no role whatsoever. There is no question during the year leading up to the case there was a massive petition and letter-writing drive. There was some sort of petition where more than 240 congressmen signed. There was that poster.

He pointed to a copy of a Teamster poster on his office wall, which showed the name *Solidarnosc* crossed out, with *Teamsters* printed crudely in red beneath. It bore the caption "Takeovers of unions are nothing new—Communists and Fascists have been doing so for decades. It's a sad day in the history of the United States and the American labor movement when such tactics are even considered."

While the Teamsters were developing and putting into action their strategy to strangle the RICO case, Mastro was recruiting his team for what would be the biggest and most significant civil racketeering case ever filed against a union.

The first to sign on was Marla Alhadeff, a twenty-nine-year-old, who, in her year on Giuliani's staff, already was a veteran of a union RICO action, the case against the mob-dominated cement workers in New York City. She followed the typical pattern of an assistant U.S. Attorney in the Southern District. After graduating from Michigan Law School in 1982, Alhadeff went to work for Debevois and Plimpton, a major law firm in New York, before winning a prized spot on the Southern District staff. "The plan was always to come here, just because of the reputation for public service and aggressiveness," Alhadeff recalled. "I was conscripted to the Teamsters case much to my delight. Randy said, 'You want to work on this?' I said, 'You bet.'"

Mastro chose an approach of dividing the nation geographically. Assigned the Northeast, Alhadeff worked primarily with FBI agents William Jenkins and Stanley Nye. Alhadeff recalled:

It was like archaeology, digging up files from archives and clerk's offices. It was quite a job. . . . We started out by doing a lot of investigative work, pulling together the work other prosecutors across the country had done. We had to pull it together and analyze it and synthesize it. What we found many times were the same players. Repeat organized crime players. That's what these civil RICO cases are all about. The criminal remedies are ineffective because you get the son, the son-in-law, cronies, a nephew. . . . Just putting these guys in jail doesn't do the trick.

The only one recruited from Kehrli's Washington team was Peter Sprung. He had a firsthand view of Teamster corruption as the prosecutor who convicted Richard Fitzsimmons, the son of the former IBT president, on racketeering charges after an eight-month trial in Michigan. Sprung had just returned to the Washington office of the Organized Crime and Racketeering Section when Paul Coffey, the deputy chief of the section, assigned him to the Teamster RICO case. He spent almost a year traveling the country to gather evidence and witnesses, only to see the prize jerked to New York.

Unlike the others who worked on the project in Washington, Sprung was anxious to continue with the case, even if it took him to New York. According to Mastro, the twenty-nine-year-old prosecutor's reputation preceded him. "The FBI agents had spoken very highly of him, and we were fortunate to get him to come to New York," Mastro said. "He had learned a tremendous amount about the Teamsters."

Mastro assigned Sprung to examine the background of Teamster vice presidents Robert Holmes of Detroit and Daniel C. Ligurotis and Donald Peters, both of Chicago. Sprung turned in a dazzling performance by coming up with a devastating piece of evidence against Peters.

An FBI bug in Allen Dorfman's Chicago insurance office had produced damaging evidence used in several racketeering cases. Sprung knew that Joseph (Joey the Clown) Lombardo, a purported capo in the Chicago organized crime family, had had a series of conversations on December 21, 1979, with Dorfman and other insiders on the question of how to assure Roy Williams's succession to the presidency, since Frank Fitzsimmons was seriously ill with cancer. "I had a strong suspicion this was important stuff," Sprung said, and it was.

In the course of the taped conversation, Peters, then head of the largest local in the Teamsters, Chicago Local 743, discussed lining up votes for Williams with Allen Dorfman, the insurance man with mob ties, and Joey Lombardo. When Fitzsimmons died in 1981, Williams succeeded him as planned, and Peters was rewarded for his services with the vice presidency vacated by Williams.

Sprung knew that Peters could not plead naïveté about the backgrounds of Dorfman and Lombardo. Peters had been a trustee of the Central States Pension Fund from 1967 until he was forced to resign in 1976 amid the IRS and Labor Department investigations.

The Mastro team expanded to include Edward Ferguson III, the lead attorney on the Fulton Fish Market civil racketeering case, Alan Taffet, who also worked on the fish-market case, Richard Mark, and Steve Bennett.

THE SALERNO SETBACK

The unofficial deadline for producing the final civil RICO complaint against the Teamsters was the return of verdicts in the Genovese organized crime family case, known informally as Salerno II. There were two reasons. Giuliani didn't want the anticipated blast of publicity certain to be generated by the filing of the IBT civil RICO to be used by defense attorneys as an excuse for a mistrial in Salerno II. The chief target in Salerno II was Fat Tony Salerno, boss of the Genovese crime family.

The second reason was that Mastro expected the Salerno II jury to convict the crime boss and his allies of the charge of wire fraud—that is, telephone conversations—for arranging the election of first Roy Williams and then Jackie Presser as Teamster presidents. Mastro explained: "If you already had a jury finding beyond a reasonable doubt that Tony Salerno and other organized crime figures had done this, you had a pretty damned good chance of convincing a federal judge that as a matter of preliminary relief in the case he should assume those facts and grant appropriate relief accordingly."

Mastro anticipated a jury verdict in the Salerno II case sometime early in 1988. That gave the Mastro team about three to four months to prepare for the filing of the Teamster RICO case. "There was a lot of work to be done," Mastro recalled, "because our theory of the case was there had been two-hundred or more cases of Teamster corruption in the last ten years. We had to collect the relevant documents related to those cases and be prepared to produce them. We were targeting about ten cases involving the highest-level Teamster officials or highest-level organized crime figures for Teamster corruption. We were going to focus on the proofs in those cases."

But the enormously complex Genovese Crime Family/Salerno II case went on and on, dragging through January 1988 into February, March, and April, finally ending on May 4. Fat Tony Salerno and his cohorts were convicted, but the jury returned a "not guilty" verdict on the wire fraud charges involving the Williams and Presser elections.

The hierarchy of the IBT was ecstatic. True to his hard-hitting style, Teamster general counsel John Climaco put out a gleefully tough statement:

> For the past two years it has been widely reported, first through calculated media leaks and then through the use of innuendo and even perjured testimony, that the elections of Teamster general presidents Roy L. Williams and Jackie Presser had been engineered and manipulated by organized crime elements. Today that myth has been once and forever shattered by the jury verdict in the Salerno case in New York.
>
> General President Presser, General Secretary-Treasurer Weldon L. Mathis, and the entire General Executive Board are gratified by the jury's verdict, feel vindicated by its action, and are comforted by the fact that after over one year of testimony, this jury was able to accurately ferret out the truth.

Whatever pap he was putting out for public consumption, however, Climaco was too experienced a criminal lawyer to believe that the feds would fade away because of the setback at the Salerno II trial.

That same day, the terminally ill Presser, too sick to keep up the charade that he was still able to run the Teamsters, took a 120-day leave of absence as general president. No one expected him to be back. In accordance with the union constitution, Secretary-Treasurer Mathis temporarily assumed Presser's office, and almost immediately the public was treated to the first glimpse of an open crack in the Teamsters' general executive board's (GEB) traditional show of solidarity.

Mathis called a special executive board meeting for May 16 at a resort near Scottsdale, Arizona, assuring the vice presidents that they could get through the necessary business in ninety minutes and have the rest of the day for golf or whatever.

In an unprecedented affront, eight of the sixteen vice presidents failed to show up. Walter Shea's excuse was that his wife was undergoing an operation. New York vice president Joseph (Joe T) Trerotola, whose life is a study of Teamster decorum and politics, told New York Teamsters that he wasn't wasting his time flying to Arizona to play golf. His words sent an unmistakable signal that he was unalterably opposed to Mathis, whom he considered a lightweight. Underlying this mini-rebellion was the suspicion that Climaco was attempting to be a kingmaker by portraying Mathis as Jackie Presser's chosen successor. They believed Climaco engineered Presser's leave to assure Mathis's ascendancy by making him the de facto president.

Mathis looked around the meeting on May 16 in Scottsdale and jumped to a false conclusion—that those who had shown up were aligned with him. All he needed to succeed the dying Presser was nine votes. There were nine men in that room— eight vice presidents and he. His miscalculation would prove costly.

BILLY McCARTHY PLAYS POLITICS

Events began to move very quickly.

On June 10, 1988, Teamster lawyer John Climaco sat down with Rudy Giuliani in his Manhattan office in a dual effort to find out whether the RICO suit was still alive and to assure the Justice Department that there no longer was a need to take such a drastic and politically unpopular step. Climaco brought with him the assurance that Mathis would bring reforms and a new era to the Teamsters. Giuliani listened attentively but remained unmoved.[24]

Less than three weeks later, William J. McCarthy, the International vice president from Boston and a man with a reputation as streetwise and tough but with a penchant for clowning around, gathered eight other International vice presidents in his suite at the exclusive Ritz Carlton Hotel in Montreal, where the GEB was holding a regularly scheduled quarterly meeting. The gathering was to nail down the votes for McCarthy's bid for the presidency.

Walter Shea, himself hungry to be president, never expected to be throwing his vote to McCarthy. Even in the strange world of Teamster politics, McCarthy wasn't presidential timber. His hijinks were legend. When the 1961 convention was held in Miami, he grabbed an idle bus and drove it all over the city. At a bar in Hawaii, by McCarthy's own account, he dropped a lighted cigarette into the pocket of a very expensive jacket worn by a Japanese businessman. "Billy hates the Japanese," Shea said.[25]

Although McCarthy had been on the GEB for nineteen years, Shea and most of the others didn't pay enough attention to him to know what he was all about. McCarthy was somewhat of a loner whose primary friends on the board were Salvatore (Sammy Pro) Provenzano and, later, Theodore Cozza, the vice president from Pittsburgh. Sammy Pro and Cozza were high on the government's list of top Teamsters with heavy mob connections.

At sixty-nine, McCarthy, who generally was called Billy, his last name pronounced Ma-kart-ee, in the fashion favored by the Boston Irish, had fifty-two years in the Teamsters behind him. He had started driving an intercity truck in 1936 at the age of seventeen. He came to the national scene unknown outside of Boston, where he had a reputation as a fierce, almost wild political infighter, one who set out to destroy those who crossed him and created dedicated enemies almost with abandon.

Few survived conflicts with McCarthy. One rebel in McCarthy's Local 25 in Boston, George Cashman, had dared to win an election as delegate to the 1976 IBT Convention. On the night the ballots were counted, someone broke his leg in a brawl in the union hall. The assault only made Cashman more determined to tumble McCarthy.

The dark rumor in Boston was that McCarthy's rise to power in the local union was fostered by his friendship with the Winter Hill Gang, a mostly Irish-American crew of mobsters, some of whom were members of Local 25. By 1946, McCarthy was a business agent, a relatively low level local union official who processes members' grievances and enforces contracts; by 1955 he was president of Local 25. Frank Fitzsimmons made him an International vice president in 1969.

While Jackie Presser had whispered to his FBI handlers that McCarthy had a relationship with Raymond Patriarca, the boss of the New England crime family, McCarthy emphatically denounced that allegation as a lie. He certainly didn't endear himself to Italian-Americans when a recorded phone conversation revealed him making derogatory remarks about "dagos." The carelessly blunt McCarthy managed to offend Jews and women, too.

Shea had been negotiating the national car haul contract in Baltimore when McCarthy broached the subject of succeeding Presser. Shea got a phone call: "Walter, I want to run for president. I know you're running, too, but by God I'm gonna win, and I want your vote."

Shea recalled, "McCarthy promised me two things. One, I would be his executive assistant, and I would be doing a lot of the work, or most of the work, of running the union. And secondly, a pay increase, which he never gave me."

Hired into the Teamsters on April 27, 1957, Shea had risen through the bureaucracy to the edge of real power in the union. He had worked with Jimmy Hoffa on some of his national union problems and had become executive assistant to Frank Fitzsimmons in 1967 and subsequently to Roy Williams in 1981. During the Fitzsimmons and Williams eras he had achieved an unofficial position as de facto president of the Teamsters because of their lack of interest in the myriad details involved in the daily routine of running the union.

"I was so involved with the office of the president for all those years," Shea said. "When Fitz was there, he called me into his office one day. He says, 'Walter. I'm going to be out of the office a lot. I'm going to be traveling more.' He says, 'When I'm out of town, I want you to sit in this office and this chair and you are me. And don't bother me unless you have a question.' I never called him."

While Fitz was off golfing, Shea plunged into running a union that stretched into every corner of North America north of the Rio Grande.

I got involved with this thing. Not only with the job itself but the people in the building and the people in the field. You talk about busy—I mean, every goddamned scrap of paper that came in that office every day I went through it. Every precious scrap of paper. Petitions, subpoenas, lawsuits, complaints, requests for financial help, jurisdictional disputes. You name it. I sat there until his death doing everything that had to be done in that office.

Roy Williams, the next president. Same thing. Roy hated the job. He hated the town. He hated the politics. He should never have taken the job. He said, "Walter, I'm not going to be here. Anytime I'm not here you come up and run the office. Any questions, call me." Never called him. I didn't have to call him.

In 1982, Williams acknowledged Shea's central role in the operation of the Teamsters by appointing him an International vice president. Four years later, Shea won his first election as a Teamster the easy way when he arrived at the 1986 convention in Las Vegas as a candidate for International vice president on the incumbent hierarchy's slate. He was unopposed.

With Presser approaching his deathbed, Shea and his mentor, Joe Trerotola, set out in the spring of 1988 to line up the votes to make him the real general president of the Teamsters. They came close, but International vice presidents John H. Cleveland of Washington, D.C., and Maurice R. Schurr of Philadelphia aligned themselves with Mathis. That came as a surprise to Joe T, who had assumed the pair would follow his directions.

Shea explained, "I needed nine [votes]. I had seven because these two guys bolted. We thought we had the East lined up pretty good. John Cleveland would have voted for me for secretary-treasurer, but he wouldn't vote for me for president. Schurr was a very close personal friend of Mathis."

Unable to close the two-vote gap and since Trerotola despised Mathis, they decided to back McCarthy. Their decision obviously was fostered by the impression that McCarthy was malleable and that through their combined talents, Joe T as a master of Teamster politics and Shea as the accomplished administrator, they would end up in control of the union.

THE RICO CASE IS FILED

If any Teamsters had gotten the message from the Salerno trial verdict that the threat of the RICO suit was past, Mastro had a very unpleasant surprise in store. Recovering from his initial disappointment at the jury's acquittal on the Williams and Presser wire-fraud charges, Mastro adjusted the case. "Now we no longer had that hook," he recalled. "We had to do a helluva lot of work over the next month to revise the complaint and the papers."

On June 28, 1988, while Jackie Presser languished in serious condition in Lakewood Hospital in suburban Cleveland and Mathis presided over the restive GEB, still in Montreal, Mastro filed the long-anticipated, historic civil racketeering case against the IBT.

Giuliani called the media to his fifth-floor office at One St. Andrew's Plaza, a stark, modern high rise behind the classic templelike U.S. District Court building in Lower Manhattan, to lay out the details of the case. While eight civil racketeering actions had been filed against businesses or local or regional unions in past years, this was the first case brought against an international union.

The 113-page complaint Mastro and his team had crafted avoided trying to clamp on the IBT an all-powerful trustee whose will would reach into seven-hundred locals, most of whose leaders were absolutely innocent of any wrongdoing. Rather, the complaint followed the gentler, more precise course recommended a year before by Labor Department investigator Mike Moroney: focusing on the hierarchy and the mob. The long-range solution sought in the action was the direct rank-and-file election of the top officers as an antidote to organized crime influence in the Teamsters.

Named as defendants were two institutions: the IBT and the Commission of La Cosa Nostra. Also named were the eighteen members of the GEB, with an emphasis on Jackie Presser; twenty-six organized crime figures, including the bosses of the five New York mob families; and Eugene Boffa, Sr., the convicted mastermind of the nationwide labor-leasing scheme. (See Appendix A for full list.)

The complaint charged in tortured legalese that organized crime had deprived Teamster members of their rights through a pattern of racketeering that included twenty murders, shootings, bombings, beatings, and misuse of union funds.

Mastro sought a preliminary injunction to bar Cosa Nostra members and associates from any dealings with the union and the appointment of a "liaison officer" to investigate and punish corruption pending the outcome of the civil racketeering trial.

The long-range goal of the suit was to remove any Teamster officials found guilty of racketeering acts and to appoint a trustee to ensure free and fair elections of new officers.

Giuliani contended that the day-to-day operations of the

Teamsters' seven-hundred locals would not be affected by the lawsuit. "The government requests court oversight only for so long as necessary to eliminate organized crime's influence over the Teamsters, to put permanent reforms into place, and to return control of the Teamsters to the many honest working men and women of the union," Giuliani said.

The outline of the complaint emphasized the foundation laid for the case by the President's Commission on Organized Crime, noting that the commission concluded that "the leaders of the nation's largest union, the International Brotherhood of Teamsters, have been firmly under the influence of organized crime since the 1950s." The complaint quoted the commission's description of former Teamster presidents Jimmy Hoffa and Roy Williams as "indisputably direct instruments of organized crime" and its conclusion that "Presser's past activities indicate that he has associated with organized crime figures and that he benefited from their support in his elevation to the IBT Presidency in 1983."

The outline offered the guts of the Southern District's case:

> The complaint alleges that the current IBT General Executive Board members have failed to remedy corruption within the Teamsters and have allowed many criminals to hold union office. The complaint charges that the board members, through various acts and failures to act, have permitted members and associates of La Cosa Nostra to maintain control over the International Union and certain of its locals and other bodies.
>
> La Cosa Nostra figures have insured the elections of the IBT's top officers, including the union's last two Presidents. In return, union officers have allowed La Cosa Nostra ready access to union funds and jobs and free reign over certain IBT Locals, which La Cosa Nostra figures have used as instrumentalities to extort monies from employers.

The complaint charged that La Cosa Nostra used Teamster locals to shake down employers and curtail competition in New York's huge air freight, construction, and commercial moving industries. Examples of the violence included the disappearance of Jimmy Hoffa and the bold daylight murder of Allen Dorfman. Central States Pension Fund loans were used to finance several Las Vegas gambling casinos from which millions of dollars were skimmed for the Milwaukee, Chicago, Cleveland, and Kansas City crime families, the complaint charged.

The complaint said the mob controlled the last four Teamster general presidents: James Hoffa, Frank Fitzsimmons, Roy Williams, and Jackie Presser.

Cited in the complaint were seven sitting members of the GEB, including Donald Peters for allegedly participating in the scheme to bribe U.S. senator Howard W. Cannon; Maurice Schurr for his conviction in 1984 for taking kickbacks from an employer; Jackie Presser, Robert Holmes, Joseph Morgan, and Donald Peters for fiduciary breaches in connection with the Central States Pension Fund; and Harold Friedman and Theodore Cozza for the felony convictions on their records as young men.

Along with the serious charges were some ridiculous ones, such as the assault flowing from a brawl Jack Cox, the California vice president, had as a young sailor, and Secretary-Treasurer Weldon Mathis's arrest record on trumped-up charges by anti-union redneck cops in Florida during his early days as an organizer.

The case raised the question of how discerning the officials of the Teamsters or any other union should be, pointing out that the GEB members ran with Williams in 1981 after he openly associated with mob figures and refused to testify before a Senate subcommittee. Should they have been willing to sacrifice their positions? The right answer obviously was yes, even if it meant risking their comfortable positions. The same test was applied to the behavior of the executive board members when the President's Commission on Organized Crime issued its report in 1986 describing the IBT as the union most controlled by organized crime. The Teamsters' executive board did nothing about the report other than pass it off as another gratuitous attack on their union.

The complaint even questioned two long-standing Teamster traditions: taking care of relatives with cushy jobs and treating themselves royally by prolifigate spending of the members' dues.

Cited as examples of such abuse were the nearly $1 million spent on the Eastern Conference and Central Conference parties at the 1986 convention in Las Vegas and the jobs ladled out to Joe T's and Mathis's sons. The complaint said that Vincent Trerotola was paid "grossly excessive salaries" for his jobs on the staff of the International, Joint Council 16, and the Eastern Conference, which in 1989 added up to $153,699[26]—not counting his income from two Teamster locals, which apparently was about another $100,000 a year.

In Montreal, after being notified of the filing of the RICO complaint, acting Teamster president Weldon Mathis issued a statement saying, "We will fight this. We will fight each and every allegation." Despite his tough talk, Mathis would be among the first to cut a deal to settle the case against him.

McCARTHY'S ELECTION

On July 9, 1988, Jackie Presser died of cardiac arrest at Lakewood Hospital in the suburbs of Cleveland, leaving behind a squabbling hierarchy fighting for his throne. The nation's mob bosses were in such turmoil from an unprecedented series of convictions and 100-year prison sentences that they were in no position this time around to dominate the selection of the next Teamster general president.

Weldon Mathis, as interim president, appeared to have a lock on the general presidency. Even he thought he had the nine necessary votes until the night before Presser's funeral, when he discovered that International vice president Daniel Ligurotis of Chicago had opted to vote for Billy McCarthy.

Mathis realized he had one hope: International vice president Walter Shea. They had worked together in Washington for more than two decades and were friends. Shea had to know that the good of the union demanded that Mathis, not McCarthy, assume the top office. The articulate Mathis had the image of a labor statesman. While Mathis was unsullied by mob connections, he was having problems in his home local, Local 728 in Atlanta, Georgia. In October 1987, Mathis had been reelected president of the local, but the U.S. Labor Department was investigating complaints from TDUers that the ballot boxes had been stuffed. However, no one in the hierarchy paid too much attention to a seemingly minor problem like a fraudulent local election.

Mathis tracked Shea to Savannah, Georgia, where he was attending a meeting of the Panama Canal Commission, of which he was a member. He asked Shea to meet him in Washington the following morning, saying he wanted to talk to him about the election. A curious Shea, sensing a renewed opportunity to thrust himself into the presidency, agreed to meet him. Mathis knew Shea was aligned with McCarthy, but he had a plum to offer that might shift his vote—to succeed him as secretary-treasurer.

Recalling the meeting, Shea said,

> We spent three hours together that morning, from eight o'clock until eleven. Never forget it. And Mathis needed one more vote. The day before the election! He thought he had Ligurotis, because Ligurotis attended that meeting he called in Arizona in Scottsdale, but he came to find out he didn't have Ligurotis. Or if he did, he lost him.
>
> So I'm sitting here having breakfast with Mathis and he says, "Walter, I'd like you to come with me. If you vote with me for the president, you can be secretary-treasurer. You and I can do a lot of good for this union. We can set up an ethical practices committee. We can clean up the union, and we can put in a lot of good programs and get this thing going in the right direction."
>
> I said, "Weldon, I like what you say, but you got the order wrong. I should be the president, and you should be the secretary-treasurer."
>
> We kept talking about it, and he kept coming back to the same thing: We could do a hell of a job putting this union back on its feet. I kept coming back to the same thing: I was still desirous of being president. I had been so close to the job for so long.

The fifty-eight-year-old Shea didn't want to be boxed into the number-two job of secretary-treasurer under the still-youthful, vigorous Mathis. Shea was willing to gamble that a little patience would eventually lead him into the presidency as McCarthy's successor.

The following morning, Mathis and the sixteen vice presidents gathered in the union's Washington headquarters for the vote whose results were now a foregone conclusion.

Arnie Weinmeister, the ex–pro football player from Seattle, nominated Mathis, but first he suggested an alternative, that the vote be delayed so a special convention could be called at which the delegates would choose the next president. It was a plea from the losing team, which had everything to gain and nothing more to lose. "It was not well received. I don't think we even took a vote on it," Shea recalled later.

The vote for general president was taken.

For McCarthy: himself; Joe T; Shea; Ligurotis; Theodore Cozza; Joseph W. Morgan of Hallandale, Florida; Presser's cohort Harold Friedman of Cleveland; Jack D. Cox of San Francisco; and Donald Peters of Chicago.

For Mathis: himself; Weinmeister; Robert Holmes of Detroit; Edward Lawson from Canada; John Cleveland of Washington, D.C.; Maurice Schurr of Philadelphia; Don West of Birmingham; and Michael Riley of Los Angeles.

The motion was made to declare the vote unanimous, to offer the membership and the public the traditional image of the Teamster hierarchy as a monolith, unified against all outsiders.

The Mathis forces refused, indicating that the battle for control of the Teamsters' presidency was not over. McCarthy was entitled to the office theoretically until the 1991 convention, but Mathis would try to unseat him again before giving up the fight.

As a gesture of reconciliation, Mathis could have switched his ballot to McCarthy, but he said he didn't want to be recorded as voting for McCarthy. He refused to explain why, although as the next two years unfolded, the reasons became crystal clear.

Mathis offered an unprecedented view of the rift at the top by supplying reporters with a tally of who voted for whom in a break with the code of silence surrounding—at least in public—the GEB's inner workings.

As Shea left the boardroom, he ran into R. V. Durham, the North Carolina Teamster leader who was an International trustee and director of the IBT's tiny Safety and Health Department. "How can you vote for this guy? He's a dinosaur," Durham said to Shea.

After his victory, McCarthy met the press. A craggy-faced man with thick glasses, McCarthy opened the news conference with a "Good morning." The reporters and television camera crews waited expectantly. McCarthy stared at them for a moment. Finally, he said: "You feel that bad, you can't say good morning?"

The silence continued until the assembled media realized that the new president of the Teamsters wasn't going to speak until they responded.

"Good morning," they said in unison, and McCarthy rolled on.

In his first press conference, McCarthy revealed himself as a rude, terse, short-tempered man in an amazingly impolitic performance. What the outside world was seeing but not yet understanding was that an incapable leader had stumbled into the presidency of the largest private-sector union in the United States. His brash style and political incompetence in setting out to punish those who had opposed him, with no thought to strengthening his grip on the union, were to set the stage for truly contested elections for the top offices of the IBT.

5

The Teamster Civil RICO Settlement

Assistant U.S. Attorney Randy Mastro scored the first coup in the civil racketeering suit against the Teamsters even before the case was filed. On June 9, 1988, a member of Mastro's team arranged for a minor criminal case against two New York Teamster leaders to be transferred to U.S. District Court judge David N. Edelstein. That seemingly routine action was a sophisticated maneuver providing the bureaucratic excuse to bring the IBT (International Brotherhood of Teamsters) RICO case before Judge Edelstein.

The IBT lawyers and their clients were aghast when they discovered that Judge Edelstein, who had a reputation for being government oriented, would be presiding over their case. The Teamster lawyers tried unsuccessfully to have the action shifted to another judge.

Appointed to the bench by Pres. Harry Truman, the seventy-eight-year-old judge could be gracious or snappish, but he was always domineering in his courtroom. The fragile-looking jurist would play a pivotal role in the IBT RICO case over the next three years, refusing to allow the Teamsters to plunge the proceedings into a legal quagmire.

The only significant victory the IBT's defense team would achieve in Judge Edelstein's courtroom came at the outset of the legal maneuverings on July 5, 1988, when the judge rejected Mastro's request to impose a court-appointed monitor on the Teamsters to review expenditures and appointments and punish wrongdoers until the RICO suit was resolved. In effect, Mastro was asking for everything without having proven anything.

But Judge Edelstein did put the case on a fast track—setting February 27 as the trial date. While years can be spent in discovery, as the pretrial examination of evidence and interrogation of witnesses under oath is called, Judge Edelstein was determined not to allow that to happen in the Teamsters' case. And it didn't.

At the same July hearing, Judge Edelstein granted the temporary injunction sought by Mastro barring members of the Teamsters' General Executive Board (GEB) from any extraordinary or improper expenditures and from associating with La Cosa Nostra members.

Mastro, anxious to press forward, had scheduled a deposition of Jackie Presser for the next day, July 6. Presser, however, was too ill to be questioned and died three days later.

In the ensuing months, Fat Tony Salerno and most of the organized crime figures listed as defendants in the RICO suit settled the case against them by agreeing never to deal with the Teamsters again. Since Salerno and the other crime bosses were serving prison sentences ranging up to 100 years, there wasn't any reason for them to go through the expensive and tedious procedures of fighting the charges.

By the end of July, Mastro and his team had begun taking depositions from the Teamster hierarchy, starting with Secretary-Treasurer Weldon Mathis. When the questions touched on mob influence on the Teamsters, Mathis and the others denied there was any. A pattern began to emerge in the depositions: the GEB had never delved into the hundreds of charges of corruption and organized crime ties leveled against officials throughout the union, from the locals to the international level.

With each deposition the underlying theme of the RICO case was being proven and reinforced: the union's top officers failed to act against corruption. In addition, dozens of local Teamster officers who were alleged crime family soldiers or associates took the Fifth Amendment, refusing to testify.

———

The end game of settling the Justice Department's racketeering case against the Teamsters had its beginning with a telephone call from IBT general counsel James T. Grady to Rudy Giuliani in December 1988. Grady suggested that perhaps they could find their way to a reasonable settlement of the suit, saving his clients and the government untold years of litigation. Grady frankly assumed that the odds of the Teamsters winning at the trial level were as close to zilch as could be imagined with Judge Edelstein sitting on the case. And that would be only the first stage. The IBT would appeal the case right up to the U.S. Supreme Court— a time-consuming and costly process.

Giuliani just as frankly assumed that the evidence was so over-whelming that the Teamsters didn't have a chance in court no matter who the judge was. But a settlement of this type of case, he knew, was always better than a trial. The Teamsters, in effect, would be voluntarily agreeing to their own sentence—without hope of appeal.

The two sides met in the U.S. Attorney's office in Lower Manhattan on December 28, 1988, the first of several meetings between Giuliani and Randy Mastro on one side and Grady with Jed Rakoff from Richard Nixon's old law firm, Mudge Rose Guthrie Alexander & Ferdon, on the other. Over the next three weeks, Grady, Rakoff, and two associates from Mudge Rose struggled with Mastro to cut a deal that the majority of the Teamsters' GEB might swallow. Billy McCarthy, the general president, was kept informed of the negotiations, but none of the other members of the GEB were told.

The negotiators hoped to come to an agreement before the January 31 departure of Guiliani from his post as U.S. Attorney. The forty-four-year-old Giuliani was taking a highly lucrative position at White and Case, a powerhouse Manhattan law firm, but the general consensus was that his political ambitions were too large to be contained in a law office, no matter how much money was involved. Giuliani was often compared to another famous New York prosecutor, Thomas Dewey, who became governor of New York and almost president of the United States. Giuliani was expected to run for whatever opportunity arose: mayor or senator or governor. A press conference announcing the voluntary settlement of the IBT RICO case, which was certain to draw the attention of the nation, would have been a nice going-away present for Giuliani.

However, the real deadline was the trial date itself—February 27, 1989—and the specter of the unyielding Judge Edelstein just waiting to rule against the Teamsters. Months of trial would cost

Billy McCarthy, Weldon Mathis, and each of the vice presidents tens and perhaps hundreds of thousands of dollars in legal fees out of their own pockets. Behind that onerous reality lay the probability that the government would punish the guilty defendants by stripping them of their lucrative severance and pension deals.

HARD BARGAINING

Mastro was dealing from a position of unassailable strength. He also was busy trying to arrive at separate settlements, again in secret, with five other International officers: Weldon Mathis and vice presidents Robert Holmes of Detroit, Edward Lawson of Vancouver, John H. Cleveland of Washington, and Don West of Birmingham.

On January 13, 1989, the first of what Grady called draft settlements evolved. The deal, pressed by Mastro, called for an all-powerful court-appointed trustee to run the union, with veto power over expenditures and appointments. That court appointee would run the next five elections for International office, meaning the court would have its clutches on the Teamsters Union until the year 2011.

The Teamster lawyers rejected that first deal—and a second one three days later in which the election process was spelled out instead of being left to the whim of a court appointee. In the second draft, the general president and general secretary-treasurer would be elected by the rank and file, while the vice presidents would continue to be elected by the delegates at the IBT conventions held every five years. That, too, was a no-go, but the negotiations continued.

Secrets are hard to keep. At a volatile meeting of the GEB in Washington on January 17, 1989, McCarthy confronted Mathis, telling him he had heard that he was meeting with the government. Mathis shot back that so was McCarthy, a revelation that confirmed the suspicions of the other board members. In a hostile atmosphere, the board passed a resolution, by a split vote of 9–4, banning individuals in the hierarchy from settling separately. Holmes, Lawson, West, and Mathis voted against the resolution.[27]

At the demand of the angry board members, Grady rapidly read the latest government offer: Not only did Giuliani want to install a watchdog in the IBT for the next ten years; he intended to carry some trophies out of office with him. Five of the vice presidents would have to retire: Joseph (Joe T) Trerotola of New York, Joseph W. Morgan of Florida, Donald Peters of Chicago, Theodore Cozza of Pittsburgh, and Harold Friedman of Cleveland, whose prospects of survival were dim, since he had been convicted that week of racketeering and embezzlement in the ghost-employee payroll-padding case in Cleveland.

A livid Joe T leapt out of his chair amid shouts of rage from the other vice presidents on the list. "What the hell is going on? I haven't done anything," said the eighty-year-old Joe T, the most powerful Teamster in the union after the general president.

Joe T and the rest of the board wanted no part of that deal. Walter Shea and Joe T argued that perhaps their attorney, Bob Baptiste, who knew more about the intricacies of the Teamster structure and the subtleties of its power than any other lawyer, should join Grady in the negotiations. No, said McCarthy in his abrupt manner. Grady and the lawyers from Mudge Rose would continue the negotiations without any interference from Baptiste or any of the other lawyers.

McCarthy got his way because he was the president, but a seed of destructive animosity had been planted in Joe T. He had put McCarthy into office expecting to run him, and now he discovered that he was dealing behind his back.

———

In a happier setting later that January day, McCarthy and the vice presidents who headed the five Teamster conferences— Trerotola (Eastern), Robert Holmes (Central), Joseph Morgan (Southern), Arnie Weinmeister (Western), and Edward Lawson (Canadian)—sat down with White House chief of staff John H. Sununu for a chat. This access to one of the most important men in the Bush administration, which reaffirmed their self-confidence and sense of power, was a perk for giving the Teamsters' endorsement to George Bush in the presidential campaign. President Bush, fresh from his inauguration, happened by to shake hands with this rare species of labor leaders willing to support Republican presidential candidates with antiunion records. There were smiles all around and possibly a welling of

94

hope among the Teamster audience that the Bush Justice Department would flex its muscles for such friends.

REJECTING A TEAMSTER FANTASY

On January 23, the Grady/Mudge Rose team offered Mastro a counterproposal watering down the powers proposed by the government and splitting the authority among three different court-appointed officers: an "independent magistrate" to hear and decide all matters using a just-cause standard; a "review officer" to investigate and file disciplinary charges; and an "election supervisor" to review—not run or supervise—the election of the IBT's top officers at the 1991 convention. That was a dream proposal, with a marshmallow quality reflected in the titles applied to the three court officers. The impact of that deal on the Teamsters Union would have been so modest that Mastro and Giuliani could not have accepted it without being accused of a political tradeoff that turned the RICO process into a joke. Judge Edelstein certainly never would have approved it.

On January 26, Mastro made another counteroffer. He agreed to three court-appointed officers—an independent administrator, an investigations officer, and an election officer—the titles reflecting appointees with authority. The independent administrator would have the same powers as the general president and the GEB. The election officer would supervise the 1991 and 1996 direct, secret-ballot, one-member/one vote election of the general president and general secretary-treasurer by all union members. The remaining International officers would be elected either at the International convention or at regional conventions by delegates also chosen by the rank and file in secret-ballot elections. The U.S. Department of Labor would supervise the elections in 2001, 2006, and 2011.

The twenty-year presence of the government and courts remained and was still unacceptable to Grady and McCarthy.

With Giuliani ready to depart within a week, Mastro and the Teamster lawyers worked out another deal on Friday, January 27.

The GEB gathered in an extraordinary session the next day for three contentious hours. Under the deal Grady brought back this time, the trio of court-appointed officers remained the same as Mastro had proposed the day before. But the investigations officer's discliplinary power would end with the 1996 election, and the election officer would supervise the next three elections, through 2001, after which the Labor Department would take over for the next two elections. Delegates to the conventions would still have to be elected by the rank and file within six months of the convention. At the International convention, the delegates would elect the vice presidents and would nominate the candidates for general president and general secretary-treasurer. The rank and file still would elect the top two officers.

The GEB unanimously rejected that settlement offer. They wanted McCarthy to add a lawyer representing each of the five IBT area conferences to the Grady/Mudge Rose negotiating team. McCarthy again said no.

After the meeting, Grady told the press: "The entire document, from page one to the last page, was totally unacceptable and an insult to the entire American labor movement and the Teamsters in particular."[28]

The same day, Mastro revealed that under the pressure of the approaching trial and mounting legal bills, individual members of the Teamster hierarchy were trying to cut separate deals. He announced that Vice Presidents Robert Holmes of Detroit and John H. Cleveland of Washington, D.C., had agreed to settle with the government and were resigning from their vice presidencies. Cleveland, who was dying of cancer, had an impeccable reputation. The seventy-six-year-old Holmes was concerned about losing his pensions if the case went to trial.[29]

Mathis, Lawson, and West, continuing to negotiate in secret with Mastro, wanted to settle but were caught in the quandary of the GEB resolution prohibiting any separate deals. They didn't want to lose their prestigious Teamster jobs.

Despite the intense efforts, Rudy Giuliani wasn't able to add the settlement of the IBT RICO case to his list of accomplishments in his six years as U.S. Attorney of the Southern District. He left with the Teamsters' suit still dangling. When Giuliani subsequently emerged as the Republican candidate for mayor, Arnold Burns, the deputy attorney general who had switched the Teamster racketeering case from Washington to New York, became Giuliani's campaign manager. But the mayoral election was a prize that Burns couldn't deliver to Giuliani. He lost to David Dinkins.

A NEW DEADLINE

Early in February, using the excuse of processing the massive amount of paperwork involved in pretrial submissions, Mastro asked for a postponement of the trial. Judge Edelstein gave him another two weeks, setting March 14, 1989 as the new date.

The pressure was becoming intense. On March 3, Mathis sent a letter to McCarthy telling him that he had agreed to sign a consent judgment with the government terminating him as a defendant. "The purpose of this letter is to ask that the General Executive Board approve this agreement," Mathis said. At the same time, Mastro went before Judge Edelstein to ask for a ruling that the GEB resolution forbidding separate settlements was invalid and could not be enforced. Judge Edelstein gave the Teamster hierarchy two days to rescind it.

They did, in the form of a new and whiny resolution saying that the majority of the board blamed Mathis, West, and Lawson, who were pursuing independent settlements, for making it easier for the government to take over the union.

On Thursday, March 10, four days before the trial was scheduled to begin, Mastro's phone rang. Grady told him he wanted to bring in a team of lawyers for another try. The young assistant U.S. Attorney responded that the basis of any discussion would have to be the government's last offer in January. There wouldn't be any considerable departures from that proposal, or they would go to trial on Monday. Grady said okay.

On Saturday morning, Grady showed up at One St. Andrews Plaza along with a contingent of lawyers representing the area conferences and some individual vice presidents. On the government side were Mastro and Associate U.S. Attorney Aaron Marcu. Mastro and Marcu consulted regularly through the long day with Benito Romano, who had succeeded Giuliani as U.S. Attorney.

Recalling that Saturday, Mastro later said:

> The negotiating session was a little bit like good cop, bad cop. Aaron didn't know the case as well and was very friendly. I would play the bad-cop role as sort of "How can you possibly say that when you know your client did this or that or the other thing?" But the negotiation session went quite amicably, really. At that point it was quite clear the Teamsters had made a

97

decision to settle and they were there to see if they could get anything out of it. They knew the basic terms on which the case would settle because they had the January proposal.

What the Teamsters wanted was to relieve the members of the GEB from the burden of paying the enormous legal bills personally. The agreement permitted the union to pick up the legal tabs. The issue of the five vice presidents on the government's hit list was resolved with a compromise. Mastro said that Harold Friedman and Donald Peters had to go. The court-appointed investigations officer could deal with the status of Joseph Trerotola, Theodore Cozza, and Joe Morgan in the future.

Conversely, the Teamsters agreed to the rank-and-file election of the entire GEB.

The Teamster lawyers scored a subtle point by inserting language in the agreement barring outside contributions to candidates for Teamster offices: "No candidates for election shall accept or use any contributions or other things of value received from any employers, representative of an employer, foundation, trust, or any similar entity." Since federal law prohibits employers from giving anything of value to a union official, the pertinent language was the bar against donations from "foundation, trust, or any similar entity." Those words obviously were aimed at Teamsters for a Democratic Union (TDU), whose information and legal arm, the Teamsters Rank and File Education and Legal Defense Foundation (TRF), received much of its funding from foundations. While the Teamster hierarchy could count on the well-paid incumbent political and bureaucratic apparatus of the union for campaign contributions, any candidate rising from the rank and file would necessarily need the backing of TDU, which has to scratch for its money from the rank and file and foundations.

This seemingly innocuous paragraph would gain the attention of Herman Benson, founder of the Association for Union Democracy, the labor civil rights organization. In analyzing the settlement in AUD's *Union Democracy Review*, Benson conjured dire consequences: "This provision goes far beyond the limitations already written into federal law and is the first explicit restriction on foundations, not to mention those elusive 'entities.' When government monitors go home in 1991, and the court relinquishes jurisdiction, this vaguely formulated restrictive clause will be enforced by union officials who will decide who and what constitute an 'entity.' "[30]

The rest of the agreement pretty much stuck to the government's last proposal:

- A trio of court-appointed officers: independent administrator, investigations officer, and elections officer;
- Election of convention delegates no longer than six months before the International convention;
- The secret-ballot, direct election of the general president, general secretary-treasurer, and International vice presidents by the rank and file.
- Following the 1991 elections, a three-member Independent Review Board, to be appointed jointly by the IBT and Justice Department, to investigate corruption and punish wrongdoers.
- No associations with organized crime figures.

The underpinnings of the agreement, specifying democratic elections, read like paragraphs from the PROD (Professional Drivers Council for Safety and Health) and TDU platforms to reform the IBT.

When the details of the agreement seemed firm, Grady went to a telephone to call Billy McCarthy.

"Well, I'm going to take a chance. I'll schedule a meeting. Where are you?" McCarthy asked.

Grady was staying at the UN Plaza Hotel.

"Fine. We'll schedule it there for two o'clock Sunday," McCarthy said.[31]

A message was flashed across the Titan, the Teamster computer network, asking the GEB to assemble at the UN Plaza Hotel in New York the following day.

THE LAST HOLDOUT

McCarthy flew into New York with his buddy Frank Hackett. Hackett, a business agent in Boston Local 25, had been elevated to International vice president on Billy McCarthy's whim; such is the power of the general president. McCarthy's enemies within

99

the hierarchy cited Hackett's appointment as evidence of their general president's erratic behavior.

No one had anything against Hackett, but in the "old boys" club of the Teamsters, an International vice president usually was appointed from the ranks of those who headed a major local or a joint council. But Hackett jumped from business agent to International vice president—an overnight promotion that admittedly surprised even him. He had been on vacation when McCarthy had called him at home to say, "Come on down here. I've got a surprise for you." When he arrived in Washington, McCarthy had told the happily astonished Hackett he was making him an International vice president.[32]

Daniel Ligurotis flew in from Chicago, and vice presidents Arnie Weinmeister, Michael J. Riley, and Jack Cox came in from the West Coast. Joe T only had to have his son Vincent drive him into Manhattan from his home in Yonkers.

Walter Shea, who had been vacationing with his wife in Florida, hitched a ride to La Guardia Airport with Joe Morgan in his Southern Conference jet plane. They arrived at the UN Plaza around 4:00 P.M. Sunday. Donald Peters and Harold Friedman were waiting in the conference room. Those who had signed separate consent agreements were missing.

The day dragged on with small talk and waiting in a conference room on the second floor of the plush hotel across the way from the United Nations on Manhattan's East Side. Bob Baptiste, the Eastern Conference lawyer, had been told by Mastro, "Your client, Walter Shea, has no problem," so Shea was a little more relaxed than some of the others. While they drank sodas and ate snack food, Sunday afternoon dragged into evening.

Around 6:00 P.M., the talks in the federal building on St. Andrews Plaza finally ended. But Mastro warned Grady to have the remaining executive board members' signatures on the document before nine o'clock the next morning—or be ready to go to trial.

Mastro recalled: "A peculiar thing happened as we were breaking up that day. I remember Jim Grady coming up to me and saying, 'Please understand, don't be offended, if McCarthy is not very supportive of this.' I thought it was an odd thing to say, since McCarthy had earlier wanted to settle and had had Grady approach us about that."

Mastro's trial team—Marla Alhadeff, James Ferguson III, and Peter Sprung—was still in the office preparing for the biggest event of their careers, the trial that was to begin in the morning. Mastro told them to keep working. A deal might be coming down, but based on the experience of the past couple of months, they couldn't be sure until it was signed by the Teamsters.

"My people were very up," Mastro recalled. "It would have been such a great trial. But I felt we gave up so little, it would have made no sense to try the case. As to fundamental reforms of the organization, I don't think we could have managed anything better even with a trial," Mastro said.

Mastro's father, a political science professor at William and Mary College in Virginia, arrived a couple of hours later to go to dinner with his son. They decided to stroll over to Little Italy, just a few blocks away. Professor Mastro was in town to see a great moment of more than passing interest, his son's opening argument in the historic Teamster RICO case the next day.

At the UN Plaza Hotel, the GEB sat at a U-shaped table, with McCarthy at the head, and Grady next to him. Joe T was in the first chair to the left, and Shea sat opposite him. Grady read aloud the tentative settlement. The Teamsters were barred from any association with organized crime. Furthermore, they were required to amend the union constitution to provide for the rank-and-file election of the hierarchy and the other reforms.

To McCarthy and the vice presidents in the room, these requirements were not as drastic as they might seem. They assumed that they had outfoxed young Mastro and his team of assistant U.S. Attorneys. The board members believed that the amendments changing the way they were elected were subject to the approval or disapproval of the delegates to the next IBT convention in 1991. Since the hierarchy had manipulated the delegates in past conventions, they had no doubt they would control the vast majority of the delegates at the next convention. They felt confident a happy ending was in sight, but they hated taking the responsibility for allowing court-appointed officers to meddle in the affairs of their union.

Reflecting on that night, Shea explained his mind-set that led him to believe the government inadvertently had built an escape hatch into the deal. "I had no problem with the prohibition against criminal associations," Shea said. "The big thing was that any change here would be subject to the convention. Any of these amendments would be presented to the delegates at the convention, including the way the election would be conducted."

It didn't turn out that way, and in ensuing years, they would blame Grady for getting them into the bind that altered the union and their lives.

But that night, on March 12, 1989, at the UN Plaza Hotel, standing behind Grady like a chorus were the vice presidents' own lawyers saying, "Sign. It's the best deal you can get." Riley and Cox remember ten or twelve lawyers saying, "Sign."

There was another threat raised by the lawyers, according to Shea. "We were told, 'You are going to be required to spend a lot of time on the case if it goes to trial.' It was a frightening thought," Shea said.

The cost of litigating the case was on everyone's mind. "That was one of the things hanging over my head," Shea said. "My bill was $65,000 so far. Some were six figures already. It would have amounted to $500,000. If we were together as a board and engaged one or two lawyers, the costs would have been dramatically less. Each one had their own lawyers," Shea said.

As in a classic contract negotiation, the clock was ticking away the final minutes of a supposedly hard deadline. The hierarchy of the Teamsters had to decide which of the grim options to choose: to capitulate by signing the settlement or to go into a costly trial with little prospect of winning. Shea said with regret, "I should have been the one who wouldn't sign it. But how could we not take a position against corruption, against association with organized crime, against wrongdoing? I had no problem with watchdogs. The most sensitive phase was the amendments to the constitution."

Everybody was exhausted by the time the actual signing began. "This is the best we're going to get," Grady said. Joe T signed first; then it went around the table. Ligurotis hesitated, thinking that he had little reason to sign, since the government's case predated his tenure on the executive board. Then he thought of being the lone defendant standing before Judge Edelstein in the morning, with the entire Justice Department arrayed against him. He signed. Shea signed, then pushed the document to McCarthy.

"I'm not going to sign it," McCarthy said.

"Nobody in this room likes this," Shea told him.

"I'm not going to sign," McCarthy said.

"What do you object to?"

"Losing autonomy," McCarthy said.

That puzzled Shea, since Grady's explanation had suggested that there would be only a loose monitoring of the election process and the delegates at the convention would vote on the amendments. But Billy McCarthy had a reputation for never putting his signature on the dotted line. That way no one could blame him.[33]

When Mastro arrived back at his office from dinner with his father, he brought cannolis, rich Italian pastries, for his hardworking team. A little celebration. To his surprise the Teamsters hadn't called. They ate the cannolis with coffee, and Mastro sent the team home to get some sleep. They might be in court in the morning.

The phone rang shortly after 1:00 A.M. "There's a problem," Grady told Mastro. "Look, we have a settlement. If McCarthy refuses to sign, what will you do?"

"Would you like to hear my opening argument?" Mastro asked, and told the Teamster general counsel to be on time for the trial in the morning.

Alone with McCarthy in his suite at the UN Plaza, Grady went around and around on the ramifications of going to trial.

"Can you represent me?" McCarthy asked Grady, his lawyer for decades.

"No, I represent the International union. I'll have to resign as general counsel to be your personal lawyer." That didn't bother McCarthy.

"What's it going to cost?" McCarthy asked.

"They are talking about a thirteen-week trial. It's going to cost you a bundle, Bill."

"Give me an idea."

"Maybe $100,000."

"I don't have $100,000," said McCarthy, a refrain that lawyers are used to hearing.

At 3:00 A.M., the phone rang. Grady picked it up to hear Mastro ask: "Do we have a deal, or don't we?"

Grady looked at McCarthy and passed on Mastro's question, "Do we have a deal, or don't we?"

"Fuck it," said McCarthy, marking this historic moment for the IBT with an exclamation from the street, and signed.

6

McCarthy Chooses
to Fight

The truce with Billy McCarthy was eleven weeks and two days old when U.S. District Court judge David N. Edelstein entered his courtroom on the eleventh floor of the imposing federal courthouse in Lower Manhattan on May 31, 1989. The aging jurist, who had spent thirty-eight years proclaiming his decisions from the bench, was about to create the setting in which McCarthy would careen like a pinball out of control, repeatedly smashing head-on into the Justice Department, the judge, and Joe T. Despite the enormous wealth, power, and influence that came with the office of general president of the International Brotherhood of Teamsters (IBT), McCarthy would stagger out the loser in every collision.

Judge Edelstein spoke to the tiny gathering of lawyers and journalists but directed his remarks that day to the broader audience of the Teamster membership and the American public:

> Just over two months ago, I signed a consent decree between the International Brotherhood of Teamsters and the government. The decree contains an acknowledgement by the Teamster leadership that there are severe shortcomings in the way it has conducted its affairs in the past, and it embodies the standards by which the leadership of the Teamsters Union should conduct its affairs in the future. It represents a commitment by the leadership of the union to adhere to democratic principles, to root out corruption within the union, and to lay a

104

foundation for a union that represents its members with undivided loyalty and zeal.

These goals alone, however, are merely statements of good intentions—and we all know where those can lead. Without a dedicated effort to put these ideals into practice, the good intentions will become empty promises and unfulfilled hopes. This court is committed to ensuring that the expectations and hope of the members of the union and the public undoubtedly raised by the decree are not dashed. The public has a significant stake in the outcome of the decree. The IBT exercises vast power and cuts across every segment of society—political, social, and economic. It affects every aspect of our lives. Such power must be insulated against corruption and criminal elements and must be reserved for legitimate use to achieve legitimate ends. To further these ends, the court is appointing today three officers, pursuant to the decree, who will be charged with implementing its provisions and, more importantly, realizing the ideal of what a union should be.

Turning these promises and hopes into reality will require hard work, ability, and integrity. The task is enormous in scope and importance. The individuals that I am appointing today are more than up to that task. Their ability, dedication, and integrity cannot be questioned. Furthermore, they will count on the assistance and cooperation of the United States government and the leadership of the Teamsters Union in fulfilling their duties. I remind the Teamsters leadership that actions speak louder than words and they have now an opportunity to speak loudly and clearly to the union members and, indeed, to the public at large by their actions. The Teamsters' leaders should join with these officers in cleansing the union of corrupt influences and establishing democratic self-governance.

. . . The conditions that have necessitated and justified such unique and unprecedented measures are extreme. The remedy therefore is necessarily extreme. The court expects that all the parties involved—the union, the government, and the three individuals I am about to appoint—live up to the spirit and letter of the laws and Constitution of the United States as well as the consent decree.

Accordingly, pursuant to paragraph twelve of the consent decree, I hereby appoint Honorable Frederick B. Lacey as independent administrator; Charles M. Carberry as investigations officer; and Michael H. Holland as election officer.

In sum, decent, honest union members and the public at large are entitled to a decent and honest union free of criminal influences and corrupt practices. Today's appointments are an important first step in that direction for the International Brotherhood of Teamsters. This court envisions that the International Brotherhood of Teamsters will become a role model, a union of the members, by the members, and for the members.

In the hallway outside the courtroom, Teamster general counsel James T. Grady, an amiable man with a perpetually pleasant expression on his face, explained to the press that although the three appointments were supposed to have been made a month before, the delay was attributable to the careful selection process. Both the Teamsters and the Justice Department had to agree on the candidates, who were then subject to Judge Edelstein's muster.

Picking Michael Holland was easy. The forty-two-year-old Holland, a partner in the Chicago law firm of Cornfield and Feldman, was at the top of both the government and Teamster lists for the election officer's job. Now a partner in the labor-oriented Chicago law firm, Holland had been the general counsel of the United Mine Workers of America (UMWA) from 1982 to 1988. The Mine Workers was one of the few unions that elect international officers through the direct vote of the rank and file. But the Teamsters would soon sour on that happy choice. Before the election process had run its course, Holland's decisions would put him in conflict with both the incumbents and the dissidents. The election officer's mission wouldn't be as perfunctory as it seemed at the outset.

Deciding on the administrative officer and the investigations officer, who had the potential of wielding substantial power, was a much tougher proposition. Grady explained, "It was a matter of getting a guy [for each position] who is balanced and has the perspective of a defense attorney as well as a prosecutor. Someone reasonable, not out just to get his name in the paper."

Both Frederick Lacey and Charles Carberry had impressive credentials from the "old boy" federal law enforcement network.

The towering sixty-eight-year-old Lacey, a partner in the prestigious multicity law firm of LeBoeuf, Lamb, Leiby & MacRae, had spent fourteen years—up until 1986—as a federal judge in New Jersey, giving him the aura of self-importance and self-confidence that imbues members of the powerful federal judiciary. As an assistant U.S. Attorney from 1953 to 1955 and later as the U.S. Attorney for New Jersey from 1969 to 1971, Lacey built an impressive record of prosecuting crooked politicians and mobsters, sending Albert Anastasia, Murder Incorporated's Lord High Executioner, to prison for income-tax evasion.

Carberry, thirty-eight, who had the presence of a Charles Laughton, made his reputation as chief of the Southern District's Securities and Commodities Fraud Unit, the stage on which he successfully pursued Wall Street finagler Dennis B. Levine. Carberry put together the plea-bargain deal under which Ivan Boesky paid $100 million to the government to settle the insider trading charges against him. After nine years in the U.S. Attorney's office in Manhattan, Carberry joined the New York office of Jones, Day, Reavis and Pogue in 1986.

The consent decree gave the independent administrator the power to sit in judgment of disciplinary and trusteeship cases, along with a veto over union expenditures, appointments, and contracts for goods and services—if they crossed into the dirty world of crime and corruption. Lacey was excluded from anything to do with collective bargaining, politics, and organizing.

As investigations officer, Carberry was to be the cop and prosecutor on the Teamster beat, nailing anyone with mob ties or corruption in his or her past—with no statute of limitations to curtail him. That was to come as a shock to the Teamster hierarchy, who had imagined that in signing the consent decree past indiscretions would be forgotten and the court-appointed honchos would be limited to grabbing them only for what they did in the future.

From the Teamsters' perspective, Lacey and Carberry were novices in the realm of organized labor, which is a specialized, complex, and convoluted field. There would be a time-consuming learning curve for both of them. Time was a precious commodity, since the consent decree limited the time span for filing charges against Teamsters to approximately thirty-four months, from the moment the consent decree was signed until certification of the 1991 election results.

The clock was ticking. Almost three months had been spent picking and approving Lacey and Carberry. Both careful men, they could be expected to lay in a solid knowledge base preparing for their new ventures of watchdogging and investigating. That would be okay with McCarthy and company.

McCARTHY SUFFERS A STROKE

The secretive McCarthy had checked into a Boston hospital in mid-June 1989 for heart surgery, hoping to slip through the experience without telling the others in the Teamster General Executive Board (GEB). An unavoidable glitch in this plan came when he failed to show up for his scheduled speech on the opening day of the Southern Conference Convention at Disney World.

Southern Conference director Joe Morgan almost had apoplexy when McCarthy didn't appear. "Where the hell is he? He's supposed to be here." Morgan demanded of Duke Zeller, the IBT director of communications.

Not even Zeller knew.

"Duke, you've got to find him," an enraged Morgan said.

Zeller tracked down James Grady, who reluctantly admitted that McCarthy was in the hospital recovering from his surgery. Grady didn't mention it, but McCarthy also had suffered a stroke while recovering from the operation.

The following day, Joe Morgan, Joseph (Joe T) Trerotola of New York, and Walter Shea of Washington, D.C., were overheard discussing McCarthy at lunch, saying something had to be done about him. The trio's conversation was reported back to McCarthy by someone who told him they were plotting a coup to oust him. That information festered in McCarthy's mind, making him suspicious of the very men who had put him in office.

CLASHING WITH LACEY

Against a background of rumor and hints that the hierarchy of the Teamsters was not going to roll over and accept the reforms agreed upon in the consent decree, Frederick Lacey traveled to Carlsbad, California, to the luxurious La Costa Hotel and Country Club, financed by Teamster loans, for his first meeting with the GEB, on July 25, 1989.

With the meeting about to begin, Lacey stopped to chat with McCarthy, Grady, and David Previant, once Jimmy Hoffa's personal lawyer. Having heard that McCarthy had recently had a heart operation, Lacey, trying to set an amiable mood, exclaimed that McCarthy had made a remarkable recovery. McCarthy responded brusquely that he was going to "fight" Lacey in his role as the independent administrator. Lacey smiled, considering it the appropriate response to a clumsy effort at humor. He referred to McCarthy's plans to "fight" him in his own remarks to the board, still stretching to keep it funny.[34]

With more and more evidence piling up of a developing fight against the court officers, Lacey soon realized that blunt Billy McCarthy seemed to be following the path laid out more than three decades earlier by Jimmy Hoffa, who had succeeded in sabotaging the work of the Board of Monitors.

Hoffa, the most famous Teamster president of them all, against whom subsequent general presidents were judged by Teamster members and the press, had confronted a Board of Monitors, imposed on the union in 1957, when he was first elected to office.

Playing only to win, Hoffa had gone into the 1957 Teamster Convention with a stacked deck of almost five hundred delegates committed to him—many with questionable credentials. Thirteen rank-and-file Teamsters in New York filed suit in federal court in Washington to block Hoffa from taking office. The case was settled on January 31, 1958, with a consent decree setting up a three-member Board of Monitors to serve as watchdogs and to recommend reforms.[35]

Hoffa and his cohorts drove the monitors to the point of ineffectiveness by challenging them constantly in the courts, harassing them verbally—with the tough-talking Hoffa making calls in the middle of the night—and just ignoring their directives. After a time, the federal judge who set up the Board of Monitors turned the union back to the Hoffa forces, and the Teamsters got worse than ever, arriving at what the Justice Department came to call the "devil's pact" with organized crime, which included turning the massive Central States Pension Fund into the mob's piggy bank.

When Lacey returned from his trip to the La Costa resort in California, he reexamined the mounting evidence of the McCarthy decision to resist rather than cooperate with the court-appointed officers. The first intimation of a Teamster plot to undermine the consent decree had come on July 19, 1989, when a union staffer had refused to permit Lacey's auditor to review financial documents at the Teamsters' Washington, D.C., headquarters. The following day, IBT general counsel James Grady refused to sign a lease for the $200,000 annual rental of office space in Manhattan for Carberry's investigative staff. And within a week Grady also rejected Holland's plans to hire three staffers, a computer consultant, and a public relations firm.

Lacey struck back in a letter to Grady on July 31, 1989. He wrote: "I can only conclude that the IBT leadership, from and after July 26, 1989, had decided that it is going to try to do everything it can to slow or impair the functions of the court-appointed officers." Lacey added that he now realized McCarthy hadn't been joshing when he said that he was going to "fight" him.

In a blitz of correspondence, memos, and motions filed with the court, Grady contended that the court officers were asking for more than they were entitled to under the consent decree. He complained, too, of the cost of the three court-appointed officers, with Lacey charging $340 an hour, Carberry, $250, and Holland, $125.

The short-tempered Judge Edelstein wasn't about to allow the McCarthy administration to bog down what had become his personal campaign to assure the cleansing of the mob and corruption from the Teamsters. Under his prodding and the threat of his punishing intervention, Lacey's auditor got access to the books, Carberry got his office space, and Holland hired his staffers.

The fight was far from over however; it had just entered the nit-picking stage. Soon it would intensify and move across a variety of fronts, beginning with the Teamster magazine in which Grady would write cutting critiques of Lacey's monthly reports to the membership.

Until the signing of the consent decree, the magazine was used as a house organ primarily to promote the incumbent president and his allies, with a sprinkling of meaningless reports on regional and trade conferences and pictures of scholarship winners and retirees. A survey showed that less than 20 percent of the Teamsters bothered to glance at their magazine.

Lacey's first report to the membership appeared in the July 1989 issue of the *International Teamster*. In the dry legalese favored by corporate lawyers and federal judges, Lacey outlined the consent decree and the powers of the three court-appointed officers. He included the full text of Judge Edelstein's comments in approving the consent decree on March 14 and in appointing Lacey, Carberry, and Holland on May 31. Still in the first blush of their relationship, the McCarthy administration printed a reference on the magazine cover: "Special Administrator's Report Inside." Lacey's message was printed on page 2 and given top billing in the table of contents.

Before the year was out, McCarthy would try to kill the magazine as a monthly in an obvious effort to block Lacey's flow of embarrassing information to the membership.

THE SELF-DESTRUCTIVE McCARTHY

Almost from the day he assumed the Teamster presidency a year before, in July 1988, McCarthy pursued a self-destructive agenda. Shortly after taking office, he spoke to a gathering of Eastern Conference lawyers and staffers. In his rambling talk about the problem of dealing with the RICO suit, McCarthy noted that only two groups had real power in Washington: the National Rifle Association and the Jews. Several of those present said McCarthy put his hand in his pocket and shook his change to illustrate the underlying reason for Jewish power.

"He did in fact make an anti-Semetic characterization," confirmed New York Teamster leader Barry Feinstein. "He didn't have enough brains to realize he is anti-Semetic."

No one confronted McCarthy. Feinstein, one of the most politically astute Teamsters in the nation, said that the meeting was an inappropriate place to take on the general president.

"It was a matter of stunned disbelief," said Feinstein. He said he left the building that day deciding never to go near McCarthy unnecessarily again. McCarthy had made a serious enemy.

According to Feinstein, Teamster leaders began exchanging stories of McCarthy's disparaging remarks about Italians and women. No one outside of Boston had paid much attention to McCarthy before. Now Teamster officials across the country listened carefully to his every word. The sounds were dismaying.

At a gathering of Teamsters in Chicago's McCormick Place convention hall in the fall of 1988, McCarthy described how he stumbled onto his career as a Teamster. After stealing a car when he was fifteen in the Charlestown section of Boston, he told the audience, a friendly truck driver had hidden young Billy from the pursuing police—and that's how it all started. He continued with a rambling speech about old-time Teamsters who beat people up and burned scab trucks.[36]

That kind of tough-guy barroom talk made his listeners nervous. Feinstein said, "It was embarrassing. Union leaders would walk away shaking their heads, saying, 'What are we going to do with him?' It was clear to me he could not continue as general president."

The brash McCarthy not only made political enemies within the Teamsters with his thoughtless words; he managed to make himself vulnerable to the forces intent on reforming the unions by his thoughtless actions. Just two weeks before the signing of the consent decree, McCarthy blundered into the grasp of the yet-to-be appointed court officers by doing what so many Teamster officials had done before him: He spread a little of the union's wealth around his family. On March 1, 1989, McCarthy dumped the printer of the *International Teamster*—the monthly magazine sent to every Teamster—and handed the multi-million-dollar contract to Windsor Graphics Inc., a company so small that it fitted neatly into the home of McCarthy's daughter, Rosemary, and her husband, Thomas J. Treacy.

And within six weeks after the signing of the consent decree, McCarthy appointed sixty-year-old George Vitale, president of Wyandotte, Michigan, Local 283, as an international vice president, ignoring his shady past. Seventeen years before, in October 1972, Vitale had pleaded guilty to a misdemeanor for accepting $500 from a Detroit firm whose workers were members of Local 283 in violation of the federal law prohibiting union officials from taking anything of value from an employer. He was fined $2,000 and given two years' probation for that crime. A month later, in November 1972, a Detroit federal grand jury convicted Vitale of embezzling union funds, a felony, in a scheme in which he purchased a Cadillac owned by Local 283 for a cut-rate price. The sentence: $1,000 fine and two years' probation.

Vitale's convictions seemed like ancient history to McCarthy, but what he and the other signers of the consent decree had not yet grasped was that Judge Edelstein and his appointees had set out to reconstruct the union with an unforgiving puritan ethic. What had been done in the past would be punished in the near future.

112

THE MAGAZINE WAR

The magazine war between the McCarthy administration and the court-appointed officers began with the September issue of the *International Teamster*. Lacey's report was no longer listed in the table of contents. The independent administrator laid out the growing conflict between the court-appointed officers and the IBT. An affidavit from Carberry that described Grady's refusal to sign the lease for office space for his staff was printed. And Judge Edelstein's ruling that the consent decree required the Teamsters Union to pay the freight for Carberry's operations was printed in full. That was to become a familiar pattern in the coming months. The Teamsters, whether lawyers, officials, or members, would fight the court-appointed officers, and Judge Edelstein would order them to obey Lacey, Carberry, or Holland. Often Judge Edelstein would spice his decision with his favorite point: "The explicit and implicit purpose of the consent decree is to rid the union of the hideous cloud of corruption that envelops it."

In the same September issue, Grady struck back. In a memorandum to McCarthy printed in the magazine, Grady said:

"The IBT does not believe that a satellite office in downtown Manhattan costing $200,000 a year in rent is reasonable or necessary given the fact that the IBT is willing and able to provide more than adequate space for Mr. Carberry and his entire staff in Washington, D.C., at the IBT headquarters as provided for in the Consent Order.

"The IBT is also deeply troubled by how freely the court-appointed officers want to spend the union members' money." He noted that Carberry was billing at the rate of $250 an hour, which would add up to $500,000 a year, assuming he worked a forty-hour week. On top of the investigations officer's professional fees, he had hired a seven-member staff for the New York operation at approximately $470,000 a year. "The cost of Mr. Carberry's unit therefore already totals by my estimate over $1.1 million a year, and Mr. Carberry tells us this is only the beginning," Grady said.

Grady complained that Lacey was billing at the rate of $340 an hour, which could come out to $680,000 a year, while Holland's rate was a more modest $125 an hour, which could add up to $250,000 a year.

And that wasn't all. Lacey's first hire, an auditor/investigator, would be getting $110,000 a year, Grady said. Moreover, Holland was planning to hire an executive assistant at $81,000 a year and an administrative assistant at $39,000 a year.

The McCarthy administration's concerns over how the members' dues was spent was amusing. Nowhere in his complaints did Grady allude to the millions of dollars the leadership spent every year on corporate jets to ferry the general president and other Teamster officers around the country to meetings held at plush resorts, to their homes for the weekend, to golf outings, or to wherever their whims might take them. Nor, of course, did Grady mention the generous use the Teamster chieftains made of the union treasury to provide their children and their in-laws with nice jobs and expense accounts.

In time, Teamster officers at the international and local levels would wail over the high cost of holding local elections, which would run in the range of $5,000 a local when there were contested elections. Many of these same officials enjoyed—without expressing any open concern—Joe T's $647,960 bash at Caesars Palace during the 1986 convention and the Central States Conference's more modest party that same week costing only a few hundred thousand dollars.

Saving money was the excuse McCarthy offered a few months later when he decided to transform the *International Teamster* into a quarterly. Lacey, suspecting that the underlying motive was to curtail his monthly messages to the membership, turned to Judge Edelstein. The judge squelched McCarthy by ordering the IBT either to continue the magazine as a monthly or to mail Lacey's reports directly to each of the 1.6 million members every month. Either way, Lacey's reports on the latest court actions, the election procedures, and the charges filed against the hierarchy would reach the rank and file.

The *International Teamster* was continued as a monthly.

CARBERRY PURSUES THE MOB

Charles Carberry's initial effort as investigations officer bounced Nicholas (Nicky Black) Grancio, identified by federal authorities as a soldier in the Colombo organized crime family, out of New York Teamsters Local 707. The sixty-two-year-old Grancio cut a frightening figure, with his shaved, bullet-shaped head and reputation for violence. He had been the prime suspect in the 1986 murder of Bruno Bauer, a mechanic in a Queens trucking company, who had had the temerity to complain about Local 707 to the Association for Union Democracy (AUD) and to U.S. labor Department investigators.

Rather than undergo questioning by Carberry, Grancio retired in July 1989 after fourteen years as Local 707's vice president. Experienced investigators espouse the theory that once the mob latches on to a local, it never lets go. Grancio demonstrated the validity of the never-let-go principle to Carberry.

Having retired, taking with him a union-owned $25,000 Jeep as a gift from Local 707's executive board, Grancio went right to work as a consultant for Waldbaum's, a New York supermarket chain owned by A & P. Grancio had an intimate knowledge of the Waldbaum labor situation. He had negotiated the contract under which Local 707 members worked at Waldbaum's. Local 707 members, who wanted their local cleaned up, complained to Carberry's staff that Nicky Black was still a presence in the union, still showing up at Local 707's offices in Woodside, still going to shop stewards' meetings.

In his effort to end Grancio's domination of Local 707, Carberry subsequently charged him with being a member of La Cosa Nostra. Additionally, Carberry charged members of the executive board with associating with Grancio, an organized crime figure. Eventually, the local's executive board members were kicked out of the Teamsters by Lacey. Grancio was dismissed from his labor relations post at Waldbaum's and agreed to quit the IBT and stay away from Local 707.[37]

During his three years as investigations officer, Carberry, working with a staff of a dozen lawyers and investigators, brought charges against more than two hundred Teamster officials, ranging from low-level shop stewards with mob ties and no-show jobs to members of the oligarchy, including General President McCarthy and Vice Presidents Joseph Trerotola, Harold Friedman, Michael Riley, Theodore Cozza, George Vitale, and Don West.

The charges, in effect internal union charges, were based on violations of either the Teamster or AFL-CIO constitutions or the consent decree, which prohibited association with organized crime. The standard of proof needed for conviction was "just cause," which bitter Teamsters said meant "just because"—rather than the stringent criterion applied to criminal cases in state and federal courts.

Carberry was investigator, grand jury, and prosecutor rolled into one, while Lacey sat as the judge without jury. Lacey's decisions were subject to review by Judge Edelstein, who sometimes rejected punishments as too lenient. Edelstein never softened or reversed a Lacey ruling.

Those who for decades had treated the members' dues with extravagant nonchalance suddenly found their ethic being questioned. Carberry brought charges against officers who had paid their personal legal bills from the union treasury, had double-dipped on expenses, and had given retiring officers new cars purchased with the members' dues. Suddenly, Teamsters found themselves being held responsible for old crimes and old friendships with mobsters. Acts they had considered part of the Teamster norm were used as evidence to oust them from the union.

———

Harold Friedman, an appendage of Jackie Presser's throughout his career, was the highest-paid Teamster, with an annual income of $590,284. He and Anthony Hughes were the first formal targets of Carberry's investigative staff.

On July 26, 1989, Carberry filed charges against Friedman and Hughes for violating the Teamsters constitution, essentially based on their convictions the previous January in the "ghost case" in Cleveland. Friedman and Hughes turned out to be much tougher customers than Carberry had anticipated.

The judge in the criminal case had sentenced Friedman and Hughes to four years' probation and ordered them to forfeit their union positions. But they were allowed to stay in office pending their appeals. In the "ghost case," $700,000 was said to have been paid to Hughes and three others for "no-show" jobs. Carberry charged them with violating a section of the Teamsters' constitution for bringing "reproach" on the IBT.

Only the humorless or the ignorant could believe that a conviction for paying someone for a no-show job could smear the reputation of the Teamsters. But that was the charge filed by Carberry, and it would be repeated in case after case to come against many other Teamster officials.

Presser and Friedman had run Bakery Workers Local 19 and Teamsters Local 507 out of the same office in Cleveland for years. The two locals, from different international unions, shared the same staffs and benefit funds. Friedman's $590,284, including salary, allowances, and expenses, came from five payrolls, a blatant example of multiple salaries. Friedman's paychecks came from the IBT, the Ohio Conference of Teamsters, Teamsters Joint Council 41, Teamsters Local 507, and Bakery Workers Local 19. He was president of Local 507.

Hughes, Local 507's recording secretary, was on four of the same payrolls, with his income adding up to only $177,672.[38]

The pair claimed that since the embezzled funds to pay the ghosts came from a Bakery Workers local, not a Teamsters local, they fell outside of Carberry's jurisdiction: the IBT. Another defense was that the Teamster constitution precluded bringing charges against Friedman and Hughes because they had been reelected in 1987 by Local 507's members, who were well aware of the allegations against them. There was no mention of the fact that in catch all Teamster locals, such as Local 507, serious opposition to incumbents rarely jells, since the members work at separate sites, with no institutional glue or common craft to bring them together. Invariably when a dissident arises, he or she is co-opted or suddenly is dismissed from work and in effect the union.

The Teamster legal fraternity closely watching this case would soon learn that Lacey had no intention of turning the hearing process into an interminable game. He ruled that the concept of "collateral estoppel" applied, meaning that a conviction in a court would be accepted as an irrefutable fact.

Lacey's hearing on the charges, originally set for September 13, 1989, was postponed several times because of the legal maneuverings. Friedman and Hughes even questioned the right of Lacey to sit as their judge.

Carberry reacted like so many prosecutors before him. On September 20, he added a new charge to Friedman's pile: accusing him of "knowingly associating with associates of La Cosa Nostra."

After hearings and motions and submissions of papers, Lacey rejected all of Friedman's and Hughes's objections. Then they appealed to Judge Edelstein, who in turn rejected their arguments, saying in his decision:

"Throughout this matter, Friedman and Hughes seem to confuse being *accused* of criminal acts with being *convicted* of criminal

117

conduct. Despite their protestations of innocence, both are convicted felons regardless of the fact they have pending appeals."

Judge Edelstein dismissed a contention by Hughes that he wasn't bound by the consent decree because he wasn't a signatory as "ludicrous." In his decision, the judge set the tone of many more decisions to come in the succeeding two years:

> The ultimate aim of the consent decree is to guarantee free elections and to rid the IBT of the hideous influence of organized crime. These goals seem squarely in the interest of the IBT rank and file as a whole.
>
> Indeed, the consent decree appears to contravene the interests of only two classes of IBT members: The election oversight may imperil unfairly elected officers, and the prosecution scheme may ultimately suspend corrupt union members. Hughes, by virtue of his criminal conviction, falls into the latter category.

Edelstein's decision was issued on November 2. More than three months had gone by. And it wasn't over yet. The pair appealed Edelstein's ruling to the Second Circuit U.S. Court of Appeals.

THE LEGAL BRAWLS CONTINUE

The day before Edelstein issued his decision, the Teamster GEB convened a special meeting in Washington, D.C., and unanimously passed a resolution at the prompting of International Vice President Theodore Cozza of Pittsburgh. The resolution would attempt to blow away the constitutional basis for the charges against Friedman and Hughes. Cozza wasn't simply being altruistic on behalf of a comrade under fire. He had been charged by Carberry on October 24 with bringing reproach on the IBT by associating with members of Pittsburgh's La Cosa Nostra.

The GEB's resolution said: "The expression 'to bring reproach upon the Union' is so vague and indefinite that it does not sufficiently inform trade union members and officers of the specific conduct which it covers in the context of trade union principles and practice." And in case anyone missed the point that that constitutional provision wasn't meant to preclude friendships with La Cosa Nostra figures, the resolution also said, "The aforesaid term was never intended to, and does not, cover associations between union members or officers with other persons inside or outside the trade union movement based upon the reputation or reputed activities of such other persons . . ."

The same resolution reaffirmed the IBT constitutional concept that disciplinary action could not be brought against an officer who had been reelected by a local membership well aware of the charges against him.

Carberry urged Lacey to reject this resolution "as nothing more than an effort by the GEB to protect its own cronies." Lacey agreed, saying that in signing the consent decree, the leadership tied themselves and their rank and file to a new standard: "There should be no criminal element of La Cosa Nostra corruption of any part of the IBT."

Besides, McCarthy inadvertently had punched a gaping hole in the IBT's argument, since he used the same section of the Teamster constitution to dump Maurice R. Schurr out of his vice presidency in August 1988 based on his felony conviction for taking payoffs in 1984.

———

Meanwhile, Elections Officer Michael Holland also got pulled into the legal brawl. The Teamster hierarchy wanted the narrowest possible interpretation of Holland's powers under the consent decree—limiting him only to the role of "observer" of the voting at the 1991 Teamster Convention, with no power to intrude in the delegate elections at the local level. Judge Edelstein issued a decision on October 18 ruling that Holland's authority covered the whole proces., from the delegate elections to the convention to the direct elections of the IBT's top officers by the rank and file. The IBT appealed, and in what was to become an almost routine procedure, the U.S. Court of Appeals for the Second Circuit rejected the appeal.

On November 17, 1989, International Vice President Daniel C. Ligurotis and five Chicago locals (Locals 301, 705, 726, 734, and 781) filed a lawsuit in Chicago federal court challenging Holland's right to run the elections.

Friedman and Hughes opened up another front on December 1, 1989, by filing a suit in the U.S. District Court for the Northern

District of Ohio in Cleveland. This new suit challenged Carberry and Lacey's jurisdiction over the case. And on December 4, 1989, Friedman filed another motion with U.S. District Court judge George W. White in Cleveland, who had presided over his criminal trial, asking him to bar Lacey from holding his hearing.

Across the Hudson in New Jersey, Teamster Joint Council 73 and Secaucus Local 641 filed yet another lawsuit in federal court in Newark contesting Carberry's power to examine the books and records of local Teamster organizations.

In the midst of all this, Hughes and Friedman finally appeared before Lacey on December 13 for their hearing—five months after being charged by Carberry. For all the effort, the outcome seemed like a slap on the wrist. Lacey found them guilty of Carberry's charges and suspended them from the Teamsters for one year. Since the Teamster constitution requires anyone running for office to be a member in good standing for two years, Lacey effectively was killing any chance of Friedman's being resurrected as a vice presidential candidate for the 1991 elections.

Of course, they appealed. Judge Edelstein and the Court of Appeals upheld Lacey's decision.

The tangle of motions and hearings, decisions and appeals, and the added layers of lawsuits were reminiscent of the legal swamp into which Jimmy Hoffa led the Board of Monitors in the 1950s. With lawsuits blossoming everywhere across the United States and Canada, the energies and resources of the three court-appointed officers, Lacey, Carberry, and Holland, could be drained, and even the U.S. Justice Department could be strained by the magnitude of the task of dealing with this onslaught.

But this was a different era, with a decidedly different and determined set of players.

———

Assistant U.S. Attorney Randy Mastro counterattacked by obtaining restraining orders from Judge Edelstein barring the Ohio suits. He asked Judge Edelstein to hold Friedman in contempt for filing the actions. Friedman had been an original signatory to the RICO settlement in March, and now he was trying to undermine it.

Friedman broke down in tears at his contempt hearing.

Through his sobs, he said that the members of Local 507 didn't want to see him dumped out of office. Judge Edelstein gave him a week to drop his Ohio case. He did.

At Mastro's request, Judge Edelstein held Ligurotis in contempt for filing the lawsuit against Holland. As a signatory to the original consent decree, Ligurotis legally was barred from doing anything to obstruct the terms of the settlement. Judge Edelstein ordered Ligurotis either to withdraw the Chicago lawsuit by December 21 or begin paying fines that would start at $125 a day and double each day to a maximum of $512,000 on the thirteenth day. Ligurotis also was directed to pay $44,901 in legal fees and court costs out of his own pocket for bringing that action. Ligurotis appealed the contempt ruling and penalties. But he withdrew the Chicago lawsuit when the higher courts again upheld Judge Edelstein.

Deciding not to play Hercules to the IBT's legal monster, Mastro turned to a willing Judge Edelstein for a temporary restraining order to bar all Teamster locals, joint councils, conferences, and other entities from filing legal actions in any court other then the federal court in Manhattan. The nationwide show-cause order was served on seven hundred Teamster locals, joint conferences, and area conferences by overnight mail, giving them until 5:00 P.M. on December 26, 1989, to respond with arguments as to why all litigation involving the consent decree shouldn't be filed in the Southern District.

McCarthy decided to exert a little more pressure. Within a week, he telexed all Teamster locals: "I urge that you fight this unprecedented and ill-advised attempt of the government to deprive you and your members of your legal and constitutional rights." McCarthy's telex listed ten legal points that lawyers for locals and other Teamster entities could pursue in the show-cause showdown. Almost half of the IBT's locals, joint councils, and conferences answered Billy McCarthy's call to fight Mastro's request for the permanent injunction against filing court actions involving the consent decree in other jurisdictions.

After examining the Teamster lawyers' arguments against Mastro's position, Judge Edelstein delivered a crucial ruling on January 17, 1990, that would end the campaign by the Teamsters to diffuse and destroy the focus of the U.S. Attorney's office in Manhattan and the court-appointed independent administrator, investigations officer, and election officer. Edelstein's "All Writs" decision required that all legal actions connected to the RICO case be filed in his courtroom.

Judge Edelstein spiced his decision with remarks showing the goal he was pursuing:

> The Consent Decree in this IBT situation attempts to instill democratic, fair, secret ballot elections into a union not known for fairness or strict adherence to democratic principles in elections and [to] root out corrupt officials in an association historically tainted by organized crime. . . . This Consent Decree represents an unprecedented attempt to reform the nation's largest labor union. Undeniably, fair elections and honest officials are squarely in the interests of the membership as a whole.

OUTRAGEOUS ELECTION RULES

The spring day was delicious when Susan Jennik walked through Battery Park. She was more in the mood for sitting in the warm sun on a bench looking out across New York harbor than for a meeting with Michael Holland.

Holland had asked Jennik to sit down with him to discuss the Association for Union Democracy's Teamster Fair Election Project. The thirty-seven-year-old Jennik was executive director of the AUD, a shoestring, independent, nonprofit operation that survives on foundation grants and espouses the cause of civil rights for union members. In theory, the Teamster Fair Election Project would provide legal aid to any Teamster needing help in the upcoming court-ordered Teamster elections. In reality, rank and filers taking on the entrenched officers would be turning to the AUD. The incumbent officers at the local and national levels had their house lawyers. They neither needed nor wanted the AUD.

Jennik left the April sunshine behind her when she went into 17 Battery Place. That day, Holland was using Investigative Officer Charles Carberry's office in the building, with its wonderful views of the harbor. Holland came right to the point with Jennik. He wanted to know what the AUD's Teamster Fair Election Project was all about. In the hairsplitting world of election lawyers, Holland wanted to be certain that the AUD wasn't providing any sort of illegal legal aid.

In the course of the meeting, Holland handed Jennik a copy of his proposed election rules. He had distributed a draft of the rules to all IBT entities on February 22, 1990, and then held a series of hearings from March 6 through March 27 in San Francisco, Seattle, New York City, Baltimore, Chicago, Memphis, Cleveland, and Toronto to give everyone a chance to make comments and suggestions. The Teamster hierarchy essentially objected to everything in the tentative rules. The IBT took the position that Holland did not even have authority under the consent decree to promulgate election rules. The IBT objected to the plan for alternate delegates, to the idea of allowing accredited candidates to publish campaign literature in the *International Teamster* magazine, and to a secret ballot for nominations at the 1991 Teamster Convention.

Jennik waited until she got on the number 4 subway train to Brooklyn before scanning Holland's proposals. When she read them, rage surged through her. The previous October, Judge Edelstein had given Holland the power to supervise the elections, and now the rules he was promulgating were handing that power right back to the locals despite warnings from the AUD and TDU that the locals officers couldn't be trusted. "How the hell can he think these local officers in the most corrupt union in the country would run a fair election?" Jennik wondered.

She was breathing hard when she arrived at the AUD's offices. She thrust the rules into Herman Benson's hands. "He didn't change it," she said. "He's still letting the locals run the elections! It's outrageous."

Benson, who had devoted the last thirty years to the union democracy movement, read Holland's rules and exploded. "The son of a bitch!" he screamed, spewing out a string of expletives. "He's proposing turning the conduct of the election over to the local officials. The whole point of the RICO suit is these guys are so infiltrated by racketeers that you can't depend on them to run a clean union."

When he calmed down, Benson discussed the setback with Jennik. "All Holland wants to do is receive tally sheets from the locals as to how their votes went," he said bitterly. The local union officers would be in charge of printing ballots, deciding who was eligible to run, running the election, storing the ballots, and counting them. Benson was suspicious of Holland's motives. Holland was a member of a Chicago law firm whose primary business was representing unions. He muttered that Holland probably was fearful of being denounced as antilabor by the Teamsters.

Benson gave Jennik his assessment: "Holland is under a great deal of pressure to show he is a reasonable man. To me that explains why he took an absolutely shitty position. . . . It can turn the whole tide in the Teamsters union. Without tight supervision of the locals Carey won't have a chance." His cynicism was based on thirty years' experience. He had discovered that stealing elections wasn't an unusual phenomenon in the labor movement.

Jennik applied some logic to the quandary facing them: "The problem is you don't know who are the crooks and who aren't, and you can't know in advance who is going to steal and who is not. So the only way to do it is to have someone else outside the union run the election in all the locals." Jennik had her own suspicions about why Holland didn't want to exercise that power. She said in retrospect:

> It was a question of practicalities. Running the election is a massive job. There are 1.6 million members. I think Holland was worried about whether it could be done effectively. Also, he comes from a mainstream union background. I think he believes local union officers are honest, decent people. In the few cases where there are bad guys, those elections could be supervised. How do you determine who the bad guys are? Holland said you look at the history of past elections, whether there had been any problems.

The thirty-eight-year-old Jennik was born in Milwaukee, the second oldest of ten children in a Polish Catholic family. Her father, who wasn't pro-union, had been through a series of jobs, losing his positions as an appliance salesman in the recession of 1959 and again in the recession of 1970. "I used to tell him if anybody needed a union, he did," Jennik said. In 1971, Jennik's mother got a job in a chain-store warehouse, ending up being fired when she hurt her hip at work.

Against that background, Jennik spent a year at the University of Wisconsin at Madison getting caught up in student organizing groups and strike support work. She dropped out of school to

combine working as a drill press operator in a factory with playing an active role in UAW Local 180. Married in 1975, Jennik
had a baby in 1977 and earned a degree in labor economics in
1978 from Parkside College in Kenosha, Wisconsin. Then she
went to New York University Law School under a Root-Tilden
Scholarship that provided full tuition and a stipend.

As a law student, Jennik worked summers for the AUD. When
she graduated in 1981, bright law school graduates from prestigious schools like NYU could command lucrative starting salaries. Jennik chose another path. She joined the law firm of Hall,
Clifton & Schwartz, whose office was on Broadway, a block south
of Canal Street, and whose clientele were workers or union dissidents with little money to pay legal fees. "Money doesn't motivate
me very much. It's more important to do something I enjoy,"
Jennik said.

After three years, she went to the Labor Bureau of the New
York State attorney general's office. But she felt too far removed
from the union movement. After a few months as a state bureaucrat, she worked out a deal to spend half of her time working
for the AUD as a lawyer and the other half for TDU as the
organization's Northeast organizer. The two jobs added up to a
modest salary. In time, Jennik dropped the TDU post when she
succeeded Benson as executive director of the AUD. Benson,
who had founded the AUD, had decided to move toward retirement gradually. He couldn't bring himself to let go entirely, so
he became the organization's secretary treasurer and continued
as editor of its monthly publication, *Union Democracy Review*.

In the course of preparing the amicus brief she would file with
Judge Edelstein, Jennik discovered a letter from labor lawyer
Joseph Rauh to the U.S. Labor Department written shortly after
the murder of Jock Yablonski, the reform candidate for president of the United Mine Workers in January 1970. Jennik said,
"The letter basically said, 'We asked you for government help
and you turned us down. Now he's dead.' "

Jennik's brief focused on the inconsistency of relying on Teamster officials to run honest elections in their locals. The brief
argued:

> With rare exceptions, the local officials who would conduct the
> elections under the Rules have been pliant supporters of an
> international union regime that has been heavily infiltrated by

organized crime. Those local officials, taken as a whole, are essentially the same individuals who have served as convention delegates and have elected the incumbent officers. While corruption was raging around them, these local officials did nothing to oppose it. . . . In the all-pervasive lawlessness that has permeated the union, it would be foolhardy, even irresponsible, to depend upon the local union officers for safeguarding the integrity of the elections.

Jennik incorporated the bitter experience of the Mine Workers' reform movement in 1960 into the brief to urge Judge Edelstein to provide greater protection for the Teamster reformers thirty years later. "I used that letter to say, Let's hope this isn't a repeat of the Mine Workers. If there is sufficient government action, violence can be avoided," Jennik said.

The odds of winning seemed dim. Judge Edelstein had yet to overrule one of his three appointed court officers. The IBT, Lacey, and the U.S. Attorney's Office for the Southern District were backing Holland's position.

Jennik said, "It seemed hopeless, but I knew the rules as written would sandbag Carey. I said, 'We just can't let this happen.' Maybe the judge would turn us down, but at least we had to tell him it was wrong and dangerous."

JUDGE EDELSTEIN'S ELECTION DECISION

At 10:00 A.M. on July 10, 1990, Judge Edelstein entered his courtroom on the eleventh floor of the federal courthouse in Manhattan to deliver his decision. Jennik wasn't there. She had missed a phone call to her office notifying her that the ruling would be handed down that day.

"I consider these election rules one of the most critical elements in the unique attempt to remove corrupt elements from the IBT, the nation's largest labor union," Judge Edelstein began.

Since I am convinced the election rules submitted to me did not provide for sufficient supervision of this election, I have approved final election rules with certain provisions altered so that I am satisfied these elections will be successful.

These amended rules provide for a significantly increased level of supervison by the election officer. . . . It is my sincere

126

belief that these modified rules will insure that the light of democracy will shine on this great union, democratize it, and return it to its membership.

The judge ordered Holland to do what Jennik and Benson had asked—to run every facet of the election instead of leaving it to chance and the Teamsters.

Roger Nober, the judge's law clerk, reached Jennik at one o'clock. "The judge has made a decision on the rules," he said.

"Can you tell me what it says?" she asked.

"Well, basically, he adopted the recommendations of amici."

Jennik, who had been standing, sat down in shock. Chills went through her. "I'll be right over," she managed to say.

———

The following Saturday, the annual AUD/TDU picnic took place as usual in Jennik's big old brown house with a wraparound porch in Freeport, Long Island. It was a multiple celebration for the victory scored by the AUD in Judge Edelstein's court the previous Tuesday and for Herman Benson's seventy-fifth birthday.

There was a keg of beer on the porch, along with seltzer and sodas and nonalcoholic beer. There were salads and pretzels and potato chips on the dining-room table. On the wraparound porch, hot dogs, hamburgers, and sausages cooked on a grill, tended by a truck driver who had just been dismissed from his job of six months. The reason wasn't given, but apparently it was his union activism, his past as a TDU member in New England.

Benson, a man who exudes energy, had just sat down on the big couch in the living room to deliver a monologue on the triumph in the court when a birthday cake was brought out as a suprise. He passed that off quickly and immediately went into his talk for the forty or so people assembled in the room—UPS drivers, including a shop steward fired the day before for urging rejection of the national UPS contract; Teamsters Local 138 drivers wearing black shirts with "Scabs must pay" and a skull imprinted on them; a plumber from George Meany's home local, Local 2 in the Bronx; a few United Food and Commercial Workers Union members; an activist in the Taxi Drivers Union who had just begun publishing a new labor newspaper; and three labor lawyers to whom union dissidents often turned: Dan Clifton and Louie Nikolaidis from New York and Paul A. Levy from Ralph Nader's Washington-based Public Interest Group.

Benson said that there were two significant differences between the Board of Monitors Jimmy Hoffa had confronted in 1958 and the consent decree the Teamsters' oligarchy faced in 1989: TDU, which developed as a national opposition group preaching a reform message that seemed to have little chance of success until now; and Judge Edelstein, who hadn't veered an inch from his intended mission of cleaning the gangsters out of the Teamsters.

———

In West Virginia, when Eddie Burke, the ex–Mine Worker turned Carey campaign manager, heard the news of Judge Edelstein's decision, he said: "For the first time, I really think we're going to win this."

7

The Candidates

RON CAREY DECIDES TO RUN

Ron Carey was eating a tuna fish sandwich in a diner in Queens with his lawyer, Richard Gilberg, when the question that had been bothering him popped out. "Maybe I should run for something?" he said to Gilberg. "This is my chance to do something for my local, for my guys."

Gilberg paused in munching his own sandwich. He responded to Carey with a question. "What do you mean, for the Joint Council?"

"No. No. No. Maybe I should run for one of the International offices as an independent or something."

A couple of weeks earlier, on March 14, 1989, U.S. District Court judge David Edelstein approved the consent decree scrapping the old political system that had created a government by oligarchy in the Teamsters in favor of a rank-and-file-based democracy. Anyone who could put together enough votes could skyrocket to the top of the union.

Carey and Gilberg had read the consent decree with care, confirming what the newspapers said: There would be rank-and-file elections After years of frustration, at last an opportunity was at hand for Carey.

Under the unwritten rules of Teamster politics, Carey should have been limited forever to the presidency of Local 804, his

129

ambitions crippled by his high standards and scruples. Under the old politics, the movement to real power in the union required a pliant personality willing to work hard for a mentor who could bring him step by step up the ladder of success behind him. Then he would attain the good life, enjoying the prestige and extra salaries of appointed jobs as an International representative or International organizer. Maybe he would become a trade division director or get a seat on the executive board of the Joint Council. If he were among the lucky few, he would get an International vice presidency. And for the select, there would be the ultimate reward of this old boys' network: the general presidency of the International Brotherhood of Teamsters (IBT).

Carey didn't believe union leaders should collect multiple salaries. He didn't speak out against corruption, but as president of Local 804, he lived the honest life, carefully accounting for every dollar of the members' money and preventing anyone else in the local from playing the dirty game of kickbacks and shakedowns that had destroyed the reputation of the IBT.

Carey came out fighting when the IBT leadership negotiated lousy national United Parcel Service (UPS) contracts that had a direct impact on his members. In a union of silent go-along and get-along local officials, Carey openly fought the 1982, 1985, and 1988 national contracts. He tried to pull Local 804, which represents more UPS employees than any other Teamster local, out of the national agreement in 1982, but the International refused. "I was tired of people getting screwed. I made a decision I wasn't going to sit back and accept it," Carey explained.[39]

When the majority of UPS workers voted against the concessionary 1988 contract and the International still shoved the contract down the members' throats by invoking the rule requiring a two-thirds' negative vote to reject, Carey went into federal court with a suit to impose majority rule.

By standing up, he stood out, and tens of thousands of rank-and-file UPSers, as well as the Teamster hierarchy and the well-organized dissidents of Teamsters for a Democratic Union (TDU), came to know who he was.

Carey's first thoughts were to run for an International vice presidency. In the ensuing weeks, as he discussed the leadership of the IBT with Gilberg over lunch and over the phone, the two agreed that those at the top of the Teamsters were lazy and out of touch with the rank and file. "I've got to do something," Carey would say in those conversations.

Finally, Gilberg told Carey, "Why not go for the whole magilla?" The general presidency.

Carey didn't need much prodding. As the consent decree was constructed, running for a regional vice presidency in the Eastern Conference was the equivalent of running for national office. There are 500,000 members in the East. Reaching that vast number could be as difficult as going after the entire 1.5 million members.

Carey said to himself, "Let's change this thing from the top, Ron."[40]

Gilberg recalled, "I was enthusiastic about Carey running for president because I have a lot of respect for him. I'm also one of those people who don't think the corruption is rampant. I just don't see it. I just thought the Teamsters needed a new look for a new era and the members were getting shortchanged. Knowing how much energy he has, how scrupulous he is, how hardworking he is, I said, 'Who's a better guy than him to take a shot? This is his shot to make an impact on a larger canvass.' "

———

Richard N. Gilberg, a lanky thirty-eight-year-old with a shock of black hair, whom everyone called Rick, was a partner in the labor law firm of Cohen, Weiss and Simon. The firm's comfortable but worn offices in an aging skyscraper next to the Port Authority Bus Terminal on West Forty-second Street are testimony to the fact that union-oriented lawyers can make a decent living but could never hope to attract the fees and glitz of Wall Street and corporate clients. Gilberg didn't mind that. He came from a background that oriented him to progressive or working-class causes.

He and Susan Davis, another lawyer in the firm who also worked closely with Carey's local, spent their professional lives representing unions. Many of them were Teamster locals, some as good as Carey's, some with dirty backgrounds, even mob connections, which they and their clients always denied. But their lawyerly advice and skills centered on the mechanics of labor law, not ethics. In their free time, Gilberg and Davis wandered through some of labor's more interesting causes—traveling to El

Salvador to delve into the murder of labor leaders by right-wing death squads and to Nicaragua to examine the economic squeeze being applied to the Sandinista regime by the anti-Communist zealots of the Reagan administration.

What a contrast was their client, Ronald Carey, a fifty-three-year-old ex-marine and registered Republican whose idea of union activism was to work as hard as he could for the seven thousand members of Local 804, most of them drivers and package handlers for the UPS, spread across the Metropolitan area in New York City's five boroughs, Long Island, and Westchester County. "My activism has always been here, which is a full-time job. The activism has to be here" had been Carey's response to broadening his union horizons.

Carey was born on the East Side of Manhattan on March 22, 1936, to nineteen-year-old Loretta Carey and her husband, Joseph. The young family moved across the East River into Queens, eventually having six sons. They lived in the borough's inner neighborhoods: Astoria, Sunnyside, and Long Island City. Joseph Carey was a Teamster and a UPS driver for forty-five years, until retiring in 1976.

Ron Carey, who could have gone to St. John's University in Queens on a swimming scholarship after Long Island City High School, chose instead to join the marines in 1953 and marry his high school sweetheart, Barbara. He swam for the corps in Special Services and got out early after two years in an era when budgets were being slashed and the military was reduced in size.

Carey followed in his father's footsteps, hiring on at the UPS and working in the Woodside terminal. He was nineteen years old, and he quickly discovered he had chosen a life of hard work. United Parcel takes pride in being an efficient, productive company. Those qualities are earned at the price of a driven management that pushes its work force hard.

UPS Teamsters say that when you cross the line to join management, you punch in and are never off the clock, meaning you are a company man twenty-four hours a day, always on call, always thinking of the company, always pressing for production.

Carey made an early decision not to move into management but to make the union into something better. He was a shop steward within two years.

Local 804 in the late 1950s was evolving into a union that reflected the national Teamster leadership under Jimmy Hoffa.

Carey hated Hoffa's Robin Hood theory of "a little for you and a little for me and everybody's happy." There were hints of corruption in the local, reinforced by the presence of tough-guy operators like business agent Louis Sunshine and a union contract that seemed to protect the boss more than the workers.

Young Carey began hearing the irritating catchphrase "You're lucky to have a job" from Local 804's union leaders, who told those who stood up to complain at union meetings: "Sit down and shut up."

The wiry ex-marine, with his slicked-back hair and piercing eyes, talked out, anyhow. He ran as an independent for trustee in Local 804's 1962 election—and lost. He ran again in 1965 for recording secretary—and lost. He was beginning to get a reputation among his fellow drivers at the UPS package center in Woodside, Queens. Management had begun to take notice, too. Recalling that era, Carey said, "I remember one time standing outside the building and we had a problem. A UPS manager had been kicking a rock. He said, 'I wish this was your fucking head.' I just ignored it. He said, 'You're nothing but trouble.' "[41]

Carey learned from losing. In 1967, he put together a winning slate, with himself as president. At the core of his victory were two issues: member dissatisfaction with the contract and the way it was enforced and that hint of corruption.

Almost a quarter of a century later, Carey, now carrying twenty more pounds on his five-foot nine-inch frame, would run for general president of the 1.6-million-member IBT in an election whose core issues were the same: the contract and corruption.

When he took office in 1968, Carey imposed a regimen on the Local 804 staff of visiting job sites every morning to listen to the gripes of the members, to defuse problems before they became explosive, and to instruct new hires on the intricacies of working under a union contract.

The first contract Carey negotiated provided a revolutionary "twenty-five-years-and-out" pension, the dream of every worker who does hard work that tears at the body and can drain the soul.

Under Carey's presidency, Local 804 had a history of sporadic "wildcat" strikes, most lasting only a couple of hours or days, in which the workers at a UPS package center would storm off the job over the continuing confrontations, big and small, with supervisors. In 1970, Carey led all of Local 804's UPS members off the job for eleven days in an illegal strike over the issue of whether drivers could wear personal buttons on their dark brown uniforms reflecting messages of patriotism or ethnic pride. Some were wearing American flags, others Black Power, Irish Power, and Italian Power pins. Carey made a speech in front of city hall, and a federal judge imposed fines of $25,000 a day against the local and $2,500 against him personally. The strike was settled with an agreement that Carey would pay a $500 fine out of his own pocket and the drivers could wear flag pins but all others were a no-no.

Carey ended up in jail during the next strike in 1974 after Ed (Doc) Dougherty, a Local 804 trustee and a good friend of Carey's, was run down on a picket line in New Jersey by a UPS truck driven by another Teamster. In those days, Local 804 negotiated its contract directly with the UPS. On August 28, 1974, the local struck after a month without a new contract. The company used nonunion supervisors to drive the trucks from Queens and Manhattan to Secaucus, New Jersey, where members of Local 177, which was not on strike, were working. Carey dispatched pickets, who tried the tactic of standing in the way of trucks entering the facility. At 9:15 P.M. on the first day of the strike, a truck barreled right at the human wall. The others got out of the way in time, but Dougherty was run down and killed.

A shaken Carey ordered the Local 804 picket lines withdrawn. After visiting Dougherty's wife to break the ugly news directly to her and to comfort her as best he could, Carey went to Secaucus, where he cursed out a Local 177 member and then blocked another truck from entering the UPS operation with his car. The Secaucus police arrested him and held him overnight in jail.[42]

The strike ended twelve weeks later.

Carey labored on as Local 804's chief executive, making a modest salary, seldom taking a vacation, never learning to play golf, never traveling to Europe or any exotic locale, although he did manage to get to Disney World with his family—his wife, Barbara, and five children, three daughters and two sons: Ronald, Jr., Daniel, Sandra, Barbara, and Pamela. In the late 1950s, he and his parents bought a two-family house together in Kew Gardens, Queens. His mother and father moved in upstairs, and Carey's family lived downstairs.

Like many other New Yorkers, the elder Carey had a little country bungalow without running water in the wilds of northern

New Jersey, a place to escape the city's brutal summer heat. Ron Carey, who liked to work with his hands, always had plenty of work to do at his father's bungalow and at the same time a cheap vacation place for his own large brood.

In 1978, Steven Brill's book *The Teamsters* lifted Carey out of obscurity, citing his dedication to his members and his ideals as a union leader. In a chapter entitled "Ron Carey," Brill depicted Carey as a diamond in the dung heap of a union rife with corruption. If the Teamsters ever were to change, Brill predicted, it would take a person like Carey to do it.

Although Carey persistently denied that Brill's accolades were his inspiration to run for the presidency, Brill clearly did help plant the seed. The Carey chapter was a touchstone proving that his reputation as an aggressive, honest union leader with a sterling character wasn't manufactured just for the 1991 Teamster presidential campaign. Time and again, rank-and-file activists who checked Carey out to determine if he were "real" found themselves convinced after reading the Brill chapter.

UPS negotiators had maneuvered Local 804 out of the position of negotiating its own contract by agreeing to a generous settlement in 1979—at a price: From the 1982 contract on, Local 804 would fall under the national agreement. In one fell swoop, UPS had eliminated the aggressive Carey from the bargaining table but inadvertently set the stage for him to become a national presence among UPSers because of his anger over the concessionary national agreements and the refusal of the Teamster hierarchy to allow him to participate in the national negotiations. They put Carey in a box from which he exploded.

Carey came away from the 1979 negotiations under the impression that he was to be on the national negotiating team in 1982. That didn't happen. Instead, the negotiating committee, appointed by General President Frank Fitzsimmons, fell into the concessionary frenzy of the time, coming out with a contract that spurred Carey into action. He moved out of his local for the first time to campaign against the agreement. He traveled across the country urging UPSers everywhere to reject the contract. Nevertheless, it passed.

In 1985, the same scenario was repeated. Carey was denied a place on the national negotiating committee, a concessionary contract was reached, and again he campaigned for its defeat. Again the contract was approved.

In 1987, the national negotiating committee came back with a contract providing less than 2 percent a year in base wage hikes to the UPS's 140,000 Teamsters, along with a $1,000 lump-sum payment as a sweetener. Carey called the contract a "sellout" and went on the road to speak to UPS Teamsters, again urging rejection. Fifty-three percent, a majority of the rank and file, voted against the agreement, but General President Jackie Presser imposed it, anyhow. Presser contended that approval was automatic unless there was a two-thirds' negative vote.

A livid Carey filed suit in federal court seeking a ruling that the majority should prevail. He said he didn't want a strike. He wanted the company to be forced to return to the bargaining table to come up with a better offer.

To finance the court action, Carey wrote UPSers around the country asking them to contribute twenty dollars each to Teamsters for a Fair Contract, the ad hoc group formed for the purpose.

A few months later, another national contract, the Master Freight Agreement, covering 200,000 inter city truck drivers and warehouse workers, was rejected by almost two-thirds of the voters—64,101 to 36,782, or 63.5 percent against. Again, the Teamster leadership in Washington rammed the contract through despite the overwhelming opposition.

The outrage of the mass of Teamsters covered by these two contracts shook the Marble Palace. Local officials, who never openly opposed the hierarchy, joined in the screams that the majority must rule.

Al Barlow, the Teamsters' chief negotiator for the UPS contract, came to Carey to urge withdrawal of his federal court action. In return, he was promised that the Teamster constitution would be amended to provide majority rule and that Carey would have a place on the next national negotiating committee. That fall, the General Executive Board (GEB) approved the change from a two-thirds' vote to majority rule, but when the 1990 negotiations arrived there still wasn't a seat for a troublemaker like Carey on the national bargaining committee.

Since two-thousand rank and filers had sent in twenty-dollar checks to finance the Teamsters for a Fair Contract suit, Carey had a problem. Only a small portion of the money had been spent. He decided to give everyone a refund on a pro rata basis. One of his daughters sat down at home and wrote out two-thousand checks for $15.74 each. Carey had it done at home instead of the union hall to avoid providing an excuse for the International to move against him with a trusteeship on a manufactured charge of misuse of his local's facilities.

The majority-rule fight raised Carey in the consciousness of the activists and many other rank and filers among the 140,000 UPSers and the 200,000 truckers and warehouse workers covered by the National Master Freight Agreement.

The only blemish on Carey's Local 804 years came in 1987, when two FBI agents walked into his union office in Blissville to announce that they were investigating John F. Long, the local's secretary-treasurer.

Union politics had brought the two together, but they had come to despise one another. Carey's boycott of the 1976 and 1981 Teamster conventions enraged Long. In 1979, in the wake of Brill's book, Long had attempted to unseat Carey by enlisting Local 804's shop stewards in a palace coup against him, but the stewards refused to go along. One night, the hulking Long and the smaller Carey slugged it out outside their union hall, with Carey coming out bloodied. They managed to coexist after that, but not happily.

Long fitted into the mold of the swaggering, tough Teamster out to make a deal wherever he could. His braggadocio was picked up on FBI bugs planted in the offices of Jesse Hyman, a Long Island dentist with heavy mob ties. Hyman carried bags of money from Cleveland for distribution to mobsters in Buffalo, New York City, and New England. When Long hooked up with him, he was raising money for a loan-shark operation.

The deal Hyman offered looked very good: extraordinarily high interest rates for union funds invested through him and finders' fees for the union officials involved. Long's problem was Carey, who questioned every investment. He needed Carey's signature for any money to be moved. The dues money Local 804 accumulated went into certificates of deposit (CDs). Hyman arranged to blindside Carey by having a New York bank accept the money from Long as if it were going into a CD, then pass it along to him. Long managed to get $150,000 to Hyman in that fashion. Carey signed off on the investment, believing the money was going into the usual CDs.

Long eventually drew John Mahoney, Jr., president of Teamsters Local 808, another Queens-based local, into the scheme.

Mahoney arranged for $1 million of his union's pension fund to be placed with an investment firm fronting for the Hyman operation. When the Local 808 funds were put in the pot, Hyman returned Local 804's $150,000. Long must have thought he was home free.

Unfortunately, the loan-sharking operation proved to be a flop. Much of the money went into hare-brained schemes ranging from a glitzy Soho night club in Manhattan to a poster company in the Midwest. The loan sharks lost the money invested with them. The investment firm went bankrupt, and Local 808 lost its $1 million.

On December 14, 1987, Long was indicted for taking a payoff of $9,000 from Hyman; Mahoney, for taking $40,000.

As soon as the indictments came down, Carey acted to dump Long out of Local 804. "When I found out he had been involved in something, he had two choices: He could either retire, or we'd have to remove him," Carey said. Long chose retirement.

Long and Mahoney subsequently were convicted by a federal jury in Manhattan. The trial was held before U.S. District judge David N. Edelstein, who sentenced Long to twelve years in prison and Mahoney to fifteen years. The convictions later were reversed, but U.S. Attorney Rudy Giuliani used the trial of the Long and Mahoney cases as a pretext to bring the civil RICO case against the IBT before Judge Edelstein, a move that ensured that the suit would be heard by a hard-edged jurist who wouldn't flinch before organized labor's cries that government had no right to trespass on the union movement.

The Long case would be the core of the smut campaign designed to undermine Carey's reputation in the coming Teamster presidential election.

THE CAREY CAMPAIGN ORGANIZATION

Having decided to go for the presidency, Carey now had to figure out how to put together a national campaign organization. He started by talking to the people around him—his lawyers, Susan Davis and Rick Gilberg, and his old allies in Local 804: Pat Pagnanella, the secretary-treasurer; Ken Spillane, vice president; and Howie Redmond, the recording secretary.

Gilberg assumed that Carey's campaign would be a miniature

version of running for president of the United States. Gilberg recalled:

> I foolhardily had the notion this was going to be a modern political campaign. Campaign manager, fund-raisers, PR and media people, pollsters, direct-mail stuff. Not that we were going to be paying a staff of twenty professionals, but I thought there would be enough interest from the liberal, left, labor intelligentsia. We may have crossed on that, miscommunicated or whatever. I think Ron had the idea all along it was going to be rank-and-file, get-out-there, old-fashioned, meet-the-members campaign. Stripped down. Spend all the money on the campaign, not on fat salaries for staffers. So we had different ideas. I'm not a campaign professional. I had the idea there's going to be a staff.

Gilberg figured that money could be raised from the pro-labor liberal community, which had always been horrified by the crooked and conservative path the Teamster oligarchy had taken.

> Early on, Susan and I made some calls. We checked around the liberal labor community. Those ideas fell by the wayside. I don't remember what the rationale was. I just think that he [Carey] was nervous about opening it up to people he wasn't familiar with or didn't trust, or maybe it was intellectuals who would talk down to him. This is my psychoanalysis of this. I know when we start using the lawyer terms, he says, "Stop with the Ivy League education stuff." We'd draft stuff for him, as all lawyers do for clients. He'd say, "Well, you know I want to send this out to the members eventually. They're not going to understand this."
>
> It was nothing he ever said to me, but I had this gut feeling he didn't want to look like he had this sort of glamorous, slick, liberal, left campaign. I think it would have made him feel personally uncomfortable.

Carey's focus was on finding a campaign manager with a knowledge of unions and national election campaigns. The logical sources of such talent would be those connected to the Mine Workers or the Steel Workers, the two major unions whose officers were elected directly by the rank and file.

Davis and Gilberg began putting out feelers to organized labor's activist community. The first person they came up with was Steve Early, a Boston-based organizer for the Communication Workers of America (CWA), who had a rich background in labor's reform movements and in addition had a law degree. Early had worked for the Mine Workers on and off from 1973 to 1977, in Ed Sadlowski's 1976 campaign for the presidency of the Steel Workers, and for PROD (Professional Drivers Council for Safety and Health) from 1977 to 1979. He was as hardworking and dedicated to the broader "labor movement" as Carey was to Local 804.

They met on June 13, 1989, for a long discussion on the tactics used by challengers in national union elections and the labor activists who might be tapped for help or ideas. They touched on Early's possible role as campaign manager, but Early, who had spent so much of his life on subsistence wages for good causes, decided he just couldn't do it again.

"Maybe we ought to talk to a wider group to see if reality is there," Carey said to his lawyers.

The following month, on July 22, 1989, Carey held a brainstorming session at Cohen, Simon & Weiss that included Early, Gilberg, Davis, Ken Paff of TDU, and Bob Master, a New York–based CWA staffer who had once worked as a volunteer for TDU.

Carey came out of the meeting with more names and lots of ideas but still didn't have a campaign manager, someone who could deal with the mix of fund-raising, scheduling, and strategy. When he tried to tap labor-oriented public relations and marketing firms, he found that they either didn't want to risk being associated with him or had been told by other important labor clients to stay away from him.

Fingerhut and Powers, a Washington-based marketing and polling firm that had worked for the Mine Workers and Hospital Workers District 1199, considered taking on Carey but were dissuaded by the potential backlash against anyone construed to be aiding an enemy of the Teamster establishment. Organized labor generally has developed a one-party culture in which opposition candidates are equated with traitors.

Abernathy and Mitchell, a small Washington-based public relations and marketing company, was excited about the prospects of handling Carey. But Ray Abernathy said he would have to clear the assignment with his major client, the Service Employees International Union. At his suggestion, Carey called John Sweeney, president of the Service Employees, who told him he couldn't let Ray Abernathy go. Sweeney repeatedly asked Carey, "Do you think you're doing the right thing in running, Ron?"*

Someone jokingly suggested Gilberg could do the job, and Carey asked him whether he was interested. "That was floated," Gilberg said, "but it didn't make sense. In order to do it correctly, it would have meant taking an unpaid leave of absence from the law firm. It would have meant leaving my partnership responsibilities, my clients. It made sense to me that he get a full-time campaign person and still have his attorneys."

One name that kept popping up was Eddie Burke, a regional director of the United Mine Workers of America (UMWA), who currently was running the Pittston strike in the hill country of southwestern Virginia. Burke had an extensive background in union electoral politics. He had played a significant role in the Miners for Democracy dissident movement, which put Rich Trumka in the presidency of the UMWA. On Carey's short and shrinking list, Burke was one of the few remaining candidates.

CAREY'S PLATFORM

On Thursday, September 14, 1989, Carey outlined his reasons for running in an interview with *Newsday*.

"I don't like the direction the Teamsters have taken," he said. "It's very difficult when you pick up the papers every day and find the same problems about corruption. I don't think the government would be here if the Teamsters had done what they should have done."

The concessionary mode of bargaining applied by the hierarchy from 1981 on infuriated Carey.

> I think these guys are asleep behind the wheel. The results of the recent contracts with freight and UPS are clear indications of their lack of concern. Some of the major contracts are jokes. It is embarrassing. They are too sensitive to management problems. I'm not a great believer in cooperation and concessionary

---

*Sweeney denied saying this to Carey.

bargaining. Our priorities are in the opposite direction. Those agreements [with the UPS and National Freight] are bad agreements. If a company makes money, we're entitled to some of it.

Most Teamster leaders blamed the press and publicity-hungry prosecutors for the ugly image of the union, contending that the Teamsters were less corrupt than business leaders and that the tough-guy image helped organizing as much as it hurt. Carey's focus was on the rank and file's image of their own union and their leaders as fat cats filling their own pockets and taking care of their own relatives without too much concern for the members.

Carey had delivered at the bargaining table, winning a pension plan his members relished: After twenty-five years on the job, they could retire no matter what their age. In 1989, a twenty-five-year retiree received $1,340 a month; a thirty-year retiree, $1,650. That was an accomplishment that would electrify Teamsters in the coming two years.

"The first thing I would like to do is change the image, to have the members truly believe we're concerned about their problems and work in their interests," Carey said.

The jet fleet was on his mind. He said he would dump the six planes in which the Teamsters had $18 million invested, using the money instead for organizing. He would eliminate the multiple salaries, which added up to hundreds of thousands of dollars for the select few. "Money isn't my motivation. I like to have a roof over my head and enough to eat. I like to do what I do. I like helping people," he said. Those words could be passed off as the pious droppings of a union politician running for office, but in Carey's case, he lived what he said. His salary was $45,344 a year, less than a good number of his members made with overtime working for the UPS. "I don't think an official making $400,000 or $500,000 can relate to a guy who drives a truck or even care about him," he said.

"The first thing we have to think about is how much money, how much bargaining strength, has been given away as a result of the corruption problem. The way to deal with it is the way I dealt with it in my own local. Take the necessary steps to get rid of the problem," Carey said. "I don't think the Teamsters are tough anymore. I think they've lost their teeth. I think we have to get more aggressive."

Carey expressed confidence from the start, as would be expected, that he would win. "My biggest concern is we could win the election with the members and lose it at the ballot box," meaning the election could be stolen.

He summed up his platform to come: "I have a message. It is based on twenty years of experience, my record, some of the vision I have: a change in image, decent agreements, building the Teamsters through a positive plan of organizing."

That Sunday, September 17, he formally announced his candidacy to those who knew him best, a gathering of twenty-five hundred cheering Local 804 members at a meeting in Washington Irving High School, a few blocks from Union Square in Manhattan. The chemistry between Carey and his membership was evident that day in the reaction to his speech and the crowd of members who shook his hand and volunteered to work in his campaign.

A couple of weeks later, Carey and his eldest son, Ron, Jr., thirty-three, left New York on a Friday afternoon to drive to Camp Solidarity, headquarters for the Pittston strikers in Virginia. "I was very impressed by what I saw," Carey said. "I had heard so much about the Mine Workers. Folks told me, 'Ron, you have to see what is happening down there. The solidarity, the history of the Mine Workers union.'

"I felt there was some parallel between what happened in the Mine Workers union and what I think should be happening in the Teamsters'. Getting rid of the bums, getting some people back in there who care about working people, getting rid of the corruption problem."

This was a dual mission for Carey. Not only was he tasting a bit of labor history; he was able to form a quick impression of the strategist behind the Pittston strike. Carey shook hands with Eddie Burke, exchanging just a few words, explaining that he was running for general president of the Teamsters.

To Burke, Carey was just another visitor passing through. But Carey was struck by Burke, by what he had seen of Burke's accomplishments in Camp Solidarity and the strike. "You know when you talk to somebody and the chemistry is right, feels right. I always believed the eyes are mirrors of the soul. You look into somebody's eyes, you can pretty much tell where the / are coming from." Yet Carey hesitated. Burke's mustache, soft voice, and gentle expression give him the appearance more of an intellectual than a hardworking miner. Carey fostered an innate suspicion of intellectuals.

Carey spent the day wandering around the camp, meeting Burke's sidekick, Rick Blaylock, a huge man with a ready laugh and a patter of funny stories. Carey returned to New York with Burke on his mind.

"After I met Eddie and saw the kind of fight the Mine Workers were waging and the strategies put into that, I really had my mind pretty well set that this is the kind of guy I'll need, even though I didn't have a whole lot of discussion with him," Carey said.

CAREY GATHERS MOMENTUM

TDU sent invitations to speak at its annual rank-and-file convention in Pittsburgh during the second week of November 1989 to the three potential candidates for president: William J. McCarthy, the incumbent president; Weldon L. Mathis, the incumbent international secretary-treasurer, who had lost the squeaker 9–8 vote to McCarthy; and Ron Carey. Only Carey showed up to speak. No one really expected McCarthy or Mathis to come to a gathering of activists in the national dissident organization that after a decade was still exposing corrupt officials, fighting concessionary contracts, and fielding candidates in elections. The oligarchy considered TDU a pariah organization of lefties, misfits, and complainers.

The six hundred TDUers at the Westin William Penn Hotel were in high spirits. The theme of their convention was "We got the vote, and we're gonna use it."

On the opening day of the convention, Carey gave a rousing speech, punching home his points in his high-pitched, nasal, New York–accented voice, saying to cheers, "The party's over." The following night, the TDUers endorsed Carey for president.

Carey accepted the TDU's endorsement but carefully kept himself at a distance from the national dissident organization. Throughout the campaign to come, he emphasized that he was not the TDU candidate but that the group was just another Teamster organization that endorsed him and he welcomed all such endorsements.

Gilberg explained the reason for taking the endorsement:

My view about it was, and this is just hardball politics, they are going to say Carey is the TDU candidate, anyway. The downside is that for years Teamster leaders have been pounding it into the members that TDU is a bunch of complainers, dissidents, communists, employer representatives. A litany of propaganda that's now been tagged onto Ron.

Two positive notes. First, TDU and Ron share some core beliefs about the union. Ron's core belief about returning the union to the membership and having more democracy is what TDU has always claimed to be for. Second, TDU has a network of very dedicated and hardworking activists. It is the only network out there.

One immediate benefit of TDU's backing came in a hastily organized fund-raiser at the convention. Mike Ruscigno, a business agent of New York Teamsters Local 138, stood up and urged everyone to kick in $200 or more for the Carey campaign. Within ninety minutes, $22,200 had been collected.[43] Ruscigno knew all about reforming a dirty union. After he and a slate of TDUers announced they were running in the 1986 Local 138 elections, the incumbent president showed up at the warehouse where Ruscigno worked to pummel him with his fists in front of the other workers in a display of muscle consistent with the local's historical roots in the infamous Murder Incorporated. Local 138's members reacted by sweeping Ruscigno and the other reformers on his slate into power.

Among the TDUers at the convention—all of whom had paid their own way, the costs of transportation, meals, and hotel rooms coming out of their own pockets—was thirty-six-year-old Steve MacDonald, a cheerful, energetic Lucky Stores truck driver from Dixon in northern California. MacDonald shook Carey's hand, then checked him out with some Local 804 members who had come to Pittsburgh with him. "I read the chapter in Brill's book. That's the only chapter I read," MacDonald said with a smile. "Working Teamster to working Teamster, you can't bullshit a Teamster. I asked the people from 804, does Carey really come down these job sites every day? They said he did.

"That's very important, because in many areas of the country you're lucky to see a business agent once every six months. They run the local from their office. I've talked to many rank and filers and TDU activists all over the country. And it's the same story; they never see a business agent." MacDonald made a commitment in his mind to volunteer to work for Carey, and so did dozens of others.

———

After the TDU convention, Carey flew to Charleston, West Virginia, where Rick Blaylock had been dispatched to drive him to Camp Solidarity in Virginia. His hopes of speaking to Eddie Burke were dashed. He wasn't there.

Carey finally managed to catch Burke at home in Charleston toward the end of November. "I still need a campaign manager, and I'm very interested in you," Carey told him.

"I'm excited about what you're saying, Ron. I'd love to be of help, but I just can't do that. I've got this Pittston strike, and I've got to see this through. Why don't you call me back in the future."

"He left the door open," Carey told himself. He translated Burke's enthusiasm for reforming the labor movement into a strong indication he would accept the role of campaign manager the moment he was free of the Pittston strike.

Carey looked at the poster on the wall of his office that summed up his philosophy of life. The print of the breaking wave with the words emblazoned across it: "Momentum. Once you are moving in the direction of your goals . . . nothing can stop you." Another version might have been Goethe's observation: "The moment one definitely commits oneself, then Providence moves too. All sorts of things occur to help one that would never otherwise have occurred. A whole stream of events issues from the decision, raising in one's favor all manner of unforeseen incidents and meetings and material assistance, which no man could have dreamed would have come his way.

"Whatever you can do, or dream you can, begin it. Boldness has genius, power and magic in it. Begin it now."

Carey made the second call to Burke on January 4, 1990. Unaware that a tentative settlement had been reached in the Pittston strike, Carey said, "I could really use a guy like you, Ed." He had felt a sense of pressure building to get the campaign under way. He threw Burke's words of the previous November back at him: "This is another situation where you could be instrumental in change, in getting this union back to its members."

Burke said he was willing to do it, but he wanted to sit down to talk it out. They agreed he would come to New York.

Providence seemed to be in Carey's corner, but he didn't reflect on that. Thoughts of money—the lack of it—crowded his mind after he hung up the phone.

"How am I going to pay for this?" Carey asked himself. "What's it going to cost me. Holy Christ, now what do I do? I've got to start thinking about a payroll and traveling expenses."

McCARTHY MAKES MORE ENEMIES

As Ron Carey's campaign for the presidency was beginning to sprout, the incumbent general president, Billy McCarthy, was in the process of destroying the political base that might have given him a chance to be reelected.

The insecure seventy-two-year-old McCarthy started by stripping International vice president Dan Ligurotis of Chicago of his powerful offices as the chairman and director of the Central Conference of Teamsters. The chairman of a conference, which is the post of chief executive officer, is elected. The director, who is the liaison to Teamster headquarters, is appointed by the general president. The same person usually held both jobs.

Ligurotis had cast the deciding ballot in the 9–8 vote that put McCarthy in the presidency. But then Ligurotis had committed unpardonable sins in McCarthy's mind. He offended McCarthy at GEB meetings by criticizing some decisions, including his choice of Disney World in Orlando, Florida, as the site of the 1991 IBT Convention. And McCarthy was irritated by the "Ligurotis for President" poster in Ligurotis's office in Chicago, that a bunch of members had given him to show how great a guy they thought he was.

The night before the opening of the May 1989 Central Conference Convention in St. Louis, McCarthy called six members of the Central Conference Policy Committee into his hotel suite. He laid it out bluntly. He demanded that they vote against retaining Ligurotis as chairman of the Policy Committee. Two refused. Ligurotis was the seventh member of the Policy Committee, which is the governing body of the conference. That meant the vote for chairman would be 4–3 against him.

In the morning at the opening meeting of the convention, Ligurotis, who had been told of the plot against him, couldn't contain himself. With McCarthy and the entire Teamster GEB sitting behind him on the platform, Ligurotis blew up. He told the surprised delegates that McCarthy wanted him out. "If the general president doesn't want me in the conference, I will withdraw as a candidate, or I'll run and get elected and resign if he tells me he wants me out," Ligurotis said.[44]

McCarthy said, "That's not true!"

"You're a fuckin' liar," Ligurotis responded.

Robert Barnes, secretary-treasurer of Waukegan, Illinois, Local 301, rose in his chair on the floor of the convention to shout: "If that's the way you're treating Danny, then I want no part of this convention. I'm leaving." He walked out, followed by about two-thirds of the delegates, booing and screaming, "Fuck McCarthy," and, "Get rid of the old bastard."

That night, a compromise was worked out by Ligurotis and the other Central Conference leaders to resume the convention the following morning and to proceed with the election of the seven Policy Committee members but to delay the vote for chairman for a few weeks. That way they could avoid an open rupture of the delegates into factions.

The convention resumed the following day, with Ligurotis and six others being reelected without incident. Two weeks later, the Policy Committee met to oust Ligurotis and to elect Jack Yager, a Kansas City Teamster leader, as chairman. A month later, McCarthy removed Ligurotis as director of the Central Conference, putting Yager in his place.

McCarthy had humiliated Ligurotis and in the process had demonstrated the power of the general president, but at the cost of creating another influential enemy. That was not smart politics. Ligurotis was still an International vice president with a substantial following among Teamsters in Chicago and throughout the Midwest.

JOE T'S PREEMPTIVE STRIKE

Tempers were boiling as the Teamsters moved into the summer of 1990. Even the cautious Joe T signaled the struggle to come when he complained in a speech on July 16, 1990, at the Teamsters Industrial Trades Division meeting at the Chateau Champlain in Montreal, "We have spent six million dollars on Mudge Rose, and they haven't won case one. I'm going to raise that at the General Executive Board. Maybe I'm going to recommend we get a new set of lawyers," Trerotola told the delegates. McCarthy wasn't at the meeting, but his close pal, International vice president Frank Hackett, was.

The following week, at the GEB meeting in Montreal, McCarthy angrily snapped at Joe T for his remarks. "McCarthy took me on for that statement," Joe T recalled.

> He accused me of playing politics up there. I said, "Are you nuts? The only thing I said was we are paying too much money for lawyers and we're not getting anything out of it."
>
> He got sort of boisterous. It was the first time I had an argument with him. So I said, "Wait till after the meeting, I'll tell you about it."
>
> After the meeting, he didn't want to meet with me. . . . He wouldn't talk to me. He said, "I'll talk to you some other time." I said, "Now. I want to straighten this out." Never got a chance to straighten it out. From then on, that was it.[45]

Joe T, who was both chairman and director of the Eastern Conference, had no intention of arriving at his conference's convention to a nasty surprise the way Ligurotis had. He decided to move first.

As part of the process of outmaneuvering McCarthy, Joe T called in key leaders to make certain they were aligned with him and willing to go along with the dangerous program of confronting McCarthy.

Philadelphia Teamster leader John Morris, a rising star in Teamster politics who controlled a significant block of votes, described one of the insider meetings: "They called me into New York. Trerotola said, 'McCarthy's going to try to remove Walter Shea and me.' I said, 'We're against that. We'll support you on that.' "

Joe T told Morris he wanted to oust Hackett and R. V. Durham from their seats on the Eastern Conference Policy Committee, Morris had a different perspective. He was willing to cut Hackett's throat to ensure that the balance of power on the Policy Committee remained with Joe T, but he wasn't going to broaden the bloodbath to Durham without a good reason. Joe T talked and talked but couldn't convince Morris to dump Durham, too.[46]

The Eastern Conference Convention at Hilton Head, South Carolina, opened in August with a dramatic speech from General

Secretary-Treasurer Weldon Mathis that provided the Justice Department with solid evidence of the sentiment among the Teamster ruling elite that the 1991 rank-and-file election— agreed to in the consent decree—must be derailed.

At the opening session on August 20, 1990, Mathis told the 350 delegates, including Ron Carey, whose Local 804 is part of the Eastern Conference:

> Our entire democratic system is a system of delegates making decision for the masses. I am opposed to the membership vote for the officers of this international union.
>
> I really am not concerned whether you agree with me or not. I'm telling you my position. I believe that the system that this international union has had for electing officers of this international union is the best system there is. Ninety-five percent, maybe ninety-eight percent of the unions in this country elect their officers the same way that this union has elected its officers over the years.
>
> Now I expect to read tomorrow or next week in TDU that Weldon Mathis is opposed to the members voting for the officers of this international union, and that doesn't bother me, either.
>
> What does bother me is the prospect of our members, without knowing who is qualified to do a job at the national level, without knowing whether our general president is qualified, without knowing whether any of the vice presidents who are now or will be in the future are qualified, because they don't know them. They are not acquainted with them. They don't deal with them. The delegates are the people that deal with the International officers of this union. You know who's qualified. You know who's best qualified to represent the members of this International.

Delegate Ron Carey rose on a point of order: "Does this union belong to the membership?" he shouted.

When Joe T ruled Carey out of order, the audience reacted with a mixture of boos and applause.

Billy McCarthy and most of the members of the GEB were sitting on the podium behind Mathis. The delegates responded with polite applause when McCarthy spoke, telling them, "I'm running, and I'm going to be around to the year 2000." He was about to be knocked out of the box by Joe T.

Over the howls of the surprised McCarthy-aligned forces, the Rules Committee, controlled by Joe T, announced plans to use an unprecedented secret ballot for the election of the seven-member Policy Committee. A McCarthy ally from New England made a motion to change the rules. The motion was overwhelmingly defeated in a voice vote.

McCarthy realized a set-up was in the works when Barry Feinstein, the New York Teamster leader who headed the IBT's Public Employees Division, was nominated for the Policy Committee. Eight men were running for seven positions, meaning that for the first time in the thirty-eight-year history of the Eastern Conference, there would be a contested election.

McCarthy lobbied furiously for his close political ally Hackett, and the voting began. When the results of the secret ballot were tallied, McCarthy's man, Hackett, receiving only 115 votes, had been swept off the Policy Committee. But a new star of Teamster politics had been created: R. V. Durham, an International vice president from North Carolina, had led the pack with 300 votes. Durham had outscored even the popular Joe T. He and many others took this as sign of his vote-getting ability.

John Morris of Philadelphia had a different interpretation. Morris had brought 107 delegates, the largest contingent present, to the convention. Most, if not all, cast their ballots for Durham. Morris said, "R. V. got this big lift. It made him look good. It actually gave him his start, like he was a massive leader, the big vote getter."

A delegate told a reporter after the session: "What happened here is going to spread like wildfire in the Teamsters' organization. There must have been sixteen of the seventeen GEB members here. Every one of those vice presidents and observers are going to be calling home, saying, 'You won't believe what happened.' I think it's the death knell for McCarthy. How can a man win the general presidency of the Teamsters if the Eastern Conference is set against him?"

The master of the old Teamster politics, Joe T, inadvertently had illustrated how the union could be transformed once the voters—whether delegates or the mass of rank and filers—could cast their ballots in secret, without fear of retaliation.

McCarthy provided some sadly comic relief to the antagonistic proceedings. On a dare or to cool off or to amuse some youngsters—the stories vary—he jumped fully clothed into the hotel pool. The president of the most powerful and wealthy labor organization in the United States, wild Billy McCarthy was still capable of crazy stunts. He was to show that he remained vindictive, too, no matter what the political cost.

―――――

McCarthy didn't waste any time before striking back at his enemies. Within days, he used his power as president to remove International vice president Jack Cox from his assignment as the vice president in charge of northern California, stripping him of prestige and authority in his power base.

Cox, who had been one of the Big Nine who put McCarthy in office, had had the temerity to send McCarthy a letter criticizing him for his handling of the UPS contract negotiations. His letter ended with a startling statement: "Thank God we have many strong leaders who are fully qualified to serve as general president and lead our great International Union on a positive forward course. But, I must tell you that there is growing Local Union and membership sentiment that you do not number among them." Copies of the letter were distributed throughout the Teamsters union.

After McCarthy retaliated against him, Cox sent him a nastier letter, which also was widely distributed. In the letter, Cox confessed to having made a terrible mistake in voting for McCarthy as general president. He urged him to end the growing turmoil within the union by resigning.

In September, McCarthy struck again, firing Joe T's son Vincent Trerotola from his part-time $58,000-a-year job as an International representative. At the same time, McCarthy hired Weldon Mathis's son Lamar Mathis as an International representative, a signal that new deals were being cut and power blocs realigned within the GEB.

McCarthy had stung Joe T by bashing his beloved son, but his rampage of revenge wasn't over. At the October meeting of the GEB in the plush PGA National Resort in Palm Beach Gardens, Florida, McCarthy confronted Joe T, telling him he was kicking him out of his $75,000-a-year post as director of the Eastern Conference.

McCarthy told the members of the GEB, "As you know, under the constitution, the general president can appoint a director but must have the approval of the board to remove. I am making the motion Joe T be removed."

McCarthy's announcement set off an abrasive exchange:

"Why are you removing me?" Joe T demanded.

"Because you're inept," McCarthy shouted.

"That's bullshit. I've been chairman of the largest conference of Teamsters for twenty-one years and all of sudden you're gonna remove me because I'm inept?"

"I don't want to debate it," McCarthy snapped back. He commenced the roll call.[47]

The 12–5 vote ousting Joe T was to mark the division of the hierarchy into majority and minority blocs from that day.[48]

Joe T, the ex-kingmaker of the Teamsters, ended the board meeting with a zinger. He, too, apologized for having made the mistake of putting McCarthy in the presidency.[49]

R. V. DURHAM ENTERS THE RACE

That evening, McCarthy gathered the members of the majority bloc into a room at the PGA National Resort. In his direct fashion, he said without preamble, "I'm not running." McCarthy said he would continue as president until the 1991 IBT Convention. He left it to those in the room to choose his successor.

The leading contenders to replace McCarthy as the majority bloc candidate were R. V. Durham and Arnie Weinmeister, the ex-pro football player from Seattle. Weinmeister would carry some heavy baggage into a presidential race where the dressings of populism, including real union roots, would be the sine qua non of a candidate. Weinmeister could be branded a nepotist, because his path to union power had been eased by his brother, who preceded him as a Teamster official. His age, sixty-nine, and his income, $502,276 a year from four Teamster jobs, weren't pluses, either.[50]

In contrast, Durham was a youthful fifty-nine. His $160,000 annual income from two Teamster positions was more than comfortable but not extraordinary for a member of the union's Washington elite. On the positive side, the handsome, white-haired Durham came off a truck, rose through the union on his own, and had a reputation that sparkled.

After McCarthy left the room, Durham and Weinmeister stepped out into the hallway. They had anticipated McCarthy's decision and had been talking for weeks, each putting forth his reasons to be the one to head the ticket. Now Weinmeister said, "R. V., you reassure the people where you stand and where you want to take this union and I'll be with you."

Weinmeister said. "I'll back off."[51]

With Weinmeister's support, Durham emerged as the consensus candidate of the majority bloc. Weldon Mathis agreed to continue in the second spot as secretary-treasurer. Mathis's presidential ambitions had been quelled over the past two years. He had been marked as a loser at the International level in his 9–8 setback by McCarthy and back home in Georgia, where a reform slate, dominated by TDUers, ousted his family from control of Atlanta Teamsters Local 728.

The next day, Wednesday, October 10, 1990, Durham made a pitch to Joe T and Shea to back his candidacy. The usually diplomatic Joe T told Durham: "You son of a bitch, you want unity after you get rid of me [as Eastern Conference director]? You must have marbles in your head."[52]

Shea told Durham he had no intention this time around of giving away his chance to be president. Shea was convinced he could head a successful ticket himself with the backing of the big-city Teamster leaders in the East and Midwest. "You think you can win. I think I can win. I think we both would make good presidents," Shea said.[53]

In the old Teamster politics, Durham's role as the candidate of the majority bloc of the Teamsters GEB would have assured his election at the next convention.

But these were different times, and if Durham didn't realize it in the heady joy of being picked by the majority of his peers in the oligarchy amid the splendor of a resort hotel in Florida, he got the message quickly when he returned home to Local 391 in Kernersville, North Carolina.

Tom Page of Winston Salem, a shop steward at Roadway Express since Durham first ran for local office, told Durham he wouldn't support him for general president if he ran with those people from Washington. When Durham refused to back down, Page told Durham he would run against him in Local 391's election for delegates to the 1991 IBT Convention and formed an ad hoc group, Rank and File for Reform.

Two issues motivated Page and others challenging Durham: the need for a better pension program and a disenchantment with the Teamster rulers who had enriched themselves and distanced themselves from the needs of the rank and file. As Page explained, "People here weren't against Durham; it was who he was with."

Ralph Vinson Durham was born appropriately enough in Durham, North Carolina, on August 19, 1931, the son of Floyd Durham, a textile worker, whose eight-dollar-a-week paycheck was enough to feed his family, but not much more.

World War II brought a measure of prosperity to the Durhams. In 1942, the family, as did so many other poor folks from North Carolina in those days, moved to the tidewater area of Virginia to work the shipyards.

The Allied victory over the Axis brought a crashing end to war production in Virginia and everywhere else. The elder Durham emerged from this economic test of fire as a successful small-time entrepreneur, opening a series of small businesses centered on the labor he could contribute. He sold coal, then opened a fish market and a restaurant, and finally got into the trucking business, a decision that would shape his son's career.

Durham graduated from Hampton High School in 1948 and went to work driving a truck for his father, who had a combination household-moving and produce business. For about a year and a half, young Durham moved produce from the Lake Okeechobee section of Florida into the north. In 1950, Durham's father decided to return to his roots. He sold his trucking firm and restaurant and moved his family from Newport News, Virginia, back to North Carolina.

R. V., as he was now called, bought one of his father's trucks and went to work for Roadway Express. In those early days of what was to become a giant in the freight industry, drivers had to provide their own trucks. Durham leased on with Roadway and became a Teamster in October 1950. He was twenty years old.

Ironically, Durham's entry into local Teamster politics was made possible by the first federal-court effort to clean up the union. In 1957, thirteen rank-and-file Teamsters had challenged the legitimacy of the selection of delegates for the 1957 IBT Convention at which Jimmy Hoffa had been elected president.

At that time, Local 391 in North Carolina was under a union trusteeship. Durham recalled in an interview in January 1991:

> As part of the settlement (of the 1957 federal suit), there was a convention scheduled in '61. This is something probably most people don't know or forgot about. In '61 we had a delegate election just like we're going through now. As part of that settlement, every local elected their delegates to go to the convention in July of '61.
>
> So in '61 our local was given the opportunity to vote for the first time in a number of years because of this trusteeship. That's when I ran for office.

Instead of having a mentor who propelled him into his new career, Durham had a skill.

> I was driving for Roadway. I took an interest in tax law, and in between my trips I would do quite a number of the drivers' taxes. So as a result of that I had the exposure to quite a number of the members. When we finally were given an opportunity to elect officers, the guys working with me said, "Hey, you should run."
>
> Now there were thirty-three of us who ran for ten spots. There was two slates. I was one of those running independent for the number-two spot in the local. There was five of us running for that spot.
>
> When they got through counting the votes, we had four from one slate, two from the other slate, and myself as an independent. That was the makeup of the board in 1960.
>
> I served nine years until the president retired in '69. The members asked me to go for the top spot. I did, and I have served in that position ever since.

Durham developed a reputation as a good organizer and a union leader as caring and dedicated to Local 391's members as Ron Carey was to his members in New York. Durham was a daily visitor to work sites, just as Carey was.

Durham had the classic American family: a wife, a son, and a daughter. Ralph, Jr. went to work as a UPS driver after graduating from the University of North Carolina. After twelve years at the UPS, he began moving into the union structure, first elected as a trustee and then recording secretary of Teamsters Local 71 in Charlotte, North Carolina. Durham said proudly, "My boy established himself on his own." Durham's wife was employed as an office worker at Local 391.

In the radically different environment of North Carolina, Durham's hard work was rewarded. In 1969, he was elected president of Joint Council 9, which covers North Carolina and South Carolina. The presidency of a joint council is a significant power base in the world of the Teamsters and under the old politics was usually the staging ground for a leap into International office. There are only forty-three joint councils in North America.

Durham was noticed by the hierarchy.

After just two years as president of Local 391, Durham found himself being recruited by then general secretary-treasurer Murray W. (Dusty) Miller for a job as an International auditor. That would have meant giving up his positions at the local and joint council. Durham had no desire to trade his power base for a dead-end post. He turned Miller down.

General President Frank Fitzsimmons, under increasing pressure from PROD to do something about truck safety, decided to set up a Safety and Health Department in 1973. There are two versions of the story of Durham's selection as the IBT's first director of safety and health.

According to Shea, in discussing potential candidates to head the department, he asked Fitzsimmons: "Do you want a worker or a golfer?" Durham fit the bill of a worker. Shea and Fitzsimmons began talking to Durham about filling the slot as director of the new department.

Durham said that he attracted Fitzsimmons's attention because of his reputation as an advocate of trucking safety. "I took an interest in safety and health in the trucking industry from early on. So when they made a decision to bring somebody in, there were three or four guys in consideration, and they offered it to me."

Arthur Fox, the former executive director of PROD, offered a slightly different version. In 1971 or 1972, a member of Durham's local founded a PROD chapter with sixty to eighty members, all Roadway Express drivers concerned about safety. The PROD members were constantly pressing Durham on their safety concerns. As a result, according to Fox, Durham raised the question of truck safety at a 1973 national freight contract meeting in Chicago without getting a real answer.

A few months later, Fox wrote Fitzsimmons a letter informing him he was going to sue the IBT over the issue of safety and health. "Fitz gets my letter and says, 'Who was that guy who said something about truck safety? Get that guy up here.'"

Whatever version is correct, Durham negotiated a deal that enabled him to split his time between his local and his Washington-based role as director of safety and health. That meant a union with about 2 million members, most of whom worked for typical employers who paid little attention voluntarily to the safety or health of their employees, would have a part-time safety and health director. Of course, that was a giant leap from having no safety and health director.

When Durham arrived at the Marble Palace on October 1, 1973, he recalled, "There was nothing in place. They said, here's your office. I did a little soul-searching, brain storming, whatever. I was always trying to figure out what could I do? We have a helluva lot of members who are not in trucking, so there were areas I had to get up to speed on. My primary interest at that time was truck safety."

Durham's proudest accomplishments in safety and health all centered on trucking. He successfully fought the U.S. Department of Transportation's automatic disqualification of drivers who had undergone open heart surgery. Unable to get the government to move on requiring the air-conditioning of over-the-road trucks, which can be brutally hot in summer, he got the requirement included in the Teamsters' 1979 National Master Freight Agreement.

Being a former truck driver, Durham also understood the problem of the shrinking cab. State laws imposed length limitations on trucks, which were measured bumper to bumper. Responding to trucking-company demands, the manufacturers were making the trailers longer by cutting into the space allotted to the cab. Drivers were being crushed against their steering wheels.

Durham said:

> So we set out to get the law changed. We went over and testified before Congress. I took some model trucks over there. These guys didn't even know what a damned fifth wheel was. So I explained. Finally, we took some trucks over there and had Senator Kennedy and a number of the congressmen climb

in them. If they had any kind of a gut at all, it was laying over the damn steering wheel. The back of the seat was up against the back of the cab.

We convinced Congress, and the law was passed in 1982 to preempt the states from setting overall length limits. If they wanted to put length limits on the units, it had to be on the cargo-carrying part. So a result of that, the cab unit was left out of the equation.

After twelve years in Washington at his part-time post, Durham got the nudge from General President Jackie Presser in 1985 that put him on the inside track to becoming a member of the Teamster oligarchy. In 1985, Presser named Durham an International trustee. The union has three International trustees, whose constitutional role is to review the IBT's financial records every six months. In reality, the trustees are the farm team. Under the old politics they would wait patiently for a vice president to die, retire, or be imprisoned so that the most senior of them could be appointed to fill that vacancy.

At the 1986 convention, Durham was swept into office right along with the rest of the Presser slate. He sat quietly on the dais while the handful of TDU delegates were derided and cursed by loyalists on the floor for proposing reforms that included the direct election of the top officers by the rank and file, a doubling of the $45-a-week strike pay, the formation of an ethics committee, and a cap on officers' multiple salaries. Shea, who also sat on that dais as an International vice president, and Carey, who was seated with the delegation from Local 804, didn't stand up, either.

McCarthy moved Durham up to a vice presidency in January 1989 to fill the vacancy created by the forced resignation of Maurice R. Schurr of Philadelphia. McCarthy jumped Durham over two more senior trustees.

WALTER J. SHEA MAKES HIS MOVE

Courtesy demanded that he tell the boss what he was doing so that the incoming calls that were sure to flow wouldn't be a surprise. So Shea did it on the first Monday in November 1990. He walked into McCarthy's office in the Marble Palace and

handed him a sheet of paper with the letterhead "SHEA FOR GEN-
ERAL PRESIDENT COMMITTEE."

"Here it is," he said.

McCarthy didn't respond. He just glanced at the letter Shea
was mailing that day to the leaders of 621 Teamster locals in the
United States and Canada. After a brief, uncomfortable silence,
Shea returned to his own office.

He felt better. He read the letter again, going over the carefully
written line "Over the weekend, I decided to put it all on the line
and declare my candidacy for general president."

Everyone assumed that Shea would be Joe T's candidate for
president. Yet as much as he hungered for the top job, he ago-
nized over reaching this decision, taking this step. He thought
about it and talked it over with friends, including his lawyer, Bob
Baptiste; Joe Konowe, head of the Industrial Division; and Bill
Joyce, the seventy-four-year-old head of Chicago Local 710. The
sum of the advice he got was "Don't do it. Don't run. The job is
a killer."

A presidential bug is very hard to shake. Shea had come so
close to being president in 1988 that it was a painful memory to
consider how differently the union would have been had someone with his political and administrative skills been picked instead
of McCarthy. He knew he was more qualified than the men he
had served as an assistant. He wasn't going to be anyone's assistant anymore. This letter was a declaration that was all behind
him forever.

In the letter, Shea asked the local leaders to circulate petitions
for his accreditation as a presidential candidate under the rules
developed by court-appointed election officer Michael Holland.
He needed 38,500 signatures by the December 14 deadline. That
was only five weeks away, but since he was drawing on a pool of
1.6 million members, he figured, no problem.

Shea had done a lot of favors for Teamster officials across the
country, and he was sure they would come through for him. He
knew hundreds, perhaps thousands, of Teamsters. He believed
that anyone looking at the record would be as convinced as he
that Walter Shea, who had served every president from Jimmy
Hoffa to Billy McCarthy, knew more about running this huge
international union than anyone else.

Two weeks went by. On November 15, his secretary said in
passing, "By the way, Walter, McCarthy asked me if you are

going to be in tomorrow." They both knew he was. Billy was so unpredictable, he knew that it would be an exercise in frustration to mull over what he wanted. Logicially, it would be to talk about Shea's entry into the presidential race, but McCarthy's memory was so shot by his stroke, he might have forgotten that already.

At a quarter to ten the following morning, McCarthy's secretary called Shea. "He wants to see you," she said.

Shea later recalled:

> I walked up to his office and sat down. I was chatting about the freight contract when McCarthy said very quietly, "I'm going to remove you."
>
> I said, "What's that?"
>
> He said, "I'm going to remove you as my assistant. I want you out of here today. Take everything out of your office. But don't take anything that doesn't belong to you."
>
> I said, "Why are you doing this?"
>
> He said, "You're not loyal." He kept saying that over and over. After so many 'disloyals,' he said, "Well, when I was recovering from my heart surgery, you and Trerotola and Morgan got together to try to get rid of me."
>
> I said, "That's not true. That is absolutely not true." Bullshit is what I said to him.

That brief exchange cost Shea not only $75,000 a year in extra salary that went with being an assistant to the president but his union car as well. He had inherited Jackie Presser's 1989 Lincoln. "I'd like to keep the car till Monday, until I get another car," he said.

"That's all right," McCarthy said.

As he rose to leave, another thought struck Shea. "Billy, I can't get out of here in eight hours. I've been here for twenty-four years."

"I don't care. I want you out of here," McCarthy replied.

Shea had a place to fall back on. He moved into Joe T's office, with its print of *Custer's Last Stand* on the wall, in the headquarters of the Eastern Conference in Bethesda, Maryland, a surburb of Washington.

A tall, slender, gracious, gray-haired man of sixty at the time of his departure from Teamster headquarters, Shea had a longness about him in body and face. At six feet three inches and two hundred pounds, he was still athletic on the edge of old age.

Shea graduated from Brooklyn's Lafayette High School in 1947, playing end on the team that won the city high school championship. His reward was a four-year scholarship to the University of South Carolina.

There were 105 players on the first day of practice at South Carolina and only three left when he graduated four years later. Shea wanted to be a teacher, a radical departure from the family calling. He was the son, grandson, and nephew of New York City policemen.

Shea, who has a tendency to hold his ever-present long cigars right in the center of his mouth, proudly recalled that his father, Walter, joined the police department in 1918 and went on to become a detective first-grade, as did his uncle Jim, who served his time in Manhattan's Chinatown. In 1934, his other uncle, Jeffrey, became the youngest policeman ever to be made captain in the city police department.

"My cousin Jimmy Shea, who was also a policeman in New York, was responsible for the capture of Son of Sam. He just retired. He was Jim Shea's son, and if I had stayed up there, I would have done the same thing probably," said Shea reflectively in an interview in his office at the Eastern Conference. "And I would have loved it," he added.

Shea, too, has loved the career he did pursue. "Oh, it's been great. Absolutely fascinating," he said.

Being fired brought Shea in a symbolic full circle back to where his career as a Teamster began. He was hired on April 27, 1957, as a research assistant to Eastern Conference director Tom Flynn, who had been General President Dan Tobin's executive assistant for fourteen years. After graduating from college, Shea served two years in the air force as a lieutenant, then worked another year as a claims adjuster for an insurance company before signing on with the Teamsters. In 1958, Shea became a member of Washington, D.C., Teamsters Local 992.

In the late 1950s and early 1960s, Shea did the research for a freight-industry study that Hoffa used in putting together the first National Master Freight Agreement in 1963.

Shea was present at the 1961 convention in Miami Beach at which Jimmy Hoffa was reelected and pushed through constitutional amendments giving the general president enormous power and perks.

Shea recalled with relish how the tradition of the Eastern Conference throwing elaborate parties at the IBT's quinquennial conventions was born.

> At the '61 convention, we were in Florida, and they had an airline strike. Nobody could get out of town. Tom Flynn put on a luau at the Americana Hotel, now called the Sheraton Bal Harbour.
>
> That luau is remembered by everybody because it was a nice, fitting ending to a great convention. We took over the hotel. They had all these little booths behind the hotel, with palms all over the place, with bars and food. They had this put together in twenty-four hours. I'll bet we had five thousand people. I don't know how the hell it was done, but it was done in twenty-four hours. Now that cost $50,000 in 1961. This party set the tone for the Eastern Conference subsequently on things like that.
>
> It was a huge success. John English [general secretary-treasurer] walked in and said to Tom Flynn, "Who are these people?"
>
> Tom said, "They're all my friends."
>
> "Who's paying for this?"
>
> "I am," Tom said.

Perhaps Flynn could be forgiven for misspeaking. The members' dues were paying for the party. He was just treating that money as if it were his own.

A reform movement gave Shea his first grand opportunity in the Teamsters, a chance to work with the legendary Hoffa. In the early 1960s, some Teamster leaders reacted with revulsion to a combination of Hoffa's dictatorial regime and the epidemic of corruption and mobsterism that was tainting the union. In Cincinnati, James Lukens defied Hoffa and pulled Local 98 out of the Teamsters, reaffiliating with the AFL-CIO. George Meany, president of the AFL-CIO and an enemy of Hoffa's, welcomed Local 98 back into the House of Labor in a ceremony on November 3, 1961.[54]

There were similar stirrings fostered by Meany in Philadelphia, where dissidents from several locals formed the Voice of the Teamsters Democratic Organizing Committee. Shea described his involvement in crushing the reformers:

Hoffa called all of the leaders of the local making up Philadelphia Joint Council 53 to a meeting in Washington, D.C., in the winter of 1962.

He announced at that meeting he personally was coming into Philadelphia to run this campaign against this defection, because if we lost that campaign, Meany was going to charter a rival Teamsters union. Meany was going to issue federal charters in ten major cities. This was heavy potatoes.

Hoffa came on like gangbusters. He says, "We can't afford to lose this group." It was about ten or twelve thousand truck drivers, dockmen that wanted to defect. And Hoffa says, "I want that tall guy from the Eastern Conference here." He didn't know my name, but I guess he knew who I was, because I prepared the freight study.

I spent six months with him up there. Lived with him at the Warwick Hotel. What an experience that was.

The vote was in March or April of '63. He brought in eighty representatives from all over the United States to service the people, to run all over that town to win that election. We went up there January one and stayed there right through it. Nobody could go home. If anybody snuck home, he raised hell with them. And he had two federal indictments hanging over his head. One in Chattanooga and one in Nashville, or whatever, at the time.

It was the most interesting three months living with him. Seven o'clock in the morning until two in the morning. He was up before me and went to bed after me. Fascinating. Ate with him. Lived with him. Met with him. Oh, what an experience.

That was Hoffa's highest moment, the night we won the election two and a half to one.[55]

A decade after Shea joined the IBT, his dedicated work as an administrator was rewarded when Hoffa appointed him as an international general organizer. Despite the title, general organizers don't necessarily organize people. They do whatever the general president wants.

Hoffa didn't last long at the Marble Palace. His appeals exhausted from his 1964 jury tampering conviction, Hoffa began his prison term in the Lewisburg federal penitentiary in Pennsylvania, and Frank Fitzsimmons succeeded him as the IBT's ruling officer in March 1967.

Fitzsimmons immediately made Shea his executive assistant, giving him a grand opportunity to apply and hone his administrative skills at the International level. Shea's loyalty and willingness to work won Fitzsimmons's trust over the years. When he became ill, he shifted so much responsibility to Shea that he became the de facto president of the IBT while the elected president rested and golfed.

"Fitz was a cute Irishman," Shea said, thinking back to those happy days. "Fitz was a clever guy. He used to say, 'Walter, I'm not bright, but I'm a good politician.' And he was. He was a terrible speaker. His grammar was atrocious. Guys liked him. He had a nice smile. He was like an old shoe.

"Fitz had a rapport with Nixon second to no one. Nixon would call him up and say, 'Frank, come on over to the White House. I want to talk to you.' Nixon was absolutely charmed by him."

The charming Fitzsimmons, who was generous with Teamster money for Nixon's reelection campaign and with jobs and contracts for veterans of his White House staff, got something heavy in return. Shea said, "When Nixon was going to send a trucking deregulation bill in, he pulled it back because of Fitz."

When Fitzsimmons died in 1981 after fourteen years at the top of the Teamsters, Shea stayed on as executive assistant to his successor, Roy Williams, whose rise through the Teamsters had been nurtured by the Kansas City mob.

Shea said, "Roy Williams was very inarticulate. He was not terribly bright, but he knew trucking, and he knew freight. He operated on animal instinct. He never had much to say. He hated the job as general president. He hated the responsibility. He hated Washington. I don't know why he took it."

Right from the start, Williams was identified in the press as a child of the mob. When Shea asked him about allegations that he was being controlled by the Kansas City syndicate, Williams said, "Forget about it. It means nothing."

To friends who inquired, "How could you work for people like that?" Shea responded, "What am I going to do about it?"

Besides, in December 1982, Williams made Shea an International vice president. Twenty-five years after joining the Teamsters, Walter Shea had finally become an officer. In the process, he skipped all of the usual rungs in between and was promoted right to the top because of his accomplishments as an administrator and the friends he made along the way, particularly Joe T.

The transformation of Shea from a general organizer with no political base into an officer of high stature coincided with his unhappy years in the Marble Palace. Jackie Presser kept Shea nominally on the presidential staff when he succeeded Williams in 1983 but excluded Shea from the inner circles of power. "He considered me a threat," Shea said. "I had plenty to do, but I didn't have the same authority or presence with him as with his two predecessors. He kept me in my office at arm's length."

At the same time, Presser knew how to feed egos. "Presser said, 'Walter, you're the smartest guy on this board.' He'd placate me. Sent me to Taiwan for two weeks. He sent me to El Salvador to get me killed," Shea said facetiously. "He put me on the Panama Canal Commission. All very interesting things, and I enjoyed them. It was very broadening, those three trips. I relish them."

When Presser died in 1988, Shea came so close to grabbing the golden crown that the ever-suspicious McCarthy could never allow him to taste real power in his Marble Palace. Shea said, "McCarthy promised me two things. One, I would be his executive assistant and I would be doing a lot of the work or most of the work. And secondly a pay increase which he never gave me."

As the 1991 presidential campaign got under way, with its promise of a new era for the IBT, Shea said almost dreamily, "I hope it will be a good ending and not an evil one or a bad one or some of the endings we've seen. The Teamsters' legacy! Think that Dan Tobin was the president for forty-five years. He put FDR's name in nomination at the '44 Convention at the Statler Hotel here in Washington at 16th and K Street.

"You talk about clout. We were held in high esteem. We were the pinnacle of the labor movement. That's heavy stuff. That's the way it ought to be."

THE THREE OTHER CANDIDATES

Three minor candidates emerged in the presidential race: Lou Riga, secretary-treasurer of San Jose, California, Local 576; Bill Genoese, director of the Teamster Airline Division and secretary-treasurer of New York airline employees Local 732; and James

P. Hoffa, son of Jimmy Hoffa and a lawyer for several Teamster locals in Michigan.

Lou Riga, fifty-four, announcing a full year after Carey, became the second candidate to declare for the presidency. He sought to open his campaign with a splash on October 8, 1990, flying from city to city for a series of press conferences designed to spread his name through the media and to generate support.

The initial press conference at New York's Waldorf-Astoria drew a lone print reporter. A bit baffled by the lack of interest, Riga pushed on, traveling over the next week to fifteen cities.

Riga, whose political base was his comparatively small fifteen-hundred-member local of automotive workers, generated neither significant media coverage nor an upsurge of backers. Still, he was convinced that anyone with reasonable credentials who tried could generate the ninety-eight votes from the 1,942 delegates to the Teamsters Convention to be nominated and placed on the ballot.

———

Bill Genoese had a toehold on a national reputation from a twenty-eight-year career that included organizing thousands of workers at Pan American World Airway, Braniff, and other airlines.

As director of the union's 35,000-member airline division, Genoese had the potential of a following large enough to give him the ninety-eight needed delegate votes. His skill as a union politician constantly in contact with Teamster officials around the country and in his native New York was one of his strengths.

The sixty-four-year-old Genoese took pride in working a six-day week during which he collected and analyzed all available data on the IBT, along with the routine matters that consume a labor leader in running a union.

Convinced that the Hoffa name, so readily recognized and revered by many, could be a ticket to the Marble Palace, Genoese talked about his willingness to combine his candidacy with young Hoffa's.

From the start, Teamster insiders predicted Genoese would use his announced candidacy to leverage himself a slot on one of the three major slates.

On February 5, 1991, Genoese announced he was running. The following month, McCarthy fired him as director of the

Airline Division, a post that paid him $86,527 in salary and expenses in 1989. The balance of his $219,834 income came from Local 732.

———

Jimmy Hoffa, the son and lawyer, ran smack into a legalism when he finally announced after months of speculation that he was running for his father's old job as president of the Teamsters on February 20, 1991.

A rank-and-file Teamster in Detroit immediately challenged Hoffa's eligibility to run. The election rules and the Teamster constitution required two years of working as a Teamster. "He's never been a legitimate member of the union and has never worked within the craft," the challenger said.[56]

Hoffa contended that his twenty-two years of service as an attorney in a practice devoted almost entirely to individual Teamsters and locals satisfied the work requirement, and besides, he was as an administrative aide to Larry Brennan, president of Michigan Teamsters Joint Council 43, since April 9, 1990.

Election officer Michael Holland rejected Hoffa's arguments, ruling that his work as an attorney in private practice couldn't be construed as being a working Teamster. The job with Brennan didn't add up to the required twenty-four months of service, Holland said. Hoffa's supporters were disappointed. They believed the Hoffa name alone gave him the winning edge in a national election in which most of the members didn't know or didn't care who was running.

8

The Tortoise
and the Hares

Like the tortoise in the fairy tale, Ron Carey was running against heavy odds when he finally went on road campaigning in January 1990—four months after his announcement for the presidency. Although the finish line was twenty-two months away, Carey started running slowly and steadily toward that distant goal, the only candidate actively pursuing the rank-and-file vote.

The incumbents in the Marble Palace in Washington, D.C., weren't paying much attention to the self-proclaimed grass-roots candidate. Guys like him were a joke. There was always an opposition candidate popping up from the inexhaustible pool of reformers, and like a mosquito on a hot summer day, each one, while briefly irritating, was squashed.

When Carey arrived on Saturday, January 20, at the Lincoln Motor Inn in Columbus, Ohio, the general president, William J. McCarthy, was still proclaiming his intention to run for reelection. The pool of voters McCarthy would face this time would be significantly larger than the seventeen men who cast ballots at the July 1988 meeting of the General Executive Board (GEB) in Washington.

The Teamster insiders were branding Carey a maverick, calling him the TDU (Teamsters for a Democratic Union) candidate. How many members did the TDU have? Ten thousand at most. That was .625 percent of the 1.6 million Teamster members "represented" by Billy McCarthy and his cohorts. The emphasis was always on "represent." The claim by the insiders was that TDU didn't represent anybody, didn't negotiate contracts, didn't handle grievances. Just complained and stirred up trouble.

The audience of 370 Teamsters who showed up at the rally in Columbus initiating Carey's whistle-stop campaign should have stirred a sense of concern in Washington.

About 270 of those gathered in the dark, V-shaped conference room were from Local 413 in Columbus, 170 of them UPSers. The remaining 100 came from fourteen locals spread across five states: Kentucky, Michigan, West Virginia, Pennsylvania, and Ohio. They were a mix of TDUers, independent activists, members of committees formed to improve Teamster pensions, and the curious.

TDU had worked to turn out a crowd from central and southern Ohio, but a substantial number were walk-ins, drawn by a desire to change their union or to find out what Carey was all about. And some had traveled hours to be there. Not many truck drivers and factory workers living in a world of television, chores to be done at home, and family demands give up a Saturday or Sunday casually. These were people who cared.

Carey's speech was a bit flat that day; he hadn't yet learned to rouse the crowd the way he would as the campaign progressed. But he touched on the subjects that formed the unchanging core of his campaign: obtaining better pensions, getting rid of multiple salaries, ending corruption—including the failure to enforce contracts—and transforming the International Brotherhood of Teamsters (IBT) into a union that responded to the members instead of the bosses at the bargaining table.

Ken Paff, TDU's national organizer, watched Carey's performance and later wrote a critique. He noted that the agenda had been much too long: three hours and twenty minutes. "Two hours should be the normal length," he advised. By the time Carey got up to speak, the audience had already listened to two hours of local speakers and questions and answers and was understandably restless. But they stayed to the end.

Carey failed to apply the simple, ego-polishing technique of saying, "Hey, did you know that twenty people drove nearly four hours from Louisville today? Let's hear from one of you guys. What are you going to do for the Ron Carey campaign in your area?"

The pitch for money, pledges, and campaign volunteers didn't come until the end of the long meeting. "Haven't any of these people ever been to church?" Paff asked rhetorically. "The pitch needs to be in mid-meeting, while it's a peak, needs to be integrated into the meeting and weaved through it, and needs to involve people from the audience."

Paff had helped organize the meeting, but he acknowledged that they obviously were not yet a well-oiled machine. The meeting room was awful, crowded and stuffy—really two separate rooms in a *V* shape with a bad sound system.

The biggest faux pas was the failure to stress the need for volunteers to spread the word in their workplace, to sign up friends, to collect money. Campaigns eat money: travel expenses, meetings rooms, meals and hotels, not to mention buttons, literature, and the salaries of staffers.

Afterward, about fifty people remained for another meeting to discuss putting together Carey delegate slates in their locals. Naturally, these slates would be construed as threats to the entrenched local leaders, who, with the astuteness learned in "old Teamster politics," were waiting to see which way the powers in Washington leaned before committing themselves. They had learned not to take risks and wanted to be sure to be on the winning side.

The relatively unknown Carey reaped the benefit of publicity that day, getting a story about his rally in the *Columbus Dispatch* along with coverage by the local television stations.

It was a beginning. Eddie Burke, the Mine Worker, had agreed to assume his role as campaign manager on February 1. Burke's arrival would mean a more carefully organized campaign, with an emphasis on hitting the barns and factories where the Teamsters worked along with gatherings or rallies such as this first one. A veteran of several rank-and-file campaigns, Burke was a believer that touching flesh and looking into a member's eyes won elections.

Discussing the first weekend foray on the campaign trail in a telephone conversation, the new campaign manager gave Carey his quick analysis: "Hell, you can't win it on weekend meetings. You got to be out there with the people. The votes are at the plant gates and in the washhouses and at the crossroads."

"Yeah," said Carey. "You're right, buddy."

Carey returned to work at Local 804 in Queens that Monday, beginning a cycle of working through the week and traveling to a different section of the country every weekend to campaign. It would carry him to forty-four states and more than a hundred cities over the next two years. Sometimes he took a Friday or Monday as a vacation day to campaign. For the next twenty-two months, Carey spent seven days a week either trekking after votes or working as a Teamster officer and business agent at Local 804.

The persistent question would be whether his unrelenting schedule would burn out the highly energetic Carey before the ballots were cast in late 1991.

In retrospect, Burke figured it took him about two months to decide on a strategy for running a national campaign on a shoestring budget. He rented an apartment in a working-class section of Queens for a combination office and New York base. There wasn't enough money in the budget to pay for regular airfare runs between his home in Charleston, West Virginia, and New York City. Driving that distance, which he often did in the next two years, was wearing and wasteful of his time, which could be better spent organizing and planning the campaign.

That May, Burke hired Charleston-based Tom Knight as a public relations and marketing consultant and rented some space in Knight's office. With fax machines, six computers, and six laser printers, Knight had the technological tools in his office to do Carey's literature, including the layouts, and to prepare mailings. "Tom brought twenty years experience, including some years as a newspaper reporter and House of Delegates member. He had writing ability; he could lay out material; he had the computers to do the printing," Burke recalled fondly, "One stop shopping: generate it, work it out, and mail it."

THE ELECTION RULES

Election Officer Michael Holland issued the rules governing the 1991 election on April 27, 1990. As expected, they required every local to hold separate, secret rank-and-file elections to choose delegates—the number based on the size of the local— to the 1991 IBT Convention in Disney World. At the convention, the delegates would perform two crucial roles: They would vote in the open on the floor of the convention, as delegates always did, on amendments to the union constitution. The second task was something new. For the first time, the delegates would vote in secret ballots to nominate GEB candidates for the December 1991 election—the general president, the general secretary-treasurer, eleven regional vice presidents, and five at-large vice presidents. To be nominated, a candidate would be required to get the votes of at least 5 percent of delegates for his or her area. That meant the presidential candidates needed about ninety-six to ninety-eight votes, depending on how many delegates were sent to the convention, a number based on the IBT's fluctuating membership. A candidate for vice president of the relatively small Southern Conference would need only seven votes.

The departure from the past practice of having local Teamster officers automatically become convention delegates upset many incumbents. Now they would have to run for a delegate slot. Many complained bitterly that this extra election being foisted on them was an unnecessary expense. They predicted that virtually all of those elected as delegates would be the officers who would have gotten those posts automatically.

But the theory behind the new delegate elections was that members might be willing to send someone with a particular political orientation to the convention as a delegate whom they were not willing to elect as an officer responsible for negotiating and enforcing contracts. The new mix of delegates would transform the convention from a rubber stamp to a more diverse and democratic gathering.

The theorists favoring the delegate elections, which were to be held in two stages—from October 15 through December 31, 1990, and from January 15 through March 31, 1991—would prove to be right. The 1991 convention would be like nothing the Teamsters had ever seen before.

A proviso in Holland's rules gave Carey the opportunity to prove the viability of his candidacy by achieving the status of an "accredited candidate." Under the rules, those who collected the signatures of 2.5 percent of the eligible voters for their office would be declared accredited candidates. Accreditation and nomination were two separate processes.

The rewards of accreditation were significant for a dissident candidate like Carey. Accredited candidates were entitled to copies of the union membership lists, which labor organizations seldom make available to opposition candidates. And they would be allocated pages in the October 1990 and February 1991 editions of the *International Teamster*. There were two deadlines for accreditation: the first on August 31, 1990, which would entitle the qualifying candidates to ad space in both the October and February magazines; the second on December 15, 1990, which would give some candidates an extended time span to collect signatures and enable new entrants to qualify for space in the February magazine.

For presidential candidates, that meant gathering 38,533 signatures. While that sounds like a modest number in a union of 1.6 million members, Teamsters don't put their names on such petitions readily. Such an action could involve some risk, including the loss of a job for offending local union leaders. In addition, most members didn't know there was an election, didn't care, and didn't want to get involved.

THE FIRST MAJOR TEST

By May 1990, Carey was telling his audiences that he was running against apathy, not McCarthy. He and his campaign manager, Eddie Burke, figured that if Carey could achieve accreditation by the August 31, 1990 deadline, he would both establish his credentials as a viable candidate and be entitled to a full page in the October issue of the *International Teamster*, which was mailed to every member. Carey couldn't afford to reach such a large audience on his own. Passing the hat at campaign stops was financing his travel, but he had nowhere near the $250,000 a single mailing to every member would cost.

Burke, who took on the role of coordinating the petition effort, knew from experience how difficult the job could be. But he realized that the petition drive would be a form of on-the-job training for the volunteers, who would be the crucial element in turning out the vote in a grass-roots campaign. By the summer of 1990, Carey had been to thirty states, held fifty rallies, drawing anywhere from twenty-five to five hundred Teamsters, and visited hundreds of work sites to shake hands and answer questions. He had developed a cadre of volunteers and TDU activists across the country.

At the outset of the campaign to gather the signatures at the end of May 1990, Burke, in his down-home style, told Carey, "Ron, the old saying is there are only two ways to run for office. Either run unopposed or hard and scared. We got to run hard." Burke started by mailing the petitions to 112 volunteers. He worked the phone from his headquarters in Charleston, calling Teamsters all over the country and urging them to press for the names Ron Carey needed. Within six weeks, the volunteer force had grown to six hundred rank and filers. Eddie Burke liked what he was seeing.

In northern California, Steve MacDonald took a week's vacation from his job as a truck driver for Lucky Stores to coordinate 125 rank and filers gathering signatures. When the vacation was over, he rose at three or four in the morning to put in several hours hitting job sites to keep the names flowing before he began his regular workday behind the wheel of a truck at 9:00 A.M.

In Denver, J. B. McAllister, a laid-off member of Local 961 and editor of the Colorado TDU chapter, assumed the role of organizing the Carey petition drive. J.B. collected only eight or nine signatures himself, but he made sure that other TDUers, like Roy Ray, who collected three hundred signatures, got the petitions.

"The pressure we had to go through to collect those signatures!" J.B. recalled. "We're amateurs. We're truck drivers." He said the election-campaign techniques of pushing petitions were an adventure in a foreign realm to the muscular, tatooed truck drivers of his world.

J.B. called Carey volunteers across Colorado to prod them, ask them what they were doing with their petitions. "They'd say, 'Damn it, I forgot.' Then they'd go out and get them signed. We collected a little over twelve hundred signatures in Colorado. About twelve percent of the membership."

Within seven weeks, 51,048 signatures had been collected. By the August 31 deadline for the first round of certification, 58,726 names were on the petitions—some twenty thousand more than the minimum needed.

General President Billy McCarthy, still the only other declared presidential candidate, didn't bother with the accreditation process. He controlled the magazine and the membership lists.

The incumbent president certainly didn't have to worry about hustling after votes like Carey, the underdog.

———

While Eddie Burke was traveling the country in the summer of 1990, creating a network of local organizations for Carey's grassroots campaign, Teamsters general counsel James Grady was still fighting the consent decree. On July 31, Grady sent Otto Obermeier, U.S. Attorney for the Southern District, a letter saying that the IBT believed the delegates to the 1991 convention should be free to vote on whether to accept or reject the amendments to the Teamster constitution imposed by the consent decree. The assumption was that the delegates would reject the rank-and-file election and, following tradition, sweep the incumbent hierarchy back into office.

The Justice Department was having no part of that. Obermeier warned the IBT that the government was aware of the widespread speculation that there might be an attempt to derail the rank-and-file vote.

While members of the oligarchy spent their energies fighting one another and the implementation of the consent decree, Carey was rallying his forces for his next major test: the delegate elections.

THE DIRTY CAMPAIGN AGAINST CAREY

By the fall of 1990, Ron Carey's candidacy couldn't be put in a box and denied anymore. His page in the October *International Teamster* was topped by a simple headline: "RON CAREY'S ANGRY!" His political ad, well laid out and written in precise, direct language, told the magazine's mass audience that the handful of men at the top had sold out the Teamsters, first by inviting the government into the union and "then spending $12 million of our money trying to block the members from electing top national officers." Those at the top, the ad said, had given themselves multiple salaries, supported politicians who served the interests of greedy corporations, and negotiated concessionary contracts with two-tier wages, inadequate pensions, and kangaroo-court grievance procedures.

The counterattack came early in December in the form of a colorful four-page tabloid, *Teamster Election News*, designed to muddy Carey's impeccable reputation. Volume 1, number 1 used the John Long case as the basis for inflammatory headlines:

GOVERNMENT INVESTIGATION REVEALS ORGANIZED

CRIME, CORRUPTION AND "SWEETHEART CONTRACTS"

IN RON CAREY'S LOCAL 804!

and

EVIDENCE IN U.S. V LONG

SHOWS MOB INFILTRATION

OF TEAMSTERS LOCAL 804

TDU's endorsement of Carey was used as the basis of a headline:

RON CAREY'S TDU BACKERS HAVE ACCEPTED OVER ONE

MILLION DOLLARS IN EMPLOYER-LINKED CONTRIBUTIONS!

A front-page profile of Carey in the *Wall Street Journal* of November 12, 1990, was used to illustrate a fictional connection between Carey and the lords of Wall Street. The lead of the story in the *Teamster Election News* said:"The official newspaper of Corporate America, the *Wall Street Journal*, has given its unmistakable endorsement to Ron Carey's campaign to take over the Teamsters." The headline in the *Teamster Election News* said:

BIG BUSINESS SAYS:

"CAREY'S OUR MAN!"

The stories under the headlines were a mix of facts, falsehoods, and innuendos in an attempt to make Carey appear as corrupt and vile as so many other Teamster officials whose sins invariably were condoned by those who led the union.

None of the articles were signed, although the front page said, "Published by Teamsters for an Informed Membership." No further information was provided on this organization, but anyone who wanted additional copies was advised on the back page to write to a post office box in Washington, D.C. Those who inquired were told they could order more copies from RL Communications Inc. of Detroit, Michigan.

Richard Gilberg, Carey's attorney, filed a complaint with Holland, the election officer, on December 27, 1990, demanding an investigation into origins, financing, and distribution of the smut sheet. The complaint noted that in the past two weeks the smut had popped up all over the country and cited the results of his investigation:

RL Communications is the brainchild of Richard Leebove, a former associate of Lyndon LaRouche, and a longtime dirty trickster, propagandist, and smear artist who has frequently been hired to attack union reform efforts, including in Detroit-area Teamster locals.

It is certainly fair to surmise that funding for this unprecedented nationwide effort to discredit the Carey campaign has been provided by Union officials (and possibly employers) opposed to the Carey candidacy.

Leebove, who ran for attorney general of Illinois on the right-wing U.S. Labor party ticket headed by LaRouche in the late 1970s, went on to become a public relations consultant for Teamster organizations. He produced newsletters, newspapers, and magazines for major Detroit locals. He traveled the country smearing TDU and also put out the *Rank and File Defender*, a newspaper for BLAST (Brotherhood of Loyal Americans and Strong Teamsters), the organization of bully boys formed by Jackie Presser to bash TDU.

As Holland moved into his investigation, Gilberg kept adding complaints. There were allegations that Ralph Durham, son of the presidential candidate, directed a member to put copies of *Teamster Election News* in the lockers of UPS employees in Charlotte, North Carolina, and reports that International vice president Frank Hackett distributed the smut sheet at an executive board meeting of Boston Local 496.

Holland's investigation showed that Teamsters for an Informed Membership's only function was as a front for the Leebove operation. "Mr. Leebove marketed the publication by sending copies to a group of twenty-five IBT officials and by distributing copies at a charity dinner sponsored by Mercy Hospital honoring Jack Yager held in Chicago, Illinois, on December 12, 1990," the election officer's report said.

Approximately 70,800 copies of the tabloid, entirely written by Leebove, were distributed to sixty IBT members and officers in major cities across the nation. Leebove sent fifteen hundred copies without charge to two anti-Carey candidates for delegate in Atlanta Local 728 after they told him they didn't have the money—$525—to pay. The smears didn't take hold in Local 728, a TDU stronghold, which had been wrested from the Mathis family.

During the Pittston Coal strike Eddie Burke (left, with bullhorn) leads a force of ninety-eight miners on a march to occupy Moss Number Three in Virginia on September 17, 1989. Burke became Ron Carey's campaign manager. *Don Petersen*

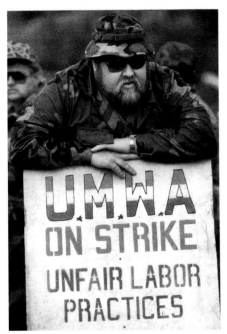

Rick Blaylock at Camp Solidarity in the hills of Virginia during the 1989 Mine Workers strike against Pittston Coal. Blaylock joined Carey as a campaign staffer. *Don Petersen*

Ron Carey at his office at Teamsters Local 804 in Queens, New York. Carey announced his candidacy for the General Presidency of the Teamsters on September 17, 1989. *Jim West/Impact Visuals*

Dave Beck, IBT General President 1952–1957. *IBT archives*

Jimmy Hoffa, IBT General President 1957–1967. *IBT archives*

Frank E. Fitzsimmons, IBT General President 1967–1981. *IBT archives*

Roy L. Williams, IBT General President 1981–1983. *IBT archives*

Jackie Presser, IBT General President 1983–1988. *IBT archives*

William J. McCarthy, IBT General President 1988–1992. *IBT archives*

Teamsters General President Jackie Presser being rolled into the lavish Eastern Conference party at Caesars Palace during the 1986 IBT Convention. *James Hamilton*

John Sikorski (at podium) speaks at 1976 PROD press conference in Washington, D.C., to announce publication of the report *Teamster Democracy and Financial Responsibility*. PROD executive director Arthur Fox is seated in the foreground on the left with his hands crossed. *John Sikorski personal collection*

TDU national organizer Ken Paff. *Jim West/Impact Visuals*

TDU staffer Steve Kindred. *Jim West/ Impact Visuals*

Susan Jennik, then a TDU organizer, leads a picket line of activists demonstrating outside the 1986 IBT Convention in Las Vegas. *Jim West/ Impact Visuals*

TDU activist Diana Kilmury. *IBT archives*

U.S. Attorney Rudolph Giuliani announces the filing of the civil RICO suit against the IBT on June 28, 1988, in Manhattan. From left are: Assistant U.S. Attorney Randy Mastro; William Doran, the special agent in charge of the FBI's New York office; Giuliani. *New York Newsday/Al Raia*

Cartoonist Mike Konopacki's prophetic portrayal of Uncle Sam arranging for TDU to deliver a magic kiss to the Teamster frog, which appeared in the *Labor Notes* issue of April 12, 1989. *Mike Konopacki*

Elections Officer Michael H. Holland tallying ballots in the delegate vote for General Presidential nominees at the 1991 IBT Convention at Disney World. *Earl Dotter*

Investigations Officer Charles M. Carberry. *Courtesy of Charles Carberry*

Independent Administrator Frederick B. Lacey. *Courtesy of Frederick B. Lacey*

Judge David Edelstein. *Courtesy of Judge David Edelstein*

Ron Carey is paraded around the convention hall at Disney World on the shoulders of his supporters. From left in the foreground: Carey running mates C. Sam Theodus, Mario Perruci, and Gene Giacumbo. *Earl Dotter*

Walter Shea making his acceptance speech after being nominated at the 1991 IBT Convention. *Earl Dotter*

Candidate R. V. Durham, in shirtsleeves at left, in the midst of a mixed demonstration of Shea, Carey, and Durham supporters at the 1991 IBT Convention. *Earl Dotter*

R. V. Durham casts his ballot. *Earl Dotter*

Ron Carey, left, speaking to supporters at the June 1991 IBT Convention. At right is Tom Sever, candidate for General Secretary-Treasurer on the Carey slate. *Jim West/ Impact Visuals*

They're Feasting

On Your Dues!

The Ron Carey Slate

General Secretary-Treasurer
Tom Sever
Jeannette, PA
Local 30

Vice President At Large
John Riojas
San Antonio, TX
Local 657

Vice President At Large
Jim Benson
Phoenix, AZ
Local 104

Vice President At Large
Diana Kilmury
Vancouver, BC
Local 155

Vice President At Large
Mario Perrucci
Hillside, NJ
Local 177

Vice President At Large
Sam Theodus
Cleveland, OH
Local 407

Central Conference Vice President
Leroy Ellis
Chicago, IL
Local 705

NOTICE:
*Your **SECRET** BALLOT will be
mailed to your home on or about
NOVEMBER 8th.*

To vote for a change, vote for the entire Carey Slate!

From the Carey slate's advertising insert in the October 1991 *International Teamster*. The flipside of the pig image reads "The Durham Slate Is Still Hungry!" An inside page of the ad shows some of Carey's running mates. *The November Group*

Ron Carey campaigning for the IBT presidency outside the UPS Center in Livonia, Michigan. *Jim West/Impact Visuals*

Ron Carey is sworn in on February 1, 1992, as the new General President of the International Brotherhood of Teamsters. *Jim West/Impact Visuals*

Ron Carey shaking hands with well-wishers outside the Marble Palace on his inauguration day. *Jim West/Impact Visuals*

Holland accepted Leebove's contention that he saw a business opportunity in smearing Carey and seized it. Leebove's books showed the project cost $8,800, sales totaled $20,000, and the profit was $11,200.

Leebove was directed to pay the Carey campaign $4,765, which was the value of either discounted or free copies given to some Teamsters. That ruling was later reversed on appeal.

While Holland didn't touch on the allegations involving Ralph Durham and Hackett, he said in his decision that penalties could not be imposed under the Teamster election rules for false and defamatory campaign statements. "The cardinal principle is that the best remedy for untrue speech is more speech, with the electorate being the final arbiter," Holland said.

Young Durham's father, R. V. Durham, said his son told him he had nothing to do with the distribution of *Teamster Election News*. He didn't care what Walter Shea or Carey did, Durham, Sr., said. He had no intention of getting involved in negative campaigning.

As the campaign heated up, Durham's good intentions soured under the pressure of the new Teamster politics. The nasty broadsides exchanged by Durham and Carey were a mix of the amusing and the downright dirty.

TWO HARES IN PURSUIT OF CAREY

The next deadline for accreditation under the election rules was December 15, 1990, almost six weeks after Shea mailed his letter to local leaders around the country announcing his candidacy and asking their help in collecting signatures.

He failed. Shea neither got the needed signatures nor realized that local Teamster leaders around the country weren't stirred to action simply because he had decided to run.

Shea offered his version of what happened: "I started too late," he said. "The locals unions that promised to get them in, got them in, but didn't get enough of them in. They were distracted. A lot of our people were going through the throes of election for delegates.

"I felt I could get those signatures even in that short period of time. But these people had another priority. So they didn't push like they would have or could have."

While Shea's effort foundered, Joe T successfully sought accreditation as a regional vice president. The conclusion to be drawn was that Shea didn't have the standing to inspire local leaders or the campaign organization to pressure them into carrying out a petition drive.

R. V. Durham didn't bother pursuing the accreditation route. Ostensibly, he had little to gain, since he had ready access to the Teamster magazine as the candidate blessed with McCarthy's backing. That point was proven by the December and January issues of the *International Teamster* in which four photos of Durham appeared in each magazine along with complimentary stories about his activities in negotiating the National Master Freight Agreement and serving with the Teamsters' Medical Advisory Committee.

Durham was confident that had he chosen to circulate petitions, his allies in the majority block of the GEB easily could have collected the necessary signatures.

Whatever the rationale, Durham didn't put himself to the voluntary accreditation test, which might have given him an early signal of the ineffectual political network on which he was basing his campaign.

––––––

Meanwhile, Carey announced his first four running mates on November 9, 1990. With a touch of innovation for the IBT, he named a woman candidate. He also struck a balance between the traditional local Teamsters Union political structure and the reformer/activists of TDU. Tom Sever, the third-term president of Local 30 in Jeannette, Pennsylvania, would run for general secretary-treasurer on the Carey ticket. Mario Perrucci, secretary-treasurer of Local 177 in Hillside, New Jersey, and Diana Kilmury, a TDUer and a truck driver–member of Local 155 in Vancouver, would run for vice presidents at large. Doug Mims, another TDUer and vice president of Local 728 in Atlanta, Georgia, would run for regional vice president in the Southern Conference.

Carey and Burke decided to have his four running mates seek accreditation. This would mean putting the volunteer network through the ordeal of another petition drive. Burke would urge the volunteers to get the signatures of different Teamsters from those who put their names on Carey's petition. The underlying strategy was to get even more people aware of the Carey campaign to oust the incumbents. This person-to-person approach that signing petitions fostered fitted into Burke's philosophy of building a rank-and-file base that could win the election.

As North America–wide candidates, Sever, Perrucci, and Kilmury would need 38,533 signatures, while Mims would only have to get 3,000 from the comparatively small Southern Conference.

Like Shea, the Carey candidates didn't have much time. Again Burke put the network of TDUers and Carey volunteers into action. This time the number of volunteers going after the signatures swelled to eight hundred.

Burke asked the volunteers to turn in their petitions by Friday, December 6, a little over a week before they were due in Holland's office. On the eve of the self-imposed deadline, he got a bit nervous. "On Thursday (December 5), we had 25,000. On Friday, 7,000 more rolled in. We needed 38,000. Between Friday and Monday, we had 42,000. Then 700 more came in. Finally, we collected 62,000 signatures," Burke said.

The effectiveness of the Carey organization should have sent shivers through the hierarchy.

Accreditation entitled the Carey slate to three and a quarter pages in the February 1991 issue of the *International Teamster*. Holland's rules gave the presidential candidate a full page, the secretary-treasurer three-quarters of a page; and vice presidential candidates a half page each—and permitted candidates to put their pages together to produce a single package. The slate's political ad, written by Burke with the help of a communications consultant, banged R. V. Durham and his running mate Weldon Mathis for sitting silently while top officers larded their salaries. It attacked Durham, Mathis, Shea, and his running mate, Daniel Ligurotis, for their cushy salaries. Just a few pages later in the same magazine, Independent Administrator Frederick B. Lacey's report to the members inadvertently reinforced Carey's message by listing the name of Mathis's son, Weldon L. Mathis, Jr., as a McCarthy appointee to International organizer.

THE FRONT RUNNER?

R. V. Durham was off to a good start. *Washington Post* labor reporter Frank Swoboda almost immediately declared him the front-runner in a news story on November 3, 1990. Swoboda apparently assumed that the "old politics" would prevail. A number of other newspapers and college professors called upon by the press for instant analysis, fell into lockstep by anointing Durham as front-runner.

To help shape his campaign, Durham turned to a longtime friend, Chris Scott, president of the North Carolina State AFL-CIO.

Late in October 1990, Scott and union political directors from around North Carolina met in Local 391's conference room to plan the final phase of what would be an unsuccessful campaign to topple conservative Republican Jesse Helms from his senate seat in the November election.

"After the meeting R. V. asked if I could stay for a few minutes," Scott said. "He said he'd like for me to come on board to run his campaign if I could get a leave of absence or if I was willing to take a flier."

The laid-back Durham suggested that Scott give the idea some thought before he made a decision.

The following Sunday, they met for a long lunch in an uncomfortable little booth in Susie's Diner near Durham's union hall in Kernersville. Scott had a lot of questions on the mechanics of the election and who was lined up for and against them. A typical question that occurs to anyone involved with the Teamsters popped into his mind: "I wanted to know if R. V. expected to be threatened or in any way intimidated. I wanted to know of any skeleton in his closet." Durham gave the right answers, but Scott still wanted a little more time to consider what would be a jolt to the comfortable life he had carved for himself.

The forty-six-year-old Scott lived with his wife and their four-month-old son in Raleigh, just a few minutes from his office. He was enjoying fatherhood and didn't want to give up this precious time in his new son's life. But at the same time, he felt a sense of excitement just thinking about the Durham campaign. Besides, this was a thunderbolt of his own making.

Scott had grown up in the comfortable suburban setting of Garden City on Long Island, where his father taught at Hofstra University from 1947 to 1987. Scott himself graduated from Hofstra in 1967, then went on to get a master's degree at the University of Texas.

Scott said:

I come out of a civil rights, antiwar background with a certain antiestablishment orientation. I've always had a sense of organized labor as a force for good. It really crystallized for me at the University of Texas, when I was involved in a strike at the student cafeteria. The employees were Hispanic. They sent in the riot squad with helmets and shields. They beat the crap out of us.

I got into the labor movement through political campaign work. During the presidential race of '72, I was issues director for the Citizens for McGovern/Shriver in North Carolina. McGovern got twenty-nine percent of the North Carolina vote. Afterwards, I looked around for the only institution less popular than McGovern, and I got a job as research director for the North Carolina State AFL-CIO.

In 1976, Scott went to work for Gov. Jim Hunt as his labor adviser. Three years later, Durham hired him as a combination public relations man, lobbyist, and organizer. "The several years I was with R. V. I began to recognize what a competent and caring leader he was. Most of the things I know about leadership I learned from R. V.," Scott said.

The Communication Workers of America, (CWA) a major force among North Carolina unions, recruited Scott away from the Teamsters late in 1980, with the goal of eventually inserting him into the presidency of the state AFL-CIO. On the day he left, Scott told Durham in a good-bye chat that he was the kind of a man the Teamsters needed as president and if the opportunity ever arose to run for the job, he should seize it.

At the time, Durham had a toehold in Teamster headquarters as safety and health director, but it seemed obvious to Scott and others that someone of his caliber would move into the inner sanctums of power. "Since I've known him, people have been saying to him, 'When the opportunity comes you need to take it,' " Scott said, admitting that this lofty goal seemed unrealistic in the context of the old Teamster politics.

In 1983, Scott became president of the state AFL-CIO and continued his warm relationship with his Teamster mentor. "R. V. and I stayed close over the years. About once a year I'd sit down and say, 'The members of this union need you,' " Scott said.

Scott said in an interview early in 1991, "Frankly, I think organized labor is in real difficulties. The Teamsters Union is one of the two or three resources that we have potentially to change things around in a dramatic fashion. The one person I met in the course of my career who I thought could accomplish that was R. V. Durham and thereby not only just affect the Teamsters union but affect, I think, the future of working people in this country."

With his wife urging him to fulfill his dream of putting Durham in the presidency of the Teamsters, Scott called him on November 15. "I'm interested," he said. "I've thought about this, and I think this is really something to do and I'll be glad to help." He arranged for a leave of absence from his post as state AFL-CIO president.

At the outset, Scott laid out a simple strategy. He anticipated that Durham would win a majority of the delegate votes at the nominating convention in June. The ultimate challenge would be the rank-and-file election. "It is really a get-out-the-vote contest," he said in an interview in January 1991.

> Basically, what we will do is mirror the existing structure of the Teamsters. The end product will be a committee in every local union, with as many committed supporters as we can get. On election day, their job is going to be to pull out that vote. Hopefully, we'll be able to say, for example, in Local 639, Here is the Unity Committee of five hundred people or a thousand people. They are willing to publicly say they are for us. That is the most effective communication device you have. No question that it will be imperfect. The more people we have, the more marginal voters will be pulled in our direction, and that's really what we want to do.
>
> We don't want to sit there on election day and wonder whether the vote is being turned out.

Underlying Scott's hunger to turn out Teamster members en masse to vote for Durham was his desire to develop a clear mandate for his candidate to reshape the IBT into something better than what it was.

It occurred to him that the opposition candidates could disappear, leaving Durham unchallenged in the December 1991 rank-and-file election. "Suppose Carey doesn't get his five percent and suppose Shea and Ligurotis merge into our slate. I'd be in favor of doing this, anyhow, and making it into an effort to get a mandate. I don't want to win this thing eight thousand votes to zero. The more votes we get, the more organization we have, the better off the union is for the future, and the more people we've identified who actually will do work and actually communicate with each other."

From the perspective of January 1991, Durham appeared on the verge of fulfilling his destiny.

The pieces began falling into place quickly with some catchy electioneering talk. The ticket was called the "Durham-Mathis Unity Team," and their platform was introduced under the slogan "New directions for a proud, powerful, and democratic union."

"Some members say we need to make the Teamsters more open and democratic. Others say we need to build on our past experience and successes to make the Teamsters more powerful than ever," said the initial piece of campaign literature in an attempt to appeal to both those unhappy with the union and those satisfied with it. The platform included support for a constitutional amendment to make direct membership voting a permanent part of IBT elections and the creation of a permanent, independent ethics review committee.

The Durham-Mathis platform illustrated how malleable a candidate could be. Just a few months earlier, Mathis had urged delegates at the Eastern Conference Convention to vote against the rank-and-file election on the theory that the average member didn't have the smarts to be trusted with a ballot selecting the IBT's top officers. Mathis refused to discuss this change of heart, but Durham said that his running mate was in accord, as were all those aligned with him.

When TDU and its allies at the 1976, 1981, and 1986 Teamster conventions raised the direct-vote and ethics-committee issues, they were accused of trying to undermine the union. Since those two concepts were centerpieces of the consent decree, which embodied them in the Teamster constitution, the Durham-Mathis Unity Team wasn't bravely pioneering reforms, but, rather, accepting reality.

The Durham-Mathis Unity Team picked up the endorsement of the Teamsters National Black Caucus on January 16, 1991. Since there were 300,000 to 400,000 black Teamsters, this seemed to be an endorsement that could transform the Unity Team into an irresistible juggernaut. But a little digging showed that the Black Caucus was a paper-thin layer of black officers and staffers—not a grass-roots organization of the mass of black

Teamster members driving trucks or working in warehouses, factories, and offices across the nation.

Aside from issuing some campaign literature, neither Durham or Shea went out to the rank and file for several months after declaring their candidacies. They focused instead on the inside baseball of the old Teamster politics, assuming that they could eventually cut a deal on a consensus slate.

In the meantime, Independent Administrator Frederick Lacey issued a series of decisions removing three International vice presidents from office in January and February. Exercising his veto power under the consent decree, Lacey canceled the appointment of Jack Yager of Kansas City as a vice president because of his close ties to the late Roy Williams throughout his career as mob puppet. Lacey dumped Vice President Theodore Cozza of Pittsburgh out of the union altogether for his organized crime connections. He suspended Vice President George Vitale of Detroit from the IBT for five years for embezzling union funds and taking a payoff from an employer.

The three were members of the majority bloc that backed Durham's candidacy, and Lacey's actions damaged Durham's campaign claim that he was the reform candidate.

TURMOIL AT THE TOP GETS WORSE

The Teamster oligarchy was in turmoil as 1991 opened. Lame-duck general president Billy McCarthy contributed to the divisiveness by either instigating, or at the very least permitting, the filing of internal union charges by two of his New England Teamster buddies against Vice President Jack Cox on January 7. Cox was accused of violating the IBT constitution by ridiculing and criticizing McCarthy the previous September. The case was never brought to a hearing.

Later the same month, on January 25, Walter Shea and five other Teamster officials or staffers who had been stripped of their appointive jobs by McCarthy struck back by filing a civil RICO suit in New York federal court demanding his ouster as general president. That case was still unresolved a year later when McCarthy left office.

A more stinging blow was delivered to McCarthy by R. V. Durham the following week, on January 31, 1991, at a GEB meeting in Palm Springs, California. In a rare moment in Teamster history, the board rejected an appointment by the general president, refusing to approve McCarthy's selection of Al Barlow, an Eastern Conference staffer, as a vice president. There were four vacancies on the board as the result of Joe Morgan's retirement in December and Lacey's removal of three others.

Going into the executive board meeting, McCarthy knew that Durham and his allies, along with the Joe T forces, were aligned against him, but he still placed Barlow's name in nomination. Barlow was rejected by a 9–5 vote.

Adding to the stress on the besieged McCarthy, Frederick Lacey chose to issue his long-awaited report on the $3.8-million-a-year contract awarded to McCarthy's son-in-law's firm, Windsor Graphics, to print the Teamster magazine.

Lacey's strident language seemed to augur another Teamster head tumbling under the consent decree:

"Regrettably, pervasive nepotism is to be found at every level of the IBT and its affiliates. . . . Here it resulted in Windsor being invited to bid without any references or credit check."

Lacey's report said that since Windsor lacked the required credit rating, the IBT guaranteed the payments for the paper and printing and gave the fledgling company $1,344,422 in cash advances between May 5, 1989, and November 2, 1989. He said:

> I find that from the beginning of the bidding process, the IBT's General President and its Director of Communications [Duke Zeller] distorted the bidding process to enable them to award the Magazine printing to Windsor.
>
> I find that Messrs. McCarthy and Zeller were guilty of extorting the rights of the members of the IBT by implementing their hidden plan to award the Magazine printing to Windsor. . . . The aforesaid scheme and conduct constituted breaches of Messrs. McCarthy and Zeller's fiduciary responsibility to the IBT membership.

That all added up, Lacey contended, to an act of racketeering by McCarthy.[57]

The contract was taken away from Windsor and awarded to another company. But despite Lacey's conclusion that the deal constituted a form of racketeering, McCarthy was permitted to serve out his term of office as general president of the Teamsters without any action against him by Lacey, the Justice Department, or court-appointed investigations officer Charles Carberry. During his remaining year as president, the usually contentious Billy McCarthy was comparatively subdued in his dealings with the court officers.

Lacey's harsh words and soft actions led Teamsters, shaped by the revelations of Jackie Presser's role as a man on a government string, to wonder whether McCarthy had cut himself a deal.

Yet Weldon Mathis seized the opening offered by Lacey's report to urge the GEB, in a message sent across the Teamster communications system on February 7, 1991, to appoint a three-member committee and a special counsel to investigate the awarding of the magazine contract to Windsor Graphics. McCarthy rejected the proposal. Mathis countered by polling the other twelve members of the GEB to determine whether a special meeting would be held to consider a review of Lacey's finding against McCarthy.

McCarthy, whose political coin was dross, risked being removed from office if the Mathis proposal was carried out. Mathis's move could be interpreted in two ways: as an effort to forestall the investigations officer from charging all of the members of the executive board for failing to act against McCarthy after Lacey's finding of racketeering or as a coup to replace wild Billy with himself.

By February 16, 1991, the vote in the electronic poll of the board was 7–6 to hold the meeting. Durham, who had yet to cast his ballot, explained his quandary: "Joe T and some board members see it as an opportunity to get McCarthy. I don't think it is appropriate. The whole issue is being appealed to Judge Edelstein, so I'm not as quick to jump in with Joe T, looking for an opportunity to go for the jugular vein, and remove McCarthy, even though he and I had some serious disagreements in the last couple of weeks. . . . I don't want to be a party to that type of move."

Durham voted in favor of McCarthy, deadlocking the board in a 7–7 tie and killing off the Mathis proposal.

Durham had saved McCarthy but had split with his running mate, Mathis, apparently beginning a process that would shatter their slate.

THE DELEGATE ELECTIONS

While the incumbents in the Marble Palace were knifing one another, Eddie Burke was focusing on the delegate elections. According to his assessment, Ron Carey had come out of the first round of delegate elections in the fall of 1990 with twenty-five or more delegates. Since there was no central clearinghouse for the results and the other two candidates weren't directly involved in those delegate elections, Burke's calculation though vague was the only information available. Burke said that the Carey forces had entered ten of the eighty elections held in the first round, from October through December.

On January 17, 1991, Burke offered reporters an admittedly conservative prediction on Carey's performance in the upcoming rounds of delegate elections in the remaining 535 Teamster locals. "I'm confident we'll get 150 to 200 delegates before this is over," he said.

In half of the elections, most of them in small locals eligible to send only a single delegate to the convention, the incumbent local president or secretary-treasurer ran unopposed. Carey slates were on the ballots in 118 of the remaining locals. TDU and Carey didn't have the resources or the connections to mount campaigns in every local. In another hundred or so locals there were slates entered by independent dissidents or competing local political factions.

Neither Shea nor Durham made an effort to develop local campaign committees for the delegate elections. Each assumed that he could lobby the incumbent officers who won for their votes. No one anticipated Carey's getting much support from those incumbents.

With rare exceptions, incumbent local officers ran as uncommitted delegates, cautiously waiting to decide at the last minute which way to jump. In contrast, those aligned with Ron Carey touted him as their candidate and openly supported his program of better pensions, elimination of multiple salaries, and an end to corruption and concessionary contracts. Their appeal was to Teamsters who wanted a change.

The first reports contained good and then stunning news. On February 1, the Carey forces swept Miami Local 769, winning eight delegate positions. Three days later, Durham's son, Ralph came in last among eight candidates competing for four delegate slots. The Carey forces swept again. Durham wasn't a magic name in North Carolina.

Burke decided to insert Carey into the battle for delegates in R. V. Durham's own Local 391 in North Carolina. Obviously, a Durham loss would sabotage his presidential ambitions—and the performance by his son in Charlotte Local 71's delegate election put such a setback in the realm of the possible.

Carey campaigned several times in the Winston-Salem, Greensboro, and High Point areas, and Durham responded by drenching the work sites with his presence day and night as the walk-in election approached in the third week of March. Both sides lashed each other with tough campaign literature, the Carey forces focusing on the greed of the hierarchy: "Compare your pension to R. V.'s. . . . It's time to put these pigs on a diet, or as Ron Carey says: 'The Party's Over!' "

Durham's literature was just as cutting: "Ron Carey lied to Teamsters about the way he handled corruption in his local union. . . . If Carey was clean in the John Long corruption case why did he need immunity from prosecution before he agreed to testify?" Carey responded that when he testified before a federal grand jury investigating Long, his lawyer advised him to demand immunity despite Carey's assertion that he had nothing to hide. Carey said that now he was sorry he followed the lawyer's advice instead of his own instincts.

Durham contended in his material, "TDU's Ron Carey is not a leader but a liar who cares more about himself than the people he represents in his own local union." He charged that Carey bolstered his local's pension plan at the expense of its health plan and that Carey enjoyed multiple salaries because he got an $11,700 expense allowance on top of his $46,000 a year salary. He said Carey deserved the "First Annual Teamster Pinocchio Award."

When the ballots were counted, Durham and his slate swept the eleven delegate positions by a 2–1 margin. While winning was certainly better than losing, it wasn't much of a victory. Carey's analysis said it all: "Durham has eighty-five hundred members. Only thirty-three hundred turned out. You had a real heated race. He beat us two to one. That was his home local!" He mused aloud, "I think we're going to fool a lot of people."

In contrast, Carey ran unopposed in his home local, and its

members endorsed him with their contributions, pouring tens of thousands of dollars into his campaign.

———

In some places the new democracy of the delegate elections was met with old-fashioned intimidation. At the nominations meeting of Chicago Local 705 on February 7, 1991, Leroy Ellis, a forty-six-year-old truck driver and TDU member running as a Carey delegate, suddenly got hit with a heavy glass ashtray, breaking his collarbone. In the brawl that ensued, racial slurs and punches were thrown at the stunned Ellis by unseen culprits in the mass of bodies pressing around him.

Ellis is a man few would want to confront toe-to-toe in a fight. Back in the 1970s, he was the World Boxing Association's fifth-ranked heavyweight contender and a sparring partner for heavyweight champ Muhammad Ali. On top of the beating he endured, he and his allies failed to win any of the nineteen delegate seats. The winners were the incumbent slate, headed by Shea's running mate, Daniel Ligurotis.

Despite the fear instilled by the bashing of Leroy Ellis and others and the suspensions and firings of dissidents openly supporting Carey, the grass-roots candidate from New York continued to pile up the delegates needed for nomination. With one-third of the races over in mid-February, Carey had eighty-six delegates of the ninety-six to ninety-eight he needed for nomination.[58]

The enthusiasm Carey inspired among rank and filers was obvious to any journalist following him on the campaign trail. David Moberg of *In These Times* captured the growing fervor when he wrote: "So far Carey has at least lit a few sparks of hope. As he got in the car to leave [a trucking company], a woman from the office—braving a 30-below-zero wind chill without a coat—dashed through the snow to shake his hand. A big smile on her face, she told him, 'You've got my vote.' "

The Carey charisma created a pool of dedicated volunteers across the nation willing to extend themselves for him and the cause of cleansing the Teamsters. Among them was Dennis Skelton, a line-haul driver for Yellow Freight in St. Louis. Concerned for Carey's safety—with good reason, given the history of the Teamsters—Skelton, a TDU member, volunteered to meet Carey whenever he was within five hundred miles of St. Louis. "I'm a pretty good-size guy," said the 325-pound, six-foot eight-inch-tall Skelton. "I don't want to depict myself as bodyguard, but if there was any trouble I was ready to do my part."

On one memorable weekend in March 1991, Skelton drove to Indianapolis to hook up with Carey, then drove him to Memphis, with the candidate sleeping en route to save money on a motel room. Carey debated Lou Riga, another announced presidential candidate, before an overflow crowd of three hundred in Memphis Local 667's union hall. Shea and Durham were too busy trying to work out an accommodation between themselves and dealing with the upper echelons of the union to respond to invitations to such gatherings. After the debate, Carey flew back to New York. Skelton drove back to St. Louis, having driven a thousand miles in thirty-six hours.

———

On March 10, 1991, the rank and file in Boston Local 25, Billy McCarthy's home base and his stomping ground for half a century, elected eight opposition candidates, including several TDUers, as delegates to the IBT Convention. International vice president Francis Hackett was the only McCarthy-aligned candidate to win. "The winds of change are here," concluded George Cashman, Local 25's recording secretary and leader of the opposition.[59]

Two days later, in what seemed at the time a nasty reaction to the evidence of Carey's steadily growing base of support—but in retrospect was the first sign of panic—Hugh J. Beins, Durham's lawyer, filed Election Protest 249, urging the removal of Carey from union office for taking money from employers. The charge, if true, was a violation of federal labor law and Holland's election rules. It stemmed from a Hollywood fund-raiser for Carey at the home of Stanley Sheinbaum, a Los Angeles publisher with a penchant for raising money for liberal political causes. The guest list was impressive: actors Ed Asner and Kris Kristofferson and director Oliver Stone, among others.

The gathering, arranged by Carey's lawyers, was very un-Carey-like. A man addicted to eating tuna fish sandwiches and listening to members' gripes wasn't that comfortable with celebrities and dainty hors d'oeuvres. Besides, after expenses, the party produced only $2,000, since the guests were warned that employers of any sort were prohibited from making contributions.[60]

In Protest 249, Beins demanded Carey's head: "Carey has been receiving money from employers and using it in his campaign on a wholesale basis. . . . Because there are criminal violations involved (Section 302 of the Labor Management Relations Act), I trust that you will alert Mr. Carberry and urge the removal of Mr. Carey from Union office."

In connection with the same protest, Beins charged that the "overwhelming majority of TDU's money comes from employers."

A few months later, Holland issued his decision. Rather than getting millions from employers, he ruled, TDU had inappropriately used $9,000, and Carey had indeed gotten some help from two employers by allowing their names to be used in the literature promoting the party. One of the names was Oliver Stone. Carey was ordered to return the $2,000 collected to the donors. Holland came to the conclusion that the sums involved were too insignificant to rule Carey off the ballot.

———

More good news arrived for Burke on March 26. On the West Coast, a coalition of TDU members and independent dissidents had scored a stunning victory, winning fourteen of seventeen delegate spots in Los Angeles Local 63. Its 13,000 members, employed by 214 separate companies, made it the sixth largest local in the Teamsters. Then Holland soured the triumph by ordering a new election in response to an appeal. His staff had screwed up the ballot by giving the TDU coalition the first line when it should have been on the second.

During the rerun, Gerald Moerler, a thirty-two-year-old truck driver, called the Association for Union Democracy's Teamsters Fair Elections Project for legal advice. He told AUD executive director Susan Jennik that he was hearing stories of business agents collecting the mail ballots in small shops where the workers were mostly Spanish speaking, with little or no understanding of English. Moerler said the business agents would mark the ballots for the incumbent-backed slate. "You're going to lose the election," Jennik agreed. "The only hope of pulling a victory out of this is to collect evidence on the ballot collecting."

Lucila Conde, a Mexican-American member of TDU's International Steering Committee, came up from San Diego to help Moerler. Speaking to the workers in Spanish, Conde was able to get statements proving that the ballot collecting had violated the election rules, which stipulated that no one was permitted to cast or collect another person's ballot. Based on this evidence, Holland sent in his own investigators. They not only gathered information supporting Moerler's claims but found a witness who saw Robert Marciel, secretary-treasurer of Local 63 and a vice presidential candidate on Shea's slate, collecting ballots and marking or voting them.

Holland disqualified the slate backed by Marciel and awarded the seventeen delegate slots to the TDU coalition.

Toward the end of March, Eddie Burke reported that Carey had 185 delegates, more than enough for nomination, with returns still coming in. "I couldn't have sat down in my wildest dreams and written the position we are in. The real story is we didn't involve ourselves in that many elections. We got mixed into 110 elections," Burke said. "We got calls from people saying, 'We got forty percent of the vote (even though they lost), and we're going to stick it out.' "

On April 1, with all but a couple of elections to go, Burke announced 245 Carey delegates from seventy-six locals would be going to the June convention, the product of a campaign that had taken the candidate to forty-one states over forty-four weekends, shaking hands wherever he could find a Teamster.

TWO CANDIDATES IN SEARCH OF A DEAL

Durham, meanwhile, had made a few visits to trucking barns, but not many. His excuse was the demands of negotiating the National Master Freight Agreement.

Shea had yet to jell as a candidate in search of rank-and-file votes, but he finally got around to creating the core of a campaign staff. On April 4, Shea announced he had hired two heavyweight companies with extensive political experience: Black, Manafort, Stone & Kelly of Alexandria, Virginia, and the Strategy Group of Chicago.

Donald R. Sweitzer, former director of finance for the Democratic National Committee and a veteran campaign staffer, was assigned from Black, Manafort to the Shea-Ligurotis slate. David Wilhelm of the Strategy Group was joining Shea and Ligurotis straight from guiding Chicago mayor Richard Daley in his successful reelection campaign.

Shea was setting up the big-ticket campaign envisioned by

Carey's lawyer Rick Gilberg, with Sweitzer and Wilhelm arranging scheduling, fund-raising, convention operations, and a road campaign for the rank-and-file vote.

On April 9, Mathis made a decision that offered Durham and Shea a grand opportunity to merge their slates. That day, Chris Scott, Durham's campaign manager, told a reporter, "There's been a little change in our ticket. Weldon Mathis has decided not to run." A fax followed giving Mathis's unctuous explanation that he wanted to spend more time with his wife, Myrtle, and their grandchildren.

The sixty-five-year-old Mathis told labor columnist Harry Bernstein of the *Los Angeles Times* that he wanted Shea to replace him, increasing the odds of the Durham slate defeating Carey. "I'm going to retire soon and decided to leave the election race now because I am no longer sure I am the running mate Durham needs to win," Mathis said.

Mathis had become a political liability to Durham. They were in conflict on moving against McCarthy over the Windsor Graphics debacle, and the delegate elections illustrated what an easy target Mathis would be in a rank-and-file election campaign. Durham's campaign manager explained, "A lot of the Carey propaganda, fair or unfair, has been aimed at Weldon. In fact, there are complete distortions about Mathis being convicted of a felony. We've picked it up in virtually every delegate race where there were Carey-oriented delegates running. They targeted in on Mathis and that charge."

Mathis was never convicted of a felony, which some election material claimed, but he was certainly not the material from which a populist candidate appealing to the rank and file could be shaped. The TDU had put out a "Wanted" poster saying Mathis was wanted for "attempted theft of our right to vote." The poster explained the reason why: "At the Eastern Conference Convention in August at Hilton Head, S.C., Mathis gave a speech in which he urged the hundreds of officials present to work to take away the membership's Right to Vote. He claimed that the members are not smart enough to elect their leaders, so the selection of IBT leadership should be left to the officials, as it has always been done."

As the acting general president, Mathis had imposed the 1988 Master Freight Agreement despite its rejection by 64 percent of the members, and the U.S. Department of Labor had ordered a new election—which TDU-backed candidates won—in Mathis's home union, Atlanta Local 728, after complaints of massive election fraud.

While the insiders would meet again and again in the coming weeks in an effort to come up with an old-fashioned consensus slate, there were three big political egos standing in the way: Both Durham and Shea wanted to be president, and Ligurotis had no intention of giving up his chance to be general secretary-treasurer.

———

The next casualty on the Durham slate was Arnie Weinmeister, the Football Hall of Fame, All-Pro, All-American tackle, who got his start in Teamster politics the old-fashioned way: through nepotism.

During a break at a meeting of the Teamsters Committee on 2000 at the end of April, the always reticent Weinmeister told Durham he was dropping off the slate. "Please keep it to yourself for a few hours," Durham said. He assigned his campaign manager, Chris Scott, to figure out a gracious way to say that another vice presidential candidate had jumped overboard.

Scott wrote a statement centering on Weinmeister's age, saying flatly that when the election was over, he would be sixty-nine and it was time to give a younger person a chance. Weinmeister rejected that. He didn't want to talk about his age despite a warning from Scott that people would then jump to other conclusions.

And they did. The towering Weinmeister made a very large target in a rank-and-file election. He had been eased into control of Seattle Teamsters Local 117 by his older brother many years before. But it wasn't nepotism that made Weinmeister easy pickings for a hard-campaigning opponent. It was the $502,000-a-year income from four Teamster payrolls, the $5 million corporate jet that hauled him around as head of the Western Conference, and finally, the $6 million loan from the International to the Western Conference, which was used to maintain the lush life-styles of those running the conference rather than for such mundane purposes as organizing.

Appointed an International vice president in 1973, Weinmeister had seldom spoken up, certainly never about the dirty dealings that smeared the union's image. He had never faced the prospect of a real election until now. He chose instead to drop out of the race and announced plans to retire to a new house being built for him overlooking Puget Sound and to the joys of his eighty-two-foot yacht and his fat pensions.[61]

———

The Strategy Group produced the first nationwide poll of the campaign late in April. It showed the Shea-Ligurotis ticket with 22 percent of the vote, Carey with 16 percent, Durham with 7 percent, and Lou Riga with 2 percent.

Interestingly, TDU came up with a 32 percent favorability rating—considerably higher than any of the candidates. "Arguments which attempt to portray TDU as some sort of fringe group simply do not work well," the Strategy Group report said.

A crucial piece of information provided by the poll was that 75 percent of the six hundred Teamsters polled didn't know who the candidates were or enough about them to offer an opinion.

Carey said he suspected the underlying motive of the poll was to convince Durham to merge with Shea. "I think the whole strategy behind this poll was to build a bridge from one slate to the other. While they're negotiating, I'll be spending my time talking to members."

The merger talks went on, but the steadfast determination of both Durham and Shea to be president and an undertone of distrust foreordained failure.

On May 29, at the Holiday Inn at O'Hare Airport near Chicago, Teamster leaders Larry Brennan of Detroit and Carmine Parise of Cleveland brought the two sides together for a two-hour meeting that spurred hope.

Durham met with Brennan, Parise, Shea, Ligurotis, Joe T, Barry Feinstein of New York, John Morris of Philadelphia, and Jack Cox. Durham was in Chicago for a meeting on the Master Freight Agreement, while Shea and his allies had been at the hotel for a meeting on the strategy and logistics of their campaign.

Durham originally was determined to keep Joe T off any merged slate, according to John Morris, but softened under the argument that the old kingmaker was the unquestioned leader of New York's 150,000 Teamsters, the biggest bloc of members in the International.

Morris was so hopeful of ending the dangerous division at the top that he told Joe T: "Joe, this you must not spoil." Knowing that Ligurotis was still intent on running for secretary-treasurer, Morris told him, "You cannot drop the ball on the ten yard line. This is an opportunity to put the whole thing together. It doesn't really make a difference who's top, who's second, if we have an understanding on how this International should be run."[62]

Pressure was building on Shea to shift to number two on Durham's slate as the negotiators met again the following week in Alexandria, Virginia. Shea, Feinstein, and Morris sat down with Durham, Brennan, Dan Darrow, and Robert Sansone of St. Louis.

According to a Shea insider, Durham told Shea he was willing to drop two McCarthy favorites, Frank Hackett and Robert DeRusha, from his slate. That was a significant development, signaling to Shea that while Durham was still unwilling to step away from the presidency, he was making a break with McCarthy.

Inside the room, however, Durham reversed direction after conferring with his associates. He told Feinstein he had decided that he couldn't dump Hackett and DeRusha, after all.

That ended the negotiations. Six days later, on June 11, Durham announced that Harold Leu of Toledo, president of the Ohio Conference of Teamsters, would be his running mate as secretary-treasurer.

THE COLORADO VOLUNTEERS

With the Teamsters Convention a month away and Shea and Durham still in the midst of their merger negotiations, Ron Carey's odyssey across the Teamster landscape brought him to Colorado on May 18 for a three-day stint that would reveal the strengths and weaknesses of his campaign.

After fifteen months of weekends spent traveling, talking, and shaking hands, Carey exhibited a seemingly boundless energy as he arrived at the Denver airport from La Guardia—on a flight that was two and a half hours late.

The highly disciplined and committed Carey was in a state of private mourning, hidden from those he dealt with on the road. Just a few weeks before, one night in April, the six Carey brothers and their mother, Loretta, sat down to discuss whether extraordinary means should be used to prolong the life of eighty-year-old

Joseph Carey, who had suffered a stroke. They came to the painful decision against using a respirator.

A few days later, Carey received a cryptic message after a candidates forum in Naples, Florida, sponsored by Cleveland Joint Council 41:"Come home immediately." Unable to reach his family by phone, he set out by car for the Miami airport. He sat in mournful silence through the hours of the drive with Eddie Burke across Florida.

At the airport, Carey called home again and was stunned to learn that the summons to return involved his mother, Loretta. A vigorous woman of seventy-four, she had died of a heart attack. He felt torn apart. Unable to control the tears that seared his face, Carey sat waiting for his flight, aching from this unexpected loss, realizing he hadn't had a chance to say good-bye. He remembered how concerned she was for his safety. "I'm so afraid they're going to kill you, Ron," she told him. "Please be careful."

Then a few weeks later, his father also passed away.

No one outside the family circle and his intimates were told of the deaths. Carey buried his mother on a Saturday morning and went to a fund-raiser that night, a dinner dance for over two hundred Local 804 members and their wives. He didn't say anything about his personal troubles. "I didn't want to put a damper on it. It was like a nightmare. I couldn't believe it was happening," he said.

"It did blow me out of the water," Carey said of the deaths of his parents. "What I had to look at was what would their decision have been? What would they have wanted me to have done? That's what I did, carry on. My mom and dad were tough folks. They would have said, 'Hey, go out there and get them!'"

Carey returned to work and back on the campaign trail, hiding his melancholy.

Carey's trip to Colorado had been laid out in detail in advance by Eddie Burke, and while he was prepared to be flexible to meet exigencies of the unexpected, he came off the plane half-expecting his hosts, the leaders of the Colorado TDU, to have given up on him after the delay.

He found two men waiting for him. They were buttons that said: "Elect Ron Carey" and "TDU." They took Carey outside to the van driven by Bry Duncan and headed out to the Embassy Suites. On the windows of the van large letters proclaimed: "Teamsters Support Ron Carey."

The man at the wheel, Bry Duncan, his wife, Molly, and their ten-year-old son, Bry II, had spent hours on their hands and knees the week before coloring in the letters red, white, blue, and gray on a fifteen-foot-long homemade banner—"Ron Carey for Teamster President"—in anticipation of the arrival of Carey in Denver that day.

The forty-nine-year-old Bry, a truck driver hauling goods around Denver, was a Local 17 shop steward and secretary-treasurer of the Colorado TDU chapter. Originally from South Carolina, the youngest of thirteen children of a farm family, Bry served in the navy before finding his way to Denver and marrying Molly, a warm, vibrant woman with aspirations to be a writer.

Bry and Molly were giving up their weekend, renting a room at their own expense at Embassy Suites, where Carey was staying. They abandoned the usual celebration of their wedding anniversary to work at the rally that Sunday, and Bry was taking off that Monday without pay because of the campaign. He was providing his van, which comfortably seated seven people, as well as serving as the driver and paying for all the gas for the three days Carey would be in Colorado.

"Two months ago, we found out he was coming," Bry said. "We distributed fliers. We started calling everybody all over the state. I've sent out fliers to New Mexico and Utah."

Molly added, "This has been a lot of work."

"I don't want nothing out of Ron Carey but to be honest and to work for the men," Bry said in explanation of his willingness to sacrifice time and money for this cause.

When the van carrying Carey arrived at the hotel, there were a dozen people waiting outside, some wearing shirts saying:"Ron Carey for President. The Party's Over." Others carried signs: "Welcome Ron Carey Candidate for President IBT 1991."

Dressed in a dark blue blazer with a "Union Yes" button, blue jeans, and a plaid sports shirt open at the neck, Carey immediately went into their midst. "It's so heartwarming to see you here after being two and a half hours late," he said in his nasal New York twang. It had taken six hours and ten minutes to reach this destination. The late arrival had cut the crowd outside the hotel and caused Carey to miss meetings scheduled with officials from Locals 267 and 435, who didn't wait around for him.

Half of the full-time staff of the Carey campaign, Rick Blaylock, an ex-miner from West Virginia and organizer for the Mine

Workers, was waiting for the candidate at the hotel. Eddie Burke, the only other full-time staffer, had to be in Disney World for Election Officer Michael Holland's walking tour of the convention facilities.

After a few minutes to brush his teeth, Carey got a briefing from J. B. McAllister, a TDU volunteer, who advised him that Denver Teamsters were interested in pensions and in avoiding strikes. With that bit of background, Carey went into a meeting with six Teamsters: four rank and filers and two business agents. For an hour, they sat talking around a big conference table in his suite. The main focus—in accordance with J. B.'s suggestion—was on pensions. But they ranged across a spectrum of complaints and questions, from Carey's position on health insurance to the hierarchy's jet fleet.

After the hotel meeting, Carey headed out in Bry Duncan's van to Yellow Freight's terminal for some plant gate campaigning, then to dinner with twenty-eight supporters at the Kings Table, where the buffet special cost six dollars. Everyone piled two plates high with salads, pasta, ribs, and pizza. Dessert was included in the price. Carey was the guest of honor, but everyone else chipped in for the modest tab.

Afterward, Carey was taken on another round of plant-gate campaigning, starting outside a terminal on a street inlaid with bricks where long-distance drivers were loading little hand carts with thermoses, blankets, radios, and personal supplies from the trunks of cars for the three or four days they would be spending on the road.

Carey stood in front of a fence topped with barbed wire that protected lines of trailers. In a moment, eleven drivers, all with big belt buckles, big bellies, and big arms with tattoos, gathered around. Amid the western drawls, Carey's high-pitched New York accent seemed even sharper. A driver who had been questioning Carey with seeming skepticism exclaimed: "I'll tell you, you're the first one I've seen where I been able to talk face-to-face since Hoffa."

Carey didn't mention it, but that's how votes are won. One of the continuing criticisms of Presser and McCarthy and the rest of the Teamsters' GEB from the TDU had been that they had no contact with the members. Hoffa won the affection of working Teamsters by suddenly appearing at a workplace in whatever area he was visiting on union business.

More and more drivers began gathering around Carey. There were twenty-eight at 7:15 P.M., then thirty-two within another minute or two.

"I'd like to see these companies not making their own contracts," a driver said, speaking in the code of the rank and file's unhappiness about givebacks at the bargaining table and the failure of the union to enforce contract language.

The drivers responded appreciatively to Carey's answer: "The union's got to get tough and say, 'Hey, the party's over.'"

By seven-thirty the following morning, Carey was outside the Roadway terminal gate. The volunteers accompanying him stuck two signs in the fence: "Vote Ron Carey for President of IBT 1991." A couple of dozen drivers dribbled in and out of the yard. It was a sleepy Sunday morning, and Carey was obviously disappointed by the turnout; the volunteers were a bit sheepish. They had predicted a large work force, but it wasn't there.

Back at the Embassy Suites, Carey met with the president and secretary-treasurer of Local 17, while J. B. McAllister, Bry, and Rick Blaylock breakfasted nearby. According to J. B., it was a breakthrough for local officers to meet with Carey. Times were really changing, he said "Wasn't too long ago people would join TDU and keep it a secret. There were only three people who wore these things," J. B. said, pointing to his TDU pin. "It's been very intimidating for people to join TDU."

J. B. explained with a chuckle the difference the TDU network made to Carey's accreditations efforts: "When the Shea petitions were delivered to the union hall, they just lay there. The officers were barred from using the union halls to collect signatures. They had to go out and get people like myself. Nobody would carry his, and that's why they failed. The business agents didn't choose to do it. There was nothing in it for them. It must have been an incredible shock to Shea."

Bry mused aloud, "If everybody shows up who says they are coming to the rally, we're going to get three hundred. We put fliers out, and a lot say they are coming." Then he added prophetically, "Saying and doing are two different things."

That Sunday afternoon at 2:15 P.M. sixty-two persons had gathered in the hotel ballroom when J. B. McAllister rose to deliver a brief but eloquent speech: "I want to trust the leadership of my union again. If we don't get Ron Carey and his slate elected, all we get is the same old tired dictatorship we've had for years. We're going to change our own union. The beginning is June 24, 1991. I'd ask you to show a big Denver, Colorado, welcome to Ron Carey."

Greeted with a standing ovation, Ron Carey, dressed in a suit, told the audience that in his travels, "I hear the same old story. Members are angry. They are frustrated." He pointed out that his Local 804 members had raised over $160,000, providing an indication of how they feel about him. He noted his members got $1,850 a month for a thirty-year pension. He emphasized pensions and organizing.

Carey compared what was happening to the Teamsters to the events in Eastern Europe. "When I first announced in 1989, people said it was a laugh; it will go nowhere." He promised to eliminate multiple salaries, deal quickly with corruption, and work to improve pensions.

Carey finished to a standing ovation.

Rick Blaylock then made a pitch for contributions as Molly and other volunteers collected pledges and donations in a cardboard bucket, raising $1,100 along with twenty pledge cards.

When the rally ended at 3:30 P.M. thirty-eight people stuck around talking. Molly and Bry were disappointed, as was J. B. The three hundred never materialized, but there were reporters from the local newspaper and television station in the room.

The following morning at breakfast, J. B. was feeling better. He read the *Denver Post* article about Carey aloud and talked with fascination about the coverage of the rally on Channel 9 the night before. Reflecting on the positive publicity that carried Carey's message across Colorado, J. B. said happily, "A bunch of truck drivers like us. We did it."

9

The 1991 Teamsters Convention

The 1991 International Brotherhood of Teamsters (IBT) Convention, which drew 1,926 delegates to the Walt Disney Dolphin Hotel and Convention Center in Buena Vista, Florida, was a theater of democracy in which the central players gathered to cross the threshold from the secretive, authoritarian politics of the old oligarchy to the uncertainty of the secret ballot.

Instead of the fierce-faced bullyboys of the Williams and Presser conventions in 1981 and 1986, delegates and visitors on their way to register on Saturday, June 22, passed through a chorus of Samoans enthusiastically chanting the name of the most obscure of the IBT's presidential hopefuls:

"Lou! Lou! Lou!"

"Riga! Riga! Riga!"

No one passed them without smiling and realizing that the new politics had really arrived.

The Samoans had attached themselves to Riga after hearing him speak at a YMCA in the San Francisco Bay Area. Twenty-eight burly Samoans, all Teamster members and unpaid volunteers, along with Riga's twenty-nine-year-old son, Michael, and another backer, had piled into five rented vans in San Francisco on June 17 with bags of homemade sandwiches as sustenance. They drove from San Francisco to the Orlando area, stopping only for one night of rest on the floor of the apartment of a sister of one of the volunteers in Fort Walton, Florida. After time out for a barbecue and a trip to the beach, they arrived in Orlando at six o'clock on the evening of June 21. The following morning, they went right to the sign-up area to advertise their candidate by chanting his name and selling "Lou Riga for President" shirts and buttons to raise money.

Louis D. Riga, secretary-treasurer of a small local in San Jose, California, had thrust himself into the presidential race without a significant political base either in his home region or nationally. Financing his effort with a combination of a home equity loan and fund-raisers that drew on the pocketbooks of sympathetic relatives and friends, the fifty-four-year-old Riga tried to make himself known through a video sent to every delegate and by occasional trips around the country.

Riga rattled off the convention costs of his shoestring campaign as he watched the chanting Samoans: "Rental of five vans, $3,000; fuel, $1,800; insurance, $1,000; five rooms, $5,200 for seven nights with six people to a room with kitchens. I'm going over to buy groceries now."

Riga took the optimistic stance that anyone with substantive credentials as a Teamster official could get the minimum ninety-six votes now needed to be nominated as a presidential candidate. And then anything, including magic or incredible luck, could happen in the rank-and-file election to come. Increasing his hopes were the delegates passing by who whispered, "I'm with you, Lou."

"I'm going to come out of here with at least three hundred votes," the optimistic Riga predicted.

R. V. Durham came into the convention confident that he would win the mass of delegate votes and prove his standing as the front-runner. His campaign manager, Chris Scott, predicted Durham would get a thousand votes or more.

Durham's staff had been carefully tracking the number of delegates committed to each candidate. Durham's figures showed that he had 883 committed delegates to 411 for Walter Shea, 237 for Ron Carey, 23 for Lou Riga, and 11 for William Genoese. He said there were 360 delegates whose sympathies were undetermined.

Shea challenged the accuracy of Durham's numbers. His advisers claimed that Shea had eight hundred delegates pledged to him coming into the convention and sneered at the prospects of Durham winning a thousand votes.

Unlike his opponents, Ron Carey came into the Disney World

complex with a bloc of 240 Teamsters, most of them rank-and-file activists, who had been elected as delegates on Carey slates in their home locals. Carey realized that he had no chance of winning the majority of the votes at the convention, for most of the delegates were local officers whose loyalties were to the old guard. Carey's primary goal at the convention, which seemed assured, was to be formally nominated. His secondary goals were to pass constitutional amendments to cap salaries and raise strike pay and to counter attempts by the Shea and Durham forces to water down the new level of democracy endowed by the consent decree.

THE CONSENT DECREE AMENDMENTS

Over the past year, there had been widespread rumors in the Teamster community that the delegates aligned with the old guard would storm out of the hotel en masse after rejecting the constitutional amendments mandated under the consent decree to require the secret-ballot election of delegates, the rank-and-file vote for the union's top officers, and the creation of the Independent Review Board to pursue corruption and racketeering.

Assistant U.S. Attorney Edward Ferguson, now in charge of the Teamster RICO case, had anticipated the possibility of a coup and had begun the process of sealing off the last hole through which the anti-rank-and-file-vote conspirators could wiggle in a motion filed with Edelstein on February 22, 1991. The motion asked for a ruling reaffirming the sanctity of the consent decree agreement amending the IBT constitution to assure the rank-and-file vote and the other changes.

Edelstein issued a decision in May saying that no matter how the delegates voted, the rank-and-file elections would be held. In his caustic ruling, the judge noted that over the past two years the IBT hierarchy had demonstrated a tendency to try to weasel out of an agreement they voluntarily signed. He said he wasn't going to let them screw up this convention. Votes against the consent-decree amendments or for any constitutional changes that clashed with those amendments would have no legal standing.

Ferguson, a tall, lean, darked-haired, thirty-four-year-old lawyer, slipped through the corridors of the Dolphin Hotel that convention week in a subtle but significant role. He was at hand for immediate action should the delegates explode in rage and try to break their union out of the democratic channels poured in concrete by the consent decree.

Judge Edelstein waited nearby in another hotel, ready to mount the bench in the federal courthouse in Orlando to squelch any attempt to renege on the consent decree. Judge Edelstein had exhibited as much rage at the betrayal of the union ideal by corrupt or timid Teamster officials as did the most fervent of the TDUers, and no one doubted he would crush anyone who led an uprising.

Carey chose to accept the reality of the consent decree, emphasizing that without it the rank-and-file vote and the ouster of mob influence never would have happened.

CLEAR AS THE LIBERTY BELL

The consent-decree amendments were to be the first order of business on the opening day of the convention, Monday, June 24. First, however, the delegates sent an immediate signal that this was really going to be a different convention. Angry over George Bush's antilabor positions, they booed through the entire three minutes of a video greeting from the president.

Billy McCarthy, who was up next, was booed as well. McCarthy delivered a rambling, disjointed speech about his past operations and his stroke, the long hours he worked, and his difficulty in expressing what he wanted to say because of the stroke. "Up here, I'm as clear as the Liberty Bell," he said, tapping his forehead to roars of laughter. "I don't know why the hell you boo. I'm getting out, anyway," he said to more laughter.

In what seemed a generous gesture at the time, McCarthy offered the use of the IBT's corporate jets to any delegate in need of a quick lift out of Disney World. In a serious tone, McCarthy told the delegates: "I also wanted to say that we have our planes standing by. Weldon and I got the two International planes that are assigned to us. If you, any member, or if you or your member delegates, any member of your family, has a problem hospitalwise, healthwise, a serious problem, emergency, our plane will be standing by to take them home."

The delegates reacted with strong applause.

McCarthy added, "But we are not going to take someone home that has got a cold."

A better understanding of McCarthy's magnanimous offer would come in a few weeks, when Independent Administrator Frederick B. Lacey issued a report on the costs and uses of McCarthy and Mathis's union-supplied jets. Since the mid-1970s, the TDU had criticized the corporate life-styles of the hierarchy, focusing on the personal jets. But beyond the shallow data provided in the annual Teamster financial reports, the dissidents weren't in a position to expose the extent of the misuse of the union's resources on such perks.

With full access to the union's books, Lacey had no such constraints, and his report was piercingly embarrassing in the new era of populism in the Teamsters. He revealed that the aircraft, a Gulfstream III and a Gulfstream II, serving the general president and the general secretary-treasurer, were purchased for about $19 million. The costs of staffing, operating, and storing them amounted to over $3.8 million, from January 1, 1989 through December 31, 1990. If depreciation costs were factored in, the price tag for those two years would have been $8.5 million, not $3.8 million.

In addition, $798,827 was spent in 1989 on the construction of a hangar to house the two planes at the Baltimore-Washington International Airport. And McCarthy used his plane for forty-eight weekend trips between Washington and Boston, his hometown—at an estimated cost of $528,000.

Teamster officers across the country had whined about the high cost of democracy—about $5,000 for each contested delegate election—while they quietly accepted without question the splashing away of the members' dues on the hierarchy's jets.

VOTING DOWN THE AMENDMENTS

The motion to reject the consent-decree package of amendments to the IBT constitution was made by Chuck Mack, a poised, well-spoken, handsome California Teamster leader and a candidate for vice president on the Durham slate. After the cheers and thunderous applause had subsided, Mack proclaimed:

A yes vote on RICO is a vote against due process. It's a vote against self-determination, and it's a vote against Teamster independence. You'd be voting for continued control by the government.

Let me at this point set the record straight concerning my position on member democracy. I support direct rank-and-file election of officers and officials. I support the existence of an ethical practices committee. I support a cap on salaries of IBT employees. I support the rooting out of organized crime influence and other forms of corruption from our organization. They have no place in the trade union movement, and particularly in the Teamsters Union.

Those were brave words from a man who had seconded the nomination of Roy Williams for general president at the 1981 IBT Convention, depicting Williams as a courageous man to run for the office. He portrayed Williams in that 1981 speech of praise as a man indicted on the flimsiest of grounds and the victim of the media, the Justice Department, and Congress.[63]

Arguing in favor of the amendments, James E. Buck, a rank-and-file delegate elected from Williams's Local 41 in Kansas City, typified the long line of speakers supporting Carey: "I know I will return to Kansas City with my head held high, knowing I have represented the rank and file. These are the people paying the freight, and this is their union. And it was a consent order that brought their voices here today." Buck's words drew loud boos from the crowd, but he continued: "No one wants government intervention in our union, but we can't forget the consent decree was forced on us because of another kind of intervention, the corruption of organized crime. We don't want the government running our union, and we sure as hell don't want the mobsters running our union, either."

The vast majority of the delegates voted to reject the consent-decree amendments, but it was a symbolic gesture because of Judge Edelstein's decision that the rejection had no legal standing.

STOP THE PRESSES

That night, the phone rang at midnight in the Carey campaign headquarters in the hotel. "Carey campaign," Eddie Burke said automatically into the phone. He was tired after the long first day of the convention.

The caller, Eugene Bennett, stirred Burke right out of his lethargy. Bennett, head of the Teamsters' parking-garage local in New York City, said he was having second thoughts about running as a vice president for the Eastern Conference on the Carey ticket.

"Mr. Bennett, I don't know if you hear those machines, but we're just about finished printing the leaflet announcing the Carey slate," Burke said, feeling a mixture of anger and anguish. In just a few hours, the nominations would be made for the vice presidential candidates.

"Stop the presses," Burke said to the two volunteers at the two copying machines. Then he rang Carey's room, awakening him. "Ron, we got a problem," Burke said as a prelude to telling him about Bennett's uncertainty. Carey responded that he would contact Bennett to straighten things out.

In the interim, Burke awakened the campaign's communications consultant, Tom Knight. "Tom, you got to fix me another flier right now," he told him.

By 2:30 A.M., the two photostat machines were churning out five thousand copies of a new flier with the latest version of the Carey slate—one name short of a full complement.

At 3:00 A.M., Carey called to say that he was meeting Bennett first thing in the morning but to cover themselves they had better print another flier without Bennett's name. "I'm one step ahead of you, buddy. They're being printed now," Burke said. They stayed up all night until the job was finished.

In the morning, Bennett dropped out. An associate said that just the thought of being a candidate had sent Bennett's blood pressure skyrocketing. His family was concerned that actually running would threaten his health.

Later in the campaign Durham allies—unaware of Bennett's last-minute pull out—spread the rumor that Carey ran only two instead of three candidates in the Eastern Conference so that his supporters could throw their votes to John Morris, who was a vice presidential candidate on the Shea ticket.

THE CONVENTION, DAY TWO

With universal agreement, the IBT constitution had been amended to create a second vice presidency for the Canadian Conference. That meant the union would have seventeen vice presidents: five at-large, three in the East, three in the Central, two in the West, two in the South, and two in Canada.

The two Canadian candidates, Charles Thibault and Louis Lacroix, who were running on the Durham slate, were so popular that Carey and Shea didn't bother fielding candidates against them. Since they were unopposed, Holland declared them elected.

Many of the fifty-five other candidates being nominated and seconded for the remaining fifteen vice presidencies received a mixture of boos and applause. Just the mention of Carey's name—and it was mentioned many times in the nominating speeches—drew boos from the old-guard delegates.

But the strongest wave of boos was reserved for Diana Kilmury during her nomination as a vice president at large on the Carey slate. The forty-four-year-old Canadian truck driver and TDU leader had endured even worse—curses and threats—at the 1981 IBT Convention when she dared to suggest the creation of an ethics committee so that the Teamsters could clean house before the government did.

McCarthy, chairing the session, could not hear Kilmury's response through the din of boos.

"Wait a minute. Hold it, will you? I can't hear her. Are you accepting the nomination?" McCarthy said.

Kilmury responded: "Brother McCarthy, I'd be happy to accept the nomination." She boomed out in a strong voice: "And I'd like to say to the delegates here, I see your manners have not improved much since 1981." The delegates reacted with cheers and boos.

The only other woman nominated was Vicki Saporta, the thirty-eight-year-old director of organizing for the IBT. Boos mingled with the applause when Saporta was nominated for vice president at large on the Shea ticket.

Durham committed a political faux pas not only in failing to put a woman on his slate but in trying to defend that omission by saying none of the 500,000 women in the union were ready for the big leagues yet.

211

William Genoese announced he was trading in his presidential bid to be candidate for vice president at large on the Shea slate.

That night, secret-ballot elections were held using voting machines. All of the vice presidential candidates on the Durham, Shea, and Carey slate received enough votes to be certified as nominated candidates for the December elections. The Durham candidates won 47 percent of the vote to the Shea candidates' 34 percent and Carey candidates' 15 percent.

DROWNING OUT CAREY

In the one debate of the week that pitted Carey directly against Durham on the third day of the convention over the issue of multiple salaries and salary caps, the old-guard delegates booed so loudly that Carey's words were drowned out six times.

Durham spoke in support of limiting the general president's salary to $225,000 and allowing no one on the International union's payroll to make more than that either from one or several salaries.

Carey countered in support of an amendment banning multiple salaries and limiting the president to $150,000 a year. As his opponents interrupted his words for the fourth time with shouts and boos, he said with irritation, "Let me finish. I haven't hit this mike once."

Carey managed to say that the Teamsters had lost over 700,000 members. "The bloated salaries, the multiple salaries, that money could be taken and put into organizing programs," he said to more boos.

Durham's version of the amendment was passed overwhelmingly.

Durham pushed through another amendment to return the IBT to the old system of making local officers automatically the delegates to the Teamster conventions held every five years. The hollow arguments in favor of the old way were that most of the delegates—about 85 percent—were officers of their locals who would have been sent under the old system and that millions of dollars would be saved by eliminating the delegate elections. The reality was that the 15 percent of the delegates who were rank and filers helped create the atmosphere of openness and debate that transformed the 1991 convention from the lockstep dance that characterized the past.

The Durham amendment also would have divorced the convention from the populist election process. He wanted to substitute a petition system in place of nominating candidates at the convention. The Durham approach would have set the stage for a future convention to eliminate the rank-and-file vote for the top officers by simply changing the constitution back to the old system of having the delegates elect those officers in the open at the convention.

Steve Lord, a rank-and-file delegate elected from Los Angeles Local 63, spoke in opposition to the return to the old way of selecting delegates. He told the convention, "This recommendation is nothing more than a smoke screen that a blind man could see through. . . . This is a new day, and the membership is no longer fooled. If we don't learn from the past, we are doomed to repeat it."

The Durham amendment passed but had no legal basis, since it violated the consent decree. But the amendment was logged onto the record to sit like a time bomb waiting to be exploded into reality in the future when the aging Judge Edelstein passed from the bench and a more understanding or naive judge succeeded to the case.

That Wednesday evening, Durham candidates swept the trustee races, with Robert Simpson, Jr., of Chicago receiving 1,076 votes; Ben Leal of San Francisco, 1,013; and Robert De-Rusha of Boston, 973. Shea's candidates lost, with Ed J. Mireles, getting 886 votes,; Eddie Kornegay of Washington, D.C., 850; and Robert N. Meidel, 768. Under Holland's rules, the three trustees were elected at the convention instead of having to run in the December elections. Under the IBT constitution, the trustees' only duty is to review the union's financial books twice a year.

Carey, realizing that the convention was the old guard's arena, hadn't fielded a delegate slate.

DURHAM TOPS 1,000

On the fourth day, June 27, with the nominations for general president at hand, the convention turned festive and exciting.

The hallways were filled with colorful banners, balloons, and delegates carrying placards promoting their candidates.

Election Officer Mike Holland warned that a tight schedule would be followed, with five minutes for the nominating speech, two minutes for a second, a quick, simple acceptance by the candidate from microphone two on the floor of the hall, and finally, a ten-minute demonstration by supporters only. No counterdemonstrations allowed.

The moment Carey pronounced his acceptance, a couple of delegates hoisted the grinning candidate onto their shoulders and led a parade around the huge convention hall. His supporters, many wearing lime-green campaign shirts, joyously chanted, "Carey! Right to vote!" as the procession sparkled with an enthusiasm missing from the other candidates' demonstrations.

As soon as the clock ran out on the Carey demonstration, an old-guard delegate from Chicago rose to complain that the ten-minute limit had been exceeded.

Convention chairman Weldon Mathis responded wittily from the podium: "Time don't go so fast when you're not having fun." Laughter filled the room.

This was to be both a triumphant and difficult day for R. V. Durham. In the delegate votes for president, Durham achieved his goal. He got 1,001 votes. Shea turned in an embarrassing 574. Carey was a distant third, but with more votes than expected: 289. And Riga fell far short of the 96 needed for nomination, receiving only 24 votes. Durham had taken 53 percent of the vote; Shea, 30 percent; and Carey, 15 percent.

Durham was glowing. He was emerging from the week-long convention as the front-runner on the basis of the delegate votes and the election of five of his slate members to International offices. He would have been whisked into the presidency if the voice of the delegates still ruled the Teamsters.

The three candidates for secretary-treasurer turned in similar margins: Durham's running mate, Harold Leu, received 984 votes; Shea's running mate, Dan Ligurotis, 615; and Carey's running mate, Tom Sever, 272.

But then came the strike-pay surprise. Because the Durham majority bloc was firmly in control of the Constitutional Committee, as incumbents always are, Durham had the power to offer those amendments he backed. On strike pay, the Constitutional

Committee recommended approval of the first increase in a decade, jumping it from $55 a week to $100.

Mario Ferenac, a truck-driver delegate from Local 385 in Orlando, rose to amend that proposal to $100 a week for the first four weeks and $150 a week thereafter. Ferenac pointed out amid cheers that the International officers are well taken care of, with their cushy salaries and benefits, and shouted it was time to share some of the wealth with members who strike. The delegates reacted with thunderous applause.

Dan Campbell, a TDU leader and delegate from Local 486 in Saginaw, Michigan, spoke in support of the $150 proposal and gave a hint that something bigger might be in the offing: "And I would say further, I would support a motion to raise it higher to $200, if that comes up." Cheers and applause again.

When Jon L. Rabine, secretary-treasurer of Local 763 in Seattle, argued against the $150 a week from the perspective of fiscal responsibility, saying, "There is no free lunch, everything has its cost," his words drew boos and derisive shouts.

"Have order!" Weldon Mathis boomed into his mike on the podium.

Then Carl Gentile of Local 170 in Worcester, Massachusetts, a convention whip for the Shea slate, upped the ante: "I think it is time that our members participate in a little bit of the wealth that we have for $200."

The Shea strategists had wanted John P. Morris, the top Teamster in Philadelphia and a vice presidential candidate on the Shea ticket, to introduce the $200-a-week amendment, but Mathis at first avoided recognizing him. Finally, he allowed him to speak on the issue.

"Nobody can live on $100 a week. That's Mickey Mouse benefits," shouted the blustery Morris, whose speaking technique invariably rouses his audience. The delegates reacted with cheers. A sense that the convention was ready to run away from discipline on this issue filled the air.

Morris jabbed his finger at Mathis. "Mr. Chairman," he screamed into his mike, "I ask you, Mr. Chairman, can you live on a hundred dollars a week if you were on strike?"

The audience jumped to its collective feet, roaring and shouting. Only the shallowest of the delegates was unaware that Mathis pulled down more than a quarter of a million dollars a year from the union and enjoyed the pleasures of an IBT-supplied corporate jet flown and maintained by an IBT-supplied pilot and crew.

"Let's have order in the hall," Mathis shouted. "If you want to sit in here and scream like a bunch of banshees, okay." When the noise subsided, Mathis told the audience he figured a $200-a-week strike benefit would cost the union $200 million a year.

In the voice vote that was overwhelmingly in favor of the $200-a-week strike benefit, Mathis ruled it was too close to call. He told the delegates in favor to stand and be counted.

They did, chanting "R.V., stand up!"

Durham remained seated on the podium.

Then the nays stood, and Mathis finally ruled the motion adopted.

The Shea forces had also scored by pushing through a resolution making local supplements to national contracts subject to rank-and-file approval.

TDU had been fighting for higher strike pay and votes on the supplements for fifteen years.

NO MORE JETS

On the final day of the convention, the transparent effort to recoup the Durham Unity Team's public relations losses on the populist issues of multiple salaries, women candidates, the $200 strike pay, election of delegates, and rank-and-file voting on the supplements to national contracts fell to Harold Leu, the candidate for general secretary-treasurer.

Leu told the convention, "The motion is very simple. The International union and all conferences shall sell all airplanes." He couched his offering in the most political of terms, saying that research by the Durham Unity Team shows that "like last year, there was in excess of $20 million spent on the use of airplanes. It is a very expensive issue. And on behalf of the Unity Team, we strongly urge all these delegates unanimously to approve this motion."

The motion sailed through. Another TDU goal had been achieved because of the insiders' concerns over the newly endowed right of the membership to vote for the top officers.

In another surprise from the floor of the convention, George

Cashman, the leader of an independent, anti-McCarthy dissident faction in Boston Local 25, made a motion to extend the secret ballot to delegates voting for the officers of the Teamsters forty-four joint councils and five area conferences. The delegates passed it with no opposition.

THE FORGOTTEN TEAMSTER

Each slate was given forty minutes to deliver acceptance speeches in the final hours of the convention on Friday, June 28, 1991.

Shea, an experienced and effective speaker, offered a vision of organizing the unorganized, working to make life better not only for Teamsters but all Americans in a talk cut short to share his block of time with Ligurotis, Saporta, Barry Feinstein of New York, and John Morris of Philadelphia. The dispersal of the Shea time among five candidates predicted things to come for the ticket in the campaign that lay ahead.

Durham used all the time himself in a speech whose fiery delivery was a radical departure from his monotones of the past. Riding high and well coached, he centered the speech on his own achievements and the bright future to which he would lead the union.

Carey spent the forty minutes delivering a memorable address focusing on "the forgotten Teamster" that brought tears to the eyes of longtime reformers.

In a style honed by a year and half on the campaign trail, Carey hammered out his words:

> Today is the beginning of a victory for hundreds of thousands of Teamsters, men and women, part-timers, full-timers, who've lost faith in their union, Teamsters who do not believe it can be reformed, that it can and will work and represent the concerns for their families, for their futures.
>
> They are forgotten Teamsters, forgotten by the top leaders who travel about this nation and the world in private jets paid for with your dues money and whose huge multiple salaries let them take home more in a single month than some of our members, who pay the dues, will earn in nearly a year.
>
> Our victory for them will be on the day when they know there is no more Marble Palace, no union official, no union abuse, no union corruption beyond their power to correct,

change, and clean up. And no dream for a better tomorrow that we cannot obtain.

They have a right to know that they never again will be forgotten Teamsters, that they are only Teamsters, brothers and sisters, working men and women, part-timers, full-timers, who stand tall and say, "I am a Teamster and I'm damn proud of it."

10

The Election Campaign

R. V. Durham came out of the 1991 IBT Convention riding high, glorying in the triumph of 1,001 votes—until he got the stunning and sobering results of a poll that would be a burning secret through the months ahead.

The nationwide poll taken in the third week of July showed that while being proclaimed the front-runner, Durham in reality was in the scut position, a close third behind Walter Shea and a long distance from Ron Carey in the three-way race for the presidency. Carey had 29 percent; Shea, 14 percent; and Durham, only 12 percent.[64]

But there was an edge of hope for the Durham camp: 88 percent of those questioned couldn't name the presidential candidates, and five months stood between this snapshot of the voters and the election. Obviously, Durham had to pursue three fronts: an intense one-on-one, handshaking, barn-and-plant-gate campaign directed at the rank and file; a strong appeal to local officers who had backed him at the convention to turn out their supporters for him; and an effort to undermine the Carey image.[65]

Durham set out with determination, knowing that the odds could sometimes be overcome. He had become the presidential candidate of the ruling majority by moving past ambitious senior General Executive Board (GEB) members because of his credentials as a dedicated Teamster with thirty years of experience across the local and national levels and as a team player who

219

had stayed clean. Durham was certain that Carey would seem a shallow opportunist to anyone comparing their accomplishments as union leaders.

Up early and campaigning hard every day, Durham plunged into the battle. He hit as many as ten work sites a day, speaking to stewards gathered by his allies at hot-dog-and-beer rallies, exhorting them to help put the Unity Team at the helm of the Teamsters.

To move away from the "millionaire team" tag that Carey nailed on the slate, his campaign created a "'91 Club" with rank and filers asked to pledge $91 to support Durham. Anyone willing to sign a form and contribute $1 could become a member of the Durham Unity Team. Harold Leu, the candidate for secretary-treasurer, put on the best of the efforts to tap the mass of members with a rally that drew one thousand people to an American Legion hall in Toledo. Admission was fifteen dollars, and the beer, soft drinks, and pretzels were free. Doc James, the vice presidential candidate from Chicago, overshadowed Durham and Leu with a display of fiery oratory at the Toledo rally.

Durham moved from a schedule of three or four days a week in July to a grueling full-time quest for votes in August. He espoused Election Officer Michael Holland's proposal for a mail ballot. Chris Scott, his campaign director, explained: "You got a couple of waves of voters who will go along with their local union presidents and with TDU; then you got lots of good people who would vote if it is convenient to vote."

Scott envisioned a well-organized support structure encouraging the mass of inattentive and uncommitted members to mark their ballots for Durham and his Unity Team. Scott claimed his candidate had the endorsement of the top officers of 225–250 locals, who would be called upon to turn out the vote.

To feed the illusion of Durham as the front-runner, Scott told the press, "Lots and lots of people see us as the probable winner. Most IBT people discount Carey. The structure, the local union presidents, look at this as a contest between Durham and Shea."

———

Shea, too, hit the pavement running in August, setting out to look as many members in the eyes as he could and to ask for their votes. He and his running mate for secretary-treasurer, Dan Ligurotis, had shed their big-time campaign consultants,

Black, Manafort, Stone & Kelly of Alexandria, Virginia, and the Strategy Group of Chicago. They couldn't afford them anymore.

Peter Giangreco of the Strategy Group said the consultants had urged the Shea slate to raise seed money for the campaign through a combination of loans for a half million dollars—with the candidates signing notes to guarantee repayment—combined with aggressive fund-raising.

Giangreco said in August:

> These guys have balked at the loan. That is indicative of two things: These guys understand union politics and the intrigue of putting somebody in under the old system. They understand inside baseball, but they don't understand retail campaign politics and how expensive it is. If they do make this commitment, they will win, because they have an organizational advantage even in excess of Durham.
>
> The base of Shea/Ligurotis is centered in the big cities, and it's a lot more accessible than getting all these little porkchop locals all over the South and the West and in Canada. We're talking about Chicago, New York, Pennsylvania, and New Jersey. That spine that reaches across from the Northeast to the Midwest. That's Shea/Ligurotis territory. And I think they understand how to organize stewards and that sort of thing—the field operation. But if they can grasp and fund the communications side of things, it is going to be a lot easier to turn their people out, because their people are together in ways that are reachable. You can use billboards or radio in Chicago, New York, or New Jersey.
>
> The bottom line is sixty percent of the rank and file don't know who anybody is. The elements are there to win if they raise the money. If they commit to the money.
>
> They can win on a million. They can win on a little less than that, but not a lot less than that. It takes money to put in full-time organizers. It takes money to communicate with people.
>
> I wouldn't spend any of that million outside the major cities. I would suggest they back-load everything, saving their bullets for the end. If you start mailing in September, the people are going to forget those messages.
>
> Going around and shaking some hands in a barn is not going to touch enough people.

With the professionals gone, Philadelphia Teamster leader John Morris effectively assumed the role of Shea's campaign director. Morris, who headed both the Philadelphia Joint Council and the Pennsylvania Conference of Teamsters, had one of the best-organized political operations in the union. He assigned Tim O'Neill, who took a leave of absence from the Pennsylvania Conference staff, to travel with Shea and coordinate his schedule.

O'Neill, who had worked on several congressional races and in the public affairs office at the Marble Palace before joining Morris, said that he began to see a phenomenon that he had seen before in candidates. Shea liked doing it. "You get a couple of smiles, a couple of people saying, 'I'm behind you,' and it is amazing what it can do to the candidate."

"Walter is tremendous one-on-one," O'Neill said. "We spent an entire week in Chicago, the week of August 12, walking the docks, hitting Consolidated Freightways, Roadway, Carolina, and Yellow. I would say he easily shook two thousand hands. Chicago isn't called the city of big shoulders for nothing."

In Chicago, Ligurotis was trying to solve the money problem by printing three thousand lottery tickets at $100 a pop, with a brand-new Lincoln Continental as the grand prize.

But fund-raising seemed trivial alongside the family crisis that exploded into a tragedy of bewildering proportions for Ligurotis on August 21, 1991. That morning, he killed his adopted son and namesake.

Ligurotis had adopted Dan, Jr., as a baby in 1955 in Greece. The towering six-foot four-inch Ligurotis and his much smaller son were very close. The younger man was being groomed to move up through the Teamsters. At the age of thirty-six, Dan, Jr., was on Teamster payrolls as a trustee and business agent in his father's Chicago Local 705, with combined salaries of $101,000 a year. But he was a troubled man, in and out of treatment centers because of addiction problems that had haunted him from his teenage years.

The father and son, who lived in adjoining town houses in suburban Westchester, began arguing at 6:30 A.M. over Dan, Jr.'s continued drinking and cocaine habits, which Dan, Sr., said were destroying his family.

The quarrel continued at Teamster City, the five-story building at 300 S. Ashland, which housed Local 705's offices on Chicago's West Side. Sometime between eight and eight-thirty, the dispute moved beyond words. Dan, Jr., drew the gun he carried for protection. "My son placed a gun to my head and said he was going to kill me," Ligurotis said in a statement. "From the look in his eyes, I knew he would. What I didn't know for sure until afterwards was that it was not my son behind those eyes. It was a deadly combination of alcohol and cocaine. I did the only thing I could under the circumstances to defend myself." Ligurotis pulled out his own pistol and shot Dan, Jr., dead.

Chicago police said that the version the sixty-three-year-old Ligurotis gave them in the course of thirteen hours of questioning was that Dan, Jr., was armed with a .25-caliber pistol, while he had a .38. The fatal bullet tore through the younger man's head, entering just above his left ear and exiting through his forehead over his right eye.

The killing had taken place in the privacy of a gym in the basement of Teamster City. Ligurotis called a close friend, then wandered through the building, chatting occasionally with staffers and other Teamsters for ninety minutes before calling the police.

Rory McGinty, a Ligurotis confidant and aide, attributed the delay in notifying the authorities to shock. He said the Ligurotises carried guns because of death threats stemming from the elder Ligurotis's assignment as the trustee in charge of Chicago Local 703, a union with a history of mob connections and violence.

After months of investigation, Ligurotis was indicted on two counts of second-degree murder at the end of November.* He attributed the charges against him to Cook County politics, contending he was being made a political football because of the upcoming contest for state's attorney, a charge that the incumbent state's attorney, Jack O'Malley, described as nonsensical.[66]

———

This was a happier time for Carey. Truck drivers were sounding their horns when they saw him campaigning. Rank and filers were reacting to him at plant gates with a gratifying fervor. At the wheel of his GMC "Jimmy" en route to Boston in mid-August, Carey roused Eddie Burke out of the torpor of a long ride on a summer afternoon by suddenly saying: "I think we're going to win."

"Don't spread that around," an alarmed Burke said. "We've got to keep everybody focused on the prize."

*Subsequently, a judge dismissed the charges against Ligurotis.

All of the candidates had been invited to George Cashman's Local 25 Leadership Team lobster-and-steak bake. Only John Morris from the Shea slate and Carey showed up.

A crowd of 650 Teamsters and their families filled a party tent that looked as long as a football field. Carey was welcomed with an ardor that was contagious. People crowded forward to see him, to shake his hand, to say he had their votes.

Watching Carey's slow progress through the enthusiastic crowd, Morris cracked to an aide: "Like Frank Sinatra."

THE DIRTY CAMPAIGN

Since none of the slates could afford to buy even a single mailing to the 1.6 million members, in large part due to the fund-raising restraints put on the candidates by Holland's election rules, the only means of reaching masses of voters was the Teamster magazine and the media. Each slate was to be given nine pages of space in the September, October, and November issues of the *International Teamster*.

The magazine was to become a battlefield in a very dirty war between Carey and Durham.

Newspapers, magazines, and television had spent decades describing the transgressions of Teamster officials that led the union into the bind of court-appointed officers, imposing democracy on the hierarchy. The sporadic accounts of the campaign that appeared tended to award Durham with his hollow title of front-runner, identify Carey as the grass-roots reformer, and tag Shea as the "old guard" candidate.

The big media blast on the Teamsters' election was expected to be delivered by "60 Minutes," the popular CBS-TV network show. While Carey anticipated a boost from the show, Durham awaited the "60 Minutes" segment with trepidation.

Shea complained with disgust to Teamsters Local 560 members at a rally in Union City that the hour and a half he spent in interviews for the *60 Minutes* program spun primarily around organized crime. "This union has been held in bondage for thirty years. It started with the McClellan Committee and Dave Beck. I told '60 Minutes' this was a great union."

No one knew on which Sunday night the Teamster story would appear, but most expected it at the point of highest impact, shortly after the ballots were mailed to members in the second or third week of November. The deadline for returning the votes was noon on December 10. Holland's staff was scheduled to begin counting that afternoon.

Ron Carey opened the nine pages alloted to his campaign material in the September issue of the *International Teamster* with a full-page color photo of three pigs feeding at a trough filled with dollar bills. "They're feasting on your dues!" said the text. The ad provoked laughter from everyone who saw it—except R. V. Durham.

He looked at the family of pigs and angrily jumped to the conclusion that the picture was intended as a personal insult to him and his family. If he, his son, and wife were not on the Teamsters' payrolls, it would not have stung so deeply.

On the next page, more pigs were pictured, including three dressed as a mother, a little boy, and little girl. That confirmed in Durham's mind that his family was the target of the jibe, since he had a daughter and a son.[67]

"I take full credit for the pigs," said Eddie Burke in a later interview. "I didn't know he had a daughter." After musing for a moment, Burke added, "Well, if the hoof fits, wear it."

Burke exclaimed, "I'm a pig man. When I left the Mine Workers, they gave me a three-foot pig with a gold necklace. That was because I was always ranting and raving about porkchoppers putting on pinky rings and gold necklaces." (A porkchopper is a derisive term for union bureaucrats.)

While Burke liked pigs, so did the November Group, a Washington, D.C.–based political marketing firm he hired to give the Carey campaign literature a hard-hitting, sophisticated edge. The November Group prepared the Carey ads in the magazine and the material used in the end game when the final pitch was made to the rank and file just before the ballots were mailed for the December election.

In the same issue of the magazine, Durham's political pages slammed Shea for never having been a working Teamster or a local union officer and supposedly not paying union dues from 1964 to 1982. Carey was accused of providing his local with a lousy health insurance plan in order to finance the pension plan. Calling Ron Carey "Mr. Immunity," the Durham material accused him of cutting a deal with the government to testify against John Long at his kickback trial and earlier failing to act against

225

Long, then Local 804's secretary-treasurer, when he knew an investigation was under way.

Burke devised a strategy of responding to Durham's attacks with ridicule, putting out a flier headlined "R. V. Durham's at it again: Lying!"

Throughout the flyer he alternated a silly statement with a denial. An example:

"Ron Carey *was not* captain of the Exxon Valdez when it ran aground in Alaska.

"Ron Carey *did not* hesitate to force a Local 804 official caught in wrongdoing out of office."

The Shea offering in the magazine had neither the stinging humor nor the battle-ax crudeness of his opponents. His pages, split among the fourteen members of his slate, gave the sense that they were all running on their own rather than as part of a formidable team headed by Shea.

Shea's magazine effort reaffirmed the general feeling that he was no longer a serious contender.

Burke tried to be bitingly funny again in the October issue of the *International Teamster* by doctoring a photo to show Durham arm in arm with a convict in chains and a gangster with a machine gun on either side of him, an allusion to both the past image of the Teamsters and the charges of corruption and organized crime ties lodged against some Durham allies.

Durham struck back in that issue with a photo of Carey with the pejorative "scab" superimposed across it. The Durham material said, "Scabbing on a Teamsters strike is as low as you can go. Ron Carey scabbed on a UPS strike."

Accusing a union leader of being a scab—one who betrays fellow workers by crossing a picket line to work—is akin to charging a gubernatorial candidate with molesting a child. It couldn't be laughed off or ignored by Carey.

"This is an out-and-out lie," Carey said.

The Durham pages contended that "Bloomingdale's department store paid Ron Carey $2 a bundle to scab." That's all. Neither the date of the strike nor any documentation in the form of records or statements from Local 804 members was included in the piece.

To reporters who inquired, Durham suggested they talk to his lawyer, Hugh Beins.

Beins said in a telephone interview: "Carey scabbed in 1962.

There was a seven-week UPS strike. He was leader of a group of members who leased trucks and hauled for Bloomingdale's and B. Altman's at two dollars a bundle. They were doing work [that] but for the strike would have been performed by UPS."

Carey said that never happened. During the 1962 strike, he said he went to work for either Rheingold or Schaeffer hauling beer, not packages for Bloomingdale's. After twenty-nine years he could recall it was a brewery, but not which one.

Beins insisted he had proof. "We have a number of statements from guys who did it with him," Bein said, but refused to produce the statements or name the people. He suggested that Carey sue if he wanted to find out who they were. "We asked him to sue so we can take his deposition," Beins said.

Janice LaChance, a public relations representative for Durham, added a little icing to the plot. She said that the people involved didn't want their names revealed unless there was a lawsuit because they feared retaliation.

Fearing retaliation in the form of either physical violence or the loss of a job because of speaking out against Ron Carey seemed like a sick joke. Neither Carey nor his local was associated with any known instances of roughing up a member. Carey's decades of militance in dealing with the UPS made it unlikely the company would punish someone undermining his candidacy.

Rick Gilberg, Carey's lawyer expressed concern that the Durham forces were anxious for Carey to sue so he could be tied up in giving time-consuming depositions that would take him off the campaign trail as the election approached. But Carey was seething, wanting to strike back, to force Durham to admit he was lying.

Carey's anger boiled over at a candidate's forum at a Western Conference meeting in Palm Springs, California. Durham came over to shake Carey's hand. "How can I shake your hand. You're a bum. You called me a scab," Carey said.

"It's true," Durham responded.

The audience of Western Conference delegates booed Carey when he revealed that Durham had asked him just before the 1991 convention in June to run on his Unity Team ticket as a vice president. "R.V., tell me you didn't ask me to run on the slate with you," Carey shouted.

Durham responded, "You're a goddamn liar."

After the forum, Carey told the press that he and Gilberg

met with Durham and Beins at Beins's law office on June 15 in Washington, D.C., just nine days before the IBT nominating convention—and not long after abandoning the effort to merge the Shea and Durham slates. Carey said Durham had offered him the vice presidency for the New York area and told him that he would be a one-term president, with Carey as his successor. Carey rejected the deal.

Gilberg confirmed Carey's story. "I remember coming out of the meeting saying, 'Man, he was offering Ron the whole barn.' Durham said he would be a one-term president. There was definitely a strong suggestion that Ron would be his successor."

Beins and Durham refused to discuss with reporters what they said was an off-the-record meeting. Carey said that he broke the agreed silence because Durham's scab charge had changed the rules of the encounter.

Gilberg satisfied the needs of the campaign and Carey's anger by instituting a $15 million libel suit against Durham and Chris Scott over the scab issue in State Supreme Court in Queens County on October 23. Under the state legal procedures, a couple of months would pass before either side could enter the discovery process, with its time-consuming depositions. The election would be over before that happened.

Durham kept up the scab attack on Carey in the November issue of the Teamster magazine. He offered as his proof an affidavit from a private investigator, Albert "Ned" Hines, who claimed to have met with several unnamed Local 804 members who said there was a seven-week strike in 1962.

That was an undisputed fact. But the carefully worded affidavit didn't contain any allegation by these unnamed members that Carey was a scab.

Hines's affidavit made the flat statement, attributed to one other than himself, that "the fact that Ron Carey was a scab was common knowledge among the members of Local 804. It was an issue when he first ran for office in the local union."

Had Carey scabbed, members of Local 804 certainly would have known back in 1963, when he first ran for office, and again in 1968, when he was elected president. Teamsters or other unionists who engaged in seven-week strikes seldom forget or forgive those who scabbed. They certainly don't elect a scab from the rank and file to the highest office in a local.

Burke, displaying his talents as a master strategist, filled

Carey's pages in the November magazine with photos of masses of Local 804 members and blaring headlines: "We won't be silent! ... A courageous man is being smeared."

"Nobody calls me a scab," said the headline over Carey's photo at the end of his block of pages in the magazine. He was quoted as saying, "The Durham crowd has stolen our money, taken kickbacks from employers, and sold out our union to organized crime."

While Durham's reputation was impeccable, he couldn't extend that claim to political allies in the union. In the midst of the mudslinging in the magazine, St. Louis Teamster leader Robert Sansone, who was running for vice president on the Durham slate, was accused by Investigations Officer Charles Carberry of failing to investigate and act against an officer in his local who was a member of organized crime.

Sansone's immediate defense was that he had delved into the purported mob ties of Anthony Parrino, a Local 682 vice president, when they first surfaced in newspaper stories in 1980 and again in 1989 and didn't come up with any substantiating evidence.[68]

Parrino's supposed mob connections surfaced in the *St. Louis Post Dispatch* in 1980 and were repeated several times through the years. Parrino denied having any organized crime ties, according to Sansone's attorney, Clyde E. Craig. "Whenever those articles appeared, he said he was absolutely not connected. He was Italian. He was raised in the same neighborhood, but he was not connected in any way. Sansone knew that Tony Perrino worked at his job and was an effective labor leader. It just seemed ludicrous."

After the consent decree was issued in 1989 prohibiting Teamster officers from associating with Cosa Nostra figures, Sansone directed Craig to reexamine Parrino's background. A special counsel, Gary M. Miller of Milwaukee, was hired to do an independent investigation. Miller issued a twenty-page report that reaffirmed that there was no solid evidence, "just unsubstantiated rumors," about Parrino.

Then the investigations officer charged Parrino, who had been a Local 682 vice president for fifteen years, with being a member of La Cosa Nostra, the *consigliere*, or adviser, of the St. Louis organized crime family. Parrino resigned from the local and the Teamsters.

Sansone complained that Carberry had been investigating the

case since December 1990 but waited until a few weeks before the election to charge him with condoning Parrino's presence in the local. Sansone said, "I find the timing of these charges to be extremely suspect." Carberry didn't respond. Investigators seldom do.

Whatever the timing, Sansone was the fifth Teamster official associated with the Durham slate to be charged. International vice presidents Michael J. Riley of Los Angeles and Don West of Birmingham, Alabama, who were running for reelection on the Durham slate, also were charged by Carberry. Riley settled a charge of an improper gift of union funds—for giving cars to seven retiring officers of his home Local 986—by agreeing to repay the local $40,760. Other charges of failing to investigate an embezzlement by another union officer and double-dipping on car expenses were dropped. West was accused of soliciting contributions from employers for a testimonial dinner for a retiring Teamster official. Lacey decided four months after the election that the charge against West was unfounded.

No charges were brought against any of those on Carey's slate, all of whom were either local union officers or rank-and-file members.

THE TRIAL OF JOE T

As the faltering Shea campaign moved into September, Joseph (Joe T) Trerotola, the octogenarian kingmaker of the Teamsters and the father of Shea's candidacy, finally succumbed to the charge that had haunted him for decades—that organized crime was all over New York Joint Council 16.

Like Durham, the eighty-two-year-old Joe T had a reputation for personal honesty. He had never been indicted, arrested, or charged with a crime, nor had he refused to testify when subpoenaed. The same couldn't be said of many of the other officers on Joint Council 16 or its fifty-one Teamster locals in New York City and Long Island.

TDU's Ken Paff liked to say with a snicker: "Joe T never met a mobster he didn't like."

The consent decree of 1989, which Joe T signed, opened the door for the internal union charge that brought him down. On May 8, 1991, the month before the Teamster nominating convention, Carberry charged Joe T with violating his fiduciary duties as an IBT officer by deliberately failing to investigate four Joint Council 16 officers who had ties to organized crime and had used the Fifth Amendment to shield themselves from testifying. The four officers made up a majority of the council's seven-member executive board.

Standing with his attorney, Robert Baptiste, at an Eastern Conference luncheon during the 1991 convention, Joe T asked rhetorically, "How the hell could they charge me with something like that?"

Baptiste said supportively: "You're supposed to be everybody's keeper, Joe."

Joe T continued, "I got fifty-one locals. Am I supposed to run the fifty-one locals in the joint council and investigate each and every one of them? And say, 'Did you take the Fifth?' or, 'Were you ever convicted of a crime?' or, 'Were you in Cosa Nostra?' That's ridiculous. Ridiculous. That's a hell of a charge to get you on. It's just, I don't know. Again I say I've been married to my woman for sixty-two years. And I tell her whatever I have to tell. And she says, 'What is this all about?' I can't even tell her, because I don't know."

The wonder was why Joe T had lingered beyond the last dance, ending his career in disgrace instead of quitting when he was still riding high.

Carberry had waited a good while to reach him, particularly when he was so prominent and easy a target. There was some division within the investigative officer's staff over whether to skip Trerotola, some figuring his age would catch up to him sooner or later.

Carberry had struck with his charge, and instead of accepting the inevitable, Joe T had stayed his course. He told a reporter in reaction to the Carberry charge, "I tell you, I have no mob connections, never had, never will, and resent very much these individuals who say we are mob controlled. I run this council with an open mind. I'm not run by anyone."

Trerotola was nominated at the convention to run for reelection as an International vice president on Shea's ticket.

On August 8, 1991, Independent Administrator Frederick B. Lacey convened the hearing on the charges against Joe T in a fourth-floor conference room at 520 Madison Avenue, which houses the New York City offices of his law firm, LeBouef, Lamb, Leiby & MacRae.

Lacey sat at the head of the U-shaped arrangement of tables. Baptiste and his associate Christie Concannon sat at the right wing of the U along with several newspaper reporters.

To Lacey's left was FBI supervisory agent R. Lindley DeVecchio, a dapper man with a flowery tie, a colorful handkerchief in his suit breast pocket, curly hair, a mustache, and expertise in organized crime. He had been an FBI agent for twenty-five years.

At the left wing table were Assistant U.S. Attorney Ed Ferguson and FBI agent Stanley Nye, whose extraordinary career had put him at the center of most of the major labor racketeering cases. Next to Nye sat Carberry, heavyset and balding, with a thick fringe of brownish hair.

In the center of the U was a "60 Minutes" camera crew, who filmed two hours of the day-long hearing.

Missing from the crowd was Joe T.

"I've been advised by Mr. Baptiste that Mr. Trerotola was suddenly taken ill last night and will not be here today," Lacey announced. The stress of a public hearing on the allegations he had denied for so many years apparently was too much for him.

Carberry presented seventy-five exhibits, most of them dealing with the presence of organized crime in the Teamsters, including dozens of newspaper clippings and extracts from the President's Commission on Organized Crime, and a deposition from Trerotola in which he said he never asked any Teamsters whether they were associated with organized crime because it was "none of my business." In the same deposition he said that the late Roy Williams lied when he testified that Joe T was controlled by organized crime.

Carberry told Lacey, "We believe the evidence will establish that for at least thirty years there has been an organized crime presence in Joint Council 16 and it was extensive and notorious. . . . Throughout this period, Mr. Trerotola was head of the joint council, and he steadfastly ignored these allegations."

DeVecchio took the stand so that his forty-four-page declaration outlining the mob ties of the four Joint Council 16 officers could be entered into the record. His declaration introduced an unsworn statement from Michael John Franzese, a capo in the Colombo organized crime family, that crudely attempted to link Joe T to the mob by hearsay.

In his statement, Franzese, who was cooperating with the government in exchange for lighter treatment for his own crimes, said that in the mid-1970s he saw Joe T at the Pan Am Diner on

Queens Boulevard in Queens talking to two crime-family soldiers. "I never personally did business with Trerotola, whom I knew by reputation to be an influential Teamsters Union official in New York City who was an associate or possible member of La Cosa Nostra," Franzese said. In effect, Franzese was accommodating his FBI handlers by floating a rumor about Joe T so shallow that he couldn't pin him to a specific mob family.

Baptiste offered a defense that swung on the point that Joe T had never been indicted, convicted, or even arrested. He pointed out that Joe T had always testified when called—not hiding behind the Fifth. He also contended that the IBT constitution did not direct officers to act against underlings who fell into the realm of corruption or organized crime. "If it is an obligation, he was not aware of it," Baptiste said.

Baptiste argued that much of the evidence had nothing to do with Joe T or was hearsay. Baptiste kept pressing for the need for a higher standard of evidence, pointing out that in arbitrations—since the hearing was governed by the rules of arbitration, not federal-court rules—a higher standard of proof is applied when someone's career and livelihood is at stake—as was Joe T's.

Originally, Joe T's hearing was to have been June 14—and Franzese's statement was made on June 6. Baptiste questioned the coincidence:

> Just on the eve of the hearing, lo and behold, this gentleman says in an unsworn statement he observed Mr. Trerotola with people involved in organized crime and suggests Mr. Trerotola may be an associate of organized crime. Even the bureau doesn't say that. . . . I think there is more to this than meets the eye. I think it may well have been instigated by one of the investigating officers, which takes us to the question of state action, which obviously raises very serious constitutional issues.

Carberry was just as quick with his counterargument: "That's not true. The Presser File makes allegations concerning Mr. Trerotola. In terms of state action, that's an argument without merit. . . . I will represent I never told anyone to go out to get a statement from Michael Franzese."

In the Presser File, the collection of the late Jackie Presser's whisperings to his FBI handlers, the ex–Teamster president said that Louis Sunshine had carried a message from an unnamed

New York mob family in 1982 that Joe T was to be retained as director of the Eastern Conference. At the same time, Sammy Pro, the International vice president from New Jersey, was challenging Joe T for control of the conference. Presser also told the FBI that mob soldier Joseph (Joe Stretch) Stracci was the liaison between Joe T and organized crime.

Lacey adjourned the hearing until September 13, saying he assumed Joe T would show up then.

Lacey didn't have to hold another hearing. Joe T surrendered to the inevitable when he agreed to end his long career with the Teamsters. In an effort to depart gracefully, he offered to drop out of his race for reelection as an International vice president and to resign as president of Joint Council 16 and chairman of the Eastern Conference. Under that proposal, Joe T would have served out the remainder of his term as an International vice president and hold on to his minor positions as vice president of New York Local 72 and as trustee of New York Local 858. His son, Vincent, headed those two locals.

But Joe T was in no position to bargain. Lacey rejected the deal. He directed Joe T to quit all of his jobs by the end of October or to take his seat in the hearing room.

Joe T went quietly.

In the wake of his departure, Barry Feinstein was appointed by Joint Council 16's executive board to succeed Joe T as president of the 150,000-member joint council, and Walter Shea was named as chairman of the 500,000-member Eastern Conference by that organization's Policy Committee. The new post gave Shea his own power base in the Teamsters for the first time in his career. Finally, he was the boss instead of somebody's assistant.

Whatever the outcome of the election, the consent decree had endowed Feinstein and Shea with two of the most important positions in the IBT.*

AT THE PEAK OF THE CAMPAIGN

The campaign reached its peak in October with rank-and-file Teamsters delivering clear signals to Carey, Shea, and Durham

---

*On September 15, 1992, Barry Feinstein was charged with misappropriating $540,000 from Local 237 by Investigations Officer Charles Carberry.

as to what to expect when the ballots were counted in December. On the campaign trail Carey was being greeted with enthusiasm everywhere, while Shea and Durham were experiencing flashes of hostility from truck drivers and warehouse workers disenchanted with their union.

On one typical campaign day Carey arrived at 4:00 A.M. at Local 804's little office building in the Blissville section of Queens, near the tunnel to Manhattan to find Mike Caffrey was waiting with containers of coffee and a bag of doughnuts. Caffrey, helper on a liquor delivery truck and a member of Local 868, had spent weeks putting the day's schedule together, pinning down locations where Teamsters worked and times when Carey could have access to them. The task was much more complex than it seemed. Most Teamsters are spread over the landscape, working in relatively small groups.

With Carey at the wheel of his GMC "Jimmy," Caffrey and Local 804 business agent Jerry Ranita set off for nearby Brooklyn.

At the first stop, Carey walked along a loading dock to shake hands with fifteen Entenmann's bakery drivers at their terminal in Flatbush. One driver, sounding like a sound bite for the Carey campaign, said, "We need a change. You go to a union meeting and the business agents are driving Lincolns."

The next stop was right around the corner at a Taystee Bread barn. To Caffrey's embarrassment, there was no one there. Carey said, "These things happen." Spotting a tractor up the street, he trotted up to it. "Teamster?" he asked, then went into his brief spiel. "I'm Ron Carey, and I'm running for general president. We got to take this union back, buddy."

At 6:40 A.M., Carey was outside the gate of Peerless Imports, near the Brooklyn end of the Kosciusko Bridge, talking to fourteen drivers at a coffee truck.

"They got a piece in the next magazine saying I'm a scab," Carey told them. Several responded they didn't believe that. "You got our support," said one.

Carey told them: "We pushed for the $200 a week, the right to vote."

A brand-new Teamster, confused by this steady patter that everyone around him seemed to understand, asked Carey what reforms he was talking about.

"You know that four general presidents have been indicted?" Carey asked.

"No," replied the young driver.

Carey continued: "There's no organizing going on in the country. We got people in there who run it like a business." He gave them a brief history of how nepotism brought Jackie Presser to the helm of the union and how Weldon Mathis had three sons on the International payroll. "There's millionaires running our union. They are making $200-and $300,000 a year.

"You now have a chance you never had before, to vote for the top leadership. There's a lot of people banking on you people not voting. If you don't vote, then it's all over."

A Teamster walking past yelled: "I worked at UPS for two years, Ron. You don't have to talk to me. You got my vote."

As Carey was about to leave, Carl Hamilton, a thirty-nine-year-old driver from Queens, rushed up. "You're the greatest. You're number one. I love you," he said. A half an hour had passed. The fifty-one-year-old Caffrey, who had been a Teamster since he was nineteen, had been distributing Carey literature to people like Hamilton and talking up his candidate for months. He was the type of Teamster who never missed a monthly union meeting.

Caffrey got involved as a Carey volunteer when he went to Local 804 to contribute $100 and started talking with the always affable Rick Blaylock. "Rick handed me some literature and said, 'Go give this to some Teamsters.' " He did and came for more, and kept coming back.

At the core of the Carey campaign were rank and filers like Caffrey who popped up all over the country, digging into their pockets to contribute hundreds of dollars and giving even more generously of their time and energy to build support in their workplaces and among friends.

The rest of the day was very much the same, with passing truck drivers tooting their horns and giving the thumbs-up sign when they saw the Carey campaign poster that Caffrey was holding.

While few of the Teamsters that day were as effusive as the truck driver at Peerless, some expressed themselves almost as strongly. At one stop a driver handed Carey a $500 contribution, a huge sum for someone making $40,000 a year.

Although almost all of the Teamsters he met were members of locals whose officers were supporting Durham or Shea, no one confronted Carey with any negative gestures or words. Durham and Shea were not enjoying a similar absence of hostility.

Walter Shea hoped to make some political coin out of the new $200-a-week strike benefit his slate helped push through at the convention. On the campaign trail in October, he showed up at a union hall in Farmingdale, Long Island, where members of Teamsters Local 138 were lined up to collect their strike pay. The Local 138 members had been on strike for eight months against White Rose, the largest grocery distributor in the New York region, over major givebacks demanded by the company. In a tactic to escape the Local 138 pickets, White Rose had shifted its distribution base across the Hudson River to New Jersey and hired a warehousing subcontractor employing members of Teamsters Local 97, working for less than half the wages and a fraction of the benefits of the Local 138 strikers. Nonunion drivers were hired to distribute the groceries to supermarkets in New York City and Long Island.

The frustrated Local 138 strikers pleaded with the Teamster hierarchy to "sanction" their picket lines in New Jersey. The "sanction" would have put the union's stamp of approval on the picket lines, meaning that other Teamsters—particularly truck drivers delivering new stock to the warehouse—could refuse to cross without risk of losing their jobs. Frank Carracino, head of New Jersey Joint Council 73, ignored the request for the sanction. Although Teamsters helping to break a Teamster strike was unusual, it was not rare in the IBT, where business unionism had been the prevailing philosophy for thirty-five years.

Local 97 president Arnold Ross told the strikers that his local had a valid contract with the subcontractor and there was no way he could break it—a common refrain of union leaders whose members are walking across another union's picket line.

The Local 138 members were standing silently, not even speaking to one another, when Shea arrived at the union hall. He had come to ask the votes of Teamsters who believed they had been betrayed by their International union and Joint Council 73.

John Hannigan, a forty-year-old warehouse worker, angrily asked Shea the question bothering all the strikers: "I can't understand how come Teamsters in New Jersey are doing our work?"

Sidestepping a direct answer, Shea responded, "It shouldn't happen." He urged Hannigan to raise the question when he spoke to the Local 138 members inside the building. As Shea continued down the line, shaking hands, Hannigan turned to his co-workers. "Guys like this showing up now. Where was he in February, March, April?"

Inside the union hall, Shea addressed the assembled strikers. "Our team alone was responsible for bringing the strike pay to the convention floor," he said, dressing up the truth a bit. He put the blame for the New Jersey situation on McCarthy. The general president should have called in the leaders of the New York and New Jersey joint councils and said, "Hey, we don't do these things," Shea told his audience of 125 Teamsters. He told them he would talk to the leaders of the joint councils.

The audience was in no mood to let Shea off the hook. "You're here to get votes. Do you expect us to vote for you if this guy Carracino is on your slate?" asked a Teamster.

Another said, "I can guarantee you three hundred to four hundred votes if you do something."

A third pleaded, "There's no way we can win this strike unless you give us some help. We need help now."

Shea responded, "I'll talk to Carracino."

When he finished speaking, only about half the audience applauded. The atmosphere was grim.

Shea hurried by car to his next appointment and a much warmer reception at lunchtime from two hundred New York City Housing Department employees, members of Barry Feinstein's Local 237, at the Queens Bridge Housing Project in Long Island City. Feinstein, obviously popular with his members, told them: "Walter Shea is clearly the guy who knows more about this union than anybody else and is the guy we're going to elect. I'm asking for your help and support as I've never asked before." The applause was strong, and several people asked for Shea buttons to distribute.

After the meeting, Shea and Feinstein left in Feinstein's chauffeur-driven Lincoln town car. The plan was to give Shea a chance to relax until a stewards' rally that night in Manhattan. This was a leisurely approach to a search for votes in the New York/ New Jersey region, which has a quarter of a million Teamsters.

The Shea campaign's top-down strategy was on display that evening at a hotel in Manhattan where Feinstein had arranged for five hundred shop stewards from Joint Council 16's fifty-one locals to gather. There were sandwiches and drinks and plenty of cheering for Shea and six of his vice presidential candidates.

Vickie Saporta implored the shop stewards to turn out their members for the Shea slate. "It's up to you. We need fifty thousand votes out of New York City, and looking at this group tonight, I'm confident we're going to get it."

Vice presidential candidate William Genoese tried to provide the audience, which was half black, with an incentive for working against Durham. Recalling his days as an organizer in the South in the 1970s, Genoese told the shop stewards, "I went in to the Carolinas and I met R. V. Durham. . . . Durham said, 'We don't organize the blacks here. It's a white man's union.' " In a subsequent interview, Durham said, "That's bullshit. I was the first, or one of the first, to integrate my staff in the 1960s. Bill Genoese has never been in my local."

R. V. Durham awoke at 1:25 A.M. the following Wednesday in his room at the Roosevelt Hotel in Manhattan five minutes before he was called for the beginning of a long day of campaigning that would take him through the Hunts Point produce market in the Bronx, two hours north of the city by car, to the huge Yellow Freight terminal in Maybrook, New York, and back to the city to the Swingline Stapling Company's big factory in Queens.

By 3:15 A.M., Durham was moving along the Hunts Point docks, filled with colorful displays of fruits and vegetables on all sides. He was accompanied by three vice presidential candidates and the leaders of Teamsters Local 202, which represented the market's workers.

Durham launched into his set patter: "We'd like to work for you guys." And, "This is the twenty-ninth state I've been in since June." And, "I joined this union when I was nineteen years old. Been a Teamster forty-one years." Every once in a while Durham would pause for a more extended chat with a Teamster loading a truck, recalling with a touch of nostalgia his own days hauling produce from Florida to the West Street Market in Manhattan.

The exchanges were positive, "You got my vote," or, "Good luck." "You got Joe's support, you got mine," said twenty-four-year-old Frank Albano of the Bronx, pointing to Joe Byers, president of Local 202.

By 5:00 A.M., Durham had shaken hands and talked to sixty Teamsters and was headed for the huge Yellow Freight operations in upstate Maybrook. The trip was a long one, but the terminal was a potential treasure trove of votes, with eleven hundred drivers, mechanics, and warehouse workers. Durham was met in the parking lot by James Buckley, president of Teamsters 707, a local with a history of an organized crime presence. Buckley was the third president of the local in two years. His predecessors had resigned under pressure from Carberry. Before the ballots were counted in the Teamsters' International election in December, Buckley was to be kicked out of office by Lacey on charges of having tolerated Colombo crime family capo Nicholas Grancio's continued visits to the local's headquarters. Grancio was an ex–Local 707 vice president.

Speaking to thirty-five mechanics in their locker room, Durham tried to create a bond by telling them his history as a Teamster, starting as a driver for Roadway and moving through the ranks of the union to the point where he negotiated the 1991 National Master Freight Agreement. That turned out to be heavy baggage rather than an impressive credential. Instead of endearing himself to the workers, he had tapped into their anger. Everyone in the nation covered by the contract got the same fifty-cent-an-hour raise, which was great for a Teamster in Mississippi, not in high-cost New York.

Several mechanics complained to Durham that the previous spring they had voted 56–0 to strike over a local issue. But Local 707's officers ignored their vote, effectively blocking the walkout. Without the officers' approval, they could be fired for participating in an unauthorized strike. Instead, the employer granted some minor concessions, and the next version of the contract was approved.

"You didn't want to strike?" Durham stated rather than asked.

"Yes, we did," responded one union member, explaining that their picket line would have closed down the terminal, a major hub for Yellow Freight's Northeast operations. The company would have been under irresistible pressure to meet their demands because the losses involved in having the terminal shut down were so heavy. These mechanics knew their potential power and were bitterly frustrated over not being able to exercise it. Like other rank and filers in similar situations, they had come to believe the union was in bed with the boss.

Durham responded with a persuasive argument on the importance of uniform wages and benefits in a national contract, including a convincing explanation of how much he had done for the

Yellow Freight workers at the bargaining table. His account so mollified one of the angry workers that after the candidate walked on, he told a reporter that he had decided to vote for Durham.

After moving through the terminal, shaking hands and being introduced by Buckley, Durham and his entourage entered a small room, where fourteen dock workers were taking a lunch break at eight in the morning. Card games were in progress at two tables, while the rest of the room held a scattering of small groups chatting over their sandwiches and individuals here and there reading a book or a newspaper.

Silence fell over the room. Durham had entered hostile territory. The atmosphere was sullen. On either side of the room were bulletin boards decorated with Carey campaign material. On the lunch tables were scatterings of fliers from a reform faction in the local.

As Durham began to speak, other workers with lunch pails or brown bags in their hands entered the room and took seats. "I like this industry, and I like this union, and I want to work for you," Durham said. Again he recounted his role in negotiating the National Master Freight Agreement.

"It might have been a decent contract for people on the West Coast, but not here, where the cost of living is higher," said a worker who had been watching Durham intently.

Durham responded with his explanation of what he won at the bargaining table and the theory behind national contracts; that if wages are higher in one area, employers will move to the places where labor costs are lower.

"How come they didn't discuss this with us? The local never talked to us about the contract," the same worker said, an acid inflection in his words. The other workers watched him with obvious respect. This was a leader.

Several workers put their heads down, not looking at Durham for the rest of his brief stay in their lunchroom. The card players at the two tables had reluctantly turned to listen to Durham speak, but before he finished, they returned to their game, first at one table, then the other, an insulting gesture lost on no one.

As he departed, Durham said to the silent men: "I never forgot where I came from. That's off a truck and off a dock."

The caravan of cars that had carried Durham's entourage upstate returned to New York City for a campaign stop at a stapling machine factory that turned out to be a pleasure for the candidate. Durham walked through the plant, next to the freight yards in Long Island City, with Chris Silvera, the top officer of Local 808. Silvera had been elected to office on a reform slate and obviously enjoyed a high standing among the factory's workers. "This is R. V. Durham, who we're going to be backing," said Silvera over the incessant clatter of the machines manufacturing staples and parts.

Adolfo Fana, the chief shop steward, bridged the language barrier for Durham's brief exchanges with the workers, most of them immigrants. Many eagerly took buttons and bumper stickers. Some said with a smile, "I'll vote for you."

THE CAREY POLL

The first and only poll released during the post convention IBT election campaign came on October 23, 1991, from Eddie Burke, Ron Carey's campaign manager.

The poll confirmed the anecdotal experience of the campaign trail: The rank and file's enthusiasm was for Ron Carey, not R. V. Durham. Walter Shea was so far behind he was out of the race.

Lauer, Lalley & Associates Inc., a Washington, D.C.–based polling firm, had questioned 605 likely voters in the United States and Canada from October 15 through October 19. (Although the number sounds small, 600 is a valid sample for a national poll.) The resulting figures sent a chill through the hierarchy's two insider candidates: Carey had 29 percent of the vote; Durham 13 percent; and Shea only 7 percent. With 51 percent of the voters undecided, uncommitted, or unwilling to respond, the outcome of the election was very much up for grabs.

Burke released only those pieces of the poll revealing Carey's 2–1 lead, which effectively deposed Durham as the "front runner," and showing that among UPS workers, Carey had 46 percent to Durham's 4 percent and Shea's 1 percent.

James W. Lauer, president of Lauer, Lalley, analyzed the results: "The election is being played out against deep member concern about corruption in the union. This plays to Carey's advantage in that Teamster members see him as the candidate for change."

The opposition reacted with the expected sneers. Tim O'Neill, Shea's campaign aide, said, "Carey paid for a poll, and he got the results that he bought. We really think that polls in this kind of an election, which is the first of its kind, really are meaningless."

Janice LaChance, a spokeswoman for Durham, said,"I think their campaign needed a shot in the arm because it was collapsing around them, and this could be it."

Two days after the release of the poll to the media, Jim Lauer sent Burke a confidential memo with some sobering information. Carey's substantial lead, he said, was tenuous, with the outcome depending on the final push to turn out likely voters.

Lauer described how Durham could position himself to win the election and proposed a counterstrategy for Carey.

"Even though Carey is leading by a good margin, this race is completely open," the Lauer memo said. "if Durham can mount a large-scale mail campaign in November, he could easily wipe out his recognition problems and beat Carey on recognition alone." Burke had good reason to fear that Durham would make a massive mail assault on the eve of the ballots being mailed out. While Carey might be winning 2–1 in the poll, Durham enjoyed a similar margin in raising funds. By the end of October, the Durham Unity Team reported $984,504 in contributions, while Carey took in $428,748—less than half.

Moreover, almost half of Carey's funds came from members of his home local, Local 804. Just twenty-three high-ranking Teamster officials gave Durham more than half a million dollars, most out of their well-larded pockets. Harold Leu, the candidate for secretary-treasurer, led the Durham list with $46,000. Billy McCarthy gave $15,475; Weldon Mathis, $10,000.[69]

"The Carey campaign must do everything it can to at least match the Durham effort in the final communications efforts of the campaign," Lauer advised Burke. "The bottom line is that 40 to 50 percent of those members who are the most likely voters know next to nothing about either candidate."

Since the poll showed the UPS vote was essentially Carey's, Lauer suggested concentrating get-out-the-vote efforts on the 140,000 UPS members. "Freight workers will also vote in large numbers, and they respond to the 'clean up corruption' and 'time for a change' messages of the Carey campaign," the memo said.

The three primary areas of concern expressed by those polled were corruption, pensions and health care, and "a sense that the union is neither representing nor servicing the average Teamster." In his two-year trek across the country, those were the issues Carey had pressed as he shook hands with tens of thousands of Teamsters.

The poll came up with some stunning figures on the Teamster electorate:

- Seventeen percent (272,000 members) were delinquent in dues or had a bad mailing address—meaning they would not be eligible to vote.
- Twenty-two percent (352,000 members) said they wouldn't vote, secret ballot or not.
- Only 61 percent of those intending to vote knew that there would be an election for President.
- Forty percent or more failed to recognize any of the candidates.

The negative campaigns waged by Durham and Carey had little significant impact, according to Lauer. He found that only 8 percent had negative feelings for Carey, while Durham's negative rating was 12 percent.

"Getting the Mafia out of the union" was the number-one priority chosen by the members from a list of issues facing the union. Lauer said, "The poll shows that the Durham slate's involvement with corruption, kickbacks, and Mafia ties represents its greatest vulnerability. Fully 64 percent of those surveyed said they are 'much less likely' to vote for Durham after learning of the charges."

Lauer discovered that very few members were aware of the "scab" and "testifying under immunity" charges against Carey. "Twenty-six percent are concerned about the scab charge and 35 percent are concerned about the immunity charge. We see little evidence in the poll that either charge is causing much damage at this point," Lauer's memo said.

On the positive side from Carey's perspective, the polling data showed he led Durham by substantial margins in each of the five Teamster area conferences, but significantly, he was way ahead in the three categories of members most likely to vote: Among freight workers, Carey led 32 percent to Durham's 15 percent; among grocery/warehouse workers Carey had 23 percent to Durham's 13 percent; and among UPSers Carey had 46 percent to Durham's 4 percent.

Perhaps the impending death knell of the Durham campaign

could be found in figures produced from Teamster officers in the election trial-heat phase of the poll: Forty-nine percent were undecided. Of those willing to commit, Durham got 26 percent to Carey's 16 percent and Shea's 9 percent.

The Durham and Shea campaigns rested on whether local union officers would turn out their members for them—and a clear majority, 65 percent, were either undecided or aligned with Carey.

PANIC IN THE DURHAM CAMP

The Durham slate began to signal a sense of panic in late October. They filed charges with Election Officer Michael Holland claiming that *Labor Notes*, a monthly publication, and the *Detroit Free Press*, a daily newspaper, had printed biased articles favoring Carey.

Larry Brennan, a vice presidential candidate on the Durham slate, complained to Holland that the *Detroit Free Press* had used the Carey campaign ad showing Durham arm in arm with a convict and a gangster on its front page and again on its business page on October 8 to illustrate an article. Brennan demanded that Holland order "cash contributions from the *Free Press* to Durham and Shea, equivalent in value to the free publicity given to Carey."

Holland quickly denied Brennan's request.

Chris Scott, Durham's campaign director, filed a protest against *Labor Notes*, a publication that focuses on and encourages activism in the American labor movement. He claimed that a report in the October issue on the three-way Teamsters' presidential race was "but one of many which are subtly structured, but 100 percent part of Carey's election campaign." The article by Phil Kwik made the point that Carey's contributions came from small donations from members, while Durham was able to tap well-paid officers, collecting $40,000 from a single fundraiser in Chicago attended by hundreds of local union officials.

Reacting to complaints from the Durham slate, Holland forced the TDU and its educational and legal arm, the Teamster Rank and File Education and Legal Defense Foundation (TRF), to file the names of all contributors of $100 or more. The TDU and the TRF gave Holland the information he demanded rather than

245

risk being banned from participating in the Teamster election campaign but immediately turned to Judge Edelstein to seek a preliminary injunction to nullify Holland's decision. The TDU and the TRF had promised contributors confidentiality, a veil sought for a variety of reasons but primarily to avoid the risk of retaliatory harassment or the loss of a job.

In a strange dialogue during a federal court hearing on the injunction, Judge Edelstein and Independent Administrator Frederick Lacey praised themselves for their role in democratizing the Teamsters while demeaning and sneering at the contributions of TDU and its rank-and-file members.

Judge Edelstein said in the courtroom, "I believe that sunshine ought to penetrate every corridor and every recess. I understand that there's always some fearfulness and apprehension about a lack of confidentiality.

"I think it is time for members of the Teamsters for a Democratic Union to stand and be counted. I do not know how many there are, but there are certainly seventeen thousand of them. I find it difficult to believe that seventeen thousand members united can be intimidated."

Plenty of Teamster dissidents had stood up through the years to assume the role of working-class hero fighting corruption— and had been crushed. A few had suffered the indignity of being punched around; many more had lost their jobs. In any repressive society—and the Teamsters Union as a whole had been a repressive organization—the members interested in survival do their jobs, pick up their pay at the end of the week, and keep their mouths shut. Only a courageous few cross the line to rebellion in an attempt to turn the world upside down.

Judge Edelstein said he wanted to see more heroes from TDU. "I would like to have them stand up and show some guts and start being unintimidated and to be confrontational, if they have to, in self-defense." The judge, of course, was speaking from the august comfort of a federal bench.

In case anyone questioned the courage of the eighty-two-year-old judge, he put that quality in perspective. "I have heard rumors about how very popular I am with this union," he said. "What am I to do? I have not acted on these rumors, and I do not intend to. I think they are a bunch of sleaze balls. The only time they are macho is when they have a bat in their hands. . . .

One of my major points when I insisted that Judge Lacey come here as administrator is because I know his quality and I know he is not going to be intimidated. Oh, I would like to see that happen, frankly."

All the while Judge Edelstein was delivering his lecture on courage, TDU's attorney, Paul A. Levy, was trying to deliver his arguments but was repeatedly interrupted as the judge made another point.

"Have you been intimidated, Judge Lacey?" Judge Edelstein asked, adding, "Even I have not been able to do that."

Lacey responded, "I have a very, very strong father. He did insist on certain rigid adherence to principle."

When Levy managed to get in his argument, he said that TDU was willing to give Holland the contributors list in confidence so he could check it out for any prohibited donors, such as employers. Levy explained that the fear of retaliation ran deep. He questioned whether the court officers could do anything about retaliation, particularly the loss of a job on a trumped-up excuse.

Holland interjected, "There's also the need for an open democratic process."

Lacey said that the IBT's June convention had convinced him that change had arrived in the Teamsters. "I was there, and the process was something that two years ago no one would have dreamed would ever happen. People were standing up on the floor and disagreeing with the leadership, attacking the leadership, deciding that Air Force One was going to be abolished." He said that TDU should "say we want to get aboard and show that we don't have any fears now because we are going to make this work."

There seemed to be an undercurrent in the Lacey/Judge Edelstein exchanges that too much credit was flowing to TDU and not enough to them for whatever transformation had occurred in the Teamsters.

"I watched a program last night, the 'Adam Smith' program on Channel thirteen," Judge Edelstein interjected. "They were extolling the TDU for the way they have been fighting for democracy well before the convention and the convention really was a culmination of their efforts, taking great credit for what had happened. And I am not going to dispute whether they are entitled to that or not."

247

Referring to his decision directing Holland to run the IBT elections, Judge Edelstein said, "They seem to forget, don't they, at this moment that I went beyond the recommendation of my own court-appointed officers in my opinion. They forget that. They have a very selective memory."

"I am glad you did what you did," Lacey responded.

Judge Edelstein ended the exchange by ruling that TDU and the TRF would have to make the filings. He announced, "My philosophy is very clear about this. I believe this is the time for the TDU to come out of the closet, stand up and be counted. Let them turn this wave of democracy and unionism into a hurricane. If they wish anonymity, that itself points a finger of suspicion about the quality of the leadership in this TDU and its members." If there were any intimidation, he said, he would order everyone who inspected the records to be investigated.

Addressing the TDU, Judge Edelstein offered a puzzling diatribe: "You have gotten far more than you ever dreamed or expected. And until this happened, where were you? This union is old. You accomplished nothing. If it hadn't been for the convention and the court officers and the government that started this by bringing on the opportunity to enter into the consent decree, where would you be?"

"And incidentally," he went on, "I have voiced this before—in many ways I'm sorry that the government ever entered into a consent decree. You all know that I had some reluctance and hesitation. I wasn't at all happy with this consent decree for one moment. I would have preferred to have gone to trial. I would have been done and finished with this a long time ago."

In his rush to judgment, Judge Edelstein failed to grasp the central role that TDU played in the democratization process. TDU offered the framework making the fulfillment of the consent decree possible. Without TDU, Ron Carey's candidacy would have been a noble gesture that went nowhere. TDU had a nationwide network of dissidents with experience in grass-roots organizing, fund-raising, and union politics awaiting the right candidate.

Without TDU, the convention would have been filled with the usual bunch of yes-men and women in Disney World to have a good time, maybe to experience another of Joe T's extraordinary parties, and to extol the virtues of the incumbent leaders.

The consent decree might have created the stress that broke the hierarchy apart, but without TDU the presidential election would have been between the two "old guard" candidates, Walter Shea and R. V. Durham—although the most likely scenario is that one of them would have been elected by acclamation at the convention, as in the good old days.

Of course, without the iron will and unassailable decisions of Judge Edelstein, the consent decree giving the rank and file the right to vote for the IBT hierarchy and the purging of the obvious elements of the mob and corruption from the Teamsters would not have been accomplished, either. He proved to be the right judge for the case.

Judge Edelstein ended the hearing by telling Levy: "And I am very disappointed in you and your [clients]. We no longer seem to be sharing the same objective and the same goals. Let them know what I think. You are now an adversary instead of an amicus. Now go to the court of appeals."

TDU did go to the Second Circuit Court of Appeals.

The AUD also filed an amicus curiae brief supporting TDU's appeal to the higher court, then found itself targeted by Holland to disclose its contributors of $100 or more, too.

AUD's founder, Herman Benson, issued a statement contending that Holland's election rules didn't apply to the AUD because the organization didn't support any candidates for election but rather extended offers of legal aid to rank and filers involved in election disputes. All of the requests came from Carey supporters, which was to be expected, since Durham and Shea backers had their union lawyers to represent them.

"They are demanding the principal organization that helps the rank and file in the fight against racketeers reveal its donors," Benson said. "Since these people—not only unionists but labor attorneys and staffers—are subject to retaliation, the idea we are to reveal our names to those who tolerated racketeers is not only an absurdity but an outrage."

The AUD's executive director, Susan Jennik, cited cases in which Carey supporters fired by the UPS claimed that the underlying reasons were retaliation for election activities, only to have Holland reject their claims. Jennik said she would give the election officer the list of foundations that provide the AUD with about $180,000 a year but no individual names. "I don't think

Holland or Lacey truly appreciate the risk taken by members who are fighting the Mafia in their union," Jennik said. "They are trying to force us to expose people who have chosen to remain anonymous about their activities, and we won't do it."

On November 13, 1991, Holland banned the AUD from any further role in the Teamster election and asked Assistant U.S. Attorney Edward Ferguson to institute contempt proceedings against the AUD. He warned that any candidate accepting assistance from the AUD could be disqualified.

Eddie Burke immediately notified the Carey team to have nothing to do with the AUD rather than risk being knocked out of the race.

Meanwhile, Holland addressed pressure coming from the Durham forces, who were unhappy that his decision hadn't dealt a death blow to the Carey candidacy. They had grown so abrasive that Holland felt compelled to confront them in writing.

On November 20, Holland sent a letter to Durham, Scott, and Beins saying:

> On November 1 and 14, 1991 (by Mr. Beins), on November 18, 1991 (by Mr. Charles Hughes of the R. V. Durham Unity Team campaign in Mr. Scott's presence), and again today, November 19, 1991 (by Mr. Durham), you have raised questions intimating that Election Office personnel might operate in some manner other than with complete objectivity, neutrality, and honesty. On each occasion when this issue has been raised, I have urged you to place before me in writing any specific facts or information you have in support of your intimations. Thus far, I have received nothing. . . . Absent any written communication from you, I will conclude that there is no substance to your intimations.

Having been told to put up or shut up, Durham and his associates offered nothing more on the matter.

On Friday, November 23, the Second Circuit Court of Appeals issued a preliminary order staying Judge Edelstein's decision forcing TDU and the TRF to disclose the contributors list. It set the stage for the first reversal of Judge Edelstein since the inception of the 1989 consent decree. Holland decided that the order applied to the AUD as well and permitted the organization to continue representing rank and filers in their election struggles.

THE END GAME

Over the Halloween weekend, Carey put his end game into play, sending 650,000 members a skillfully executed, colorful pamphlet whose cover was the picture of the cigar-smoking gangster wearing a Durham Unity Team button. "Guess who runs the Teamsters?" was the question posed on the cover. Opening the cover provided the answer in large white letters against a black background: "Starting Now, You Do." The information inside focused on the issues that the Lauer, Lalley poll had uncovered as the crucial ones—The Carey Promise: 1. Throw out the Mafia, 2. Better Pensions, 3. Better Health Care, and 4. Stop Corruption. Another page provided a simple, direct attack on Durham in three paragraphs:

> 1. Three members of the Durham Slate have been charged with corruption, kickbacks and mafia ties. R. V. Durham faces civil charges for lying about Ron Carey.
> 2. The R. V. Durham Slate is supported by the same Old Guard leaders who are destroying our union. They have contributed more than $400,000 to support R. V. Durham's campaign.
> 3. R. V. Durham pays himself two salaries totaling $160,000 per year. And his wife and son are on the Teamster payroll.

Carey phone banks went into operation in thirty cities. In some places blocks of phones were rented; in others, volunteers called from their home phones. The feedback from the members being called in New England and Detroit seemed to reflect the same margin of victory uncovered in the poll. Carey was leading Durham 2–1, and Shea wasn't even in the running.

Durham was depending on the officers and shop stewards committed to the Unity slate in at least three hundred locals to play the role of precinct captains in turning out the vote.

The specter of a TDU-backed president in the Marble Palace was used to prod the key players in those three hundred locals.

In a letter of October 31 to principal officers, Durham wrote: "While I don't agree with the numbers in their poll, unless every one of us works hard over the next month, we could wake up one morning to find Ron Carey TDU president of the IBT." He

251

urged them to organize phone banks, to do a mailing to their local's members, and to wear "I voted for the Durham Unity Team" stickers.

Almost a month later, while urging the officers to keep pressing for every vote, Durham offered an unintended tribute to the TDUers as he tried to provoke his supporters to action: "TDU's outright lies and deceptions, coupled with the antiunion media's distortions, have fired up Carey's supporters. They were the first to vote and are now spending all the time between now and December tenth as volunteers on phone banks and handing out leaflets."

WAITING FOR "60 MINUTES"

The unfulfilled hope that "60 Minutes" would blow a hole in the Durham campaign on the eve of mailing out the ballots knocked the merriment out of Eddie Burke. He had been telling Carey supporters for weeks that he had been assured that the Teamster segment on "60 Minutes" would air on the second Sunday in November.

Tens of thousands of Teamsters tuned into CBS-TV on Sunday, November 10, 1991, and were disappointed. The anticipated Teamster story wasn't shown.

That Tuesday, Holland's staff began mailing the 1.56 million ballots. The deadline for returning a vote was noon on December 10, 1991.

On Thursday, November 14, Burke faxed a letter to Don Hewitt, executive producer of the show, saying that he had heard the Teamster story wouldn't be shown on the coming Sunday, either. Burke said he didn't know the final content of the Teamsters piece, but he urged Hewitt to put it on that Sunday.

Burke wrote:

> 60 Minutes is in a position to play a significant role in this historic process. I hope you would agree this is an opportunity that should not be missed. If the program is not aired, many Teamsters may well wonder why 60 Minutes, which they know has spent months preparing a piece on the election (including with much visibility at the union's June convention in Orlando), has decided not to broadcast the piece at the time of optimum

252

interest, i.e., at the actual time of the election. Indeed, since it is expected that most ballots will be returned within the next 10 days, broadcasting the piece after November 17 will be interesting only as a postelection footnote.

That Sunday, November 17, "60 Minutes" again failed to show the Teamster story.

By the following Friday, about 250,000 ballots, almost 60 percent of the votes that would be cast, had been returned to the election officer.

Finally, "60 Minutes" put the Teamster election story on the air on November 24. The piece opened with a quick survey of the union's crooked history and the jailed Teamster presidents. Shea and Durham were shown lamely claiming they were reformers. Carey called them "the born-again reformers." Carey projected the image of a fierce campaigner intent on transforming the union. He dismissed their claims of experience with the telling question "What has their experience done for this membership?"

Far from having a minimal impact on the election, "60 Minutes" had the potential of spurring thousands of the 1.25 million Teamsters who hadn't voted to mark their ballots, most likely for Carey, if they were influenced by the program. The Teamsters who were committed to one candidate or another probably had voted by the time the show appeared, but the mass of members who didn't care, who were vacillating, or who had forgotten they had received a ballot were available to feel the impact of the unspoken message of "60 Minutes" that Carey was the candidate of change.

The following day, Durham offered his critique of the show in a letter to his key supporters: "Some of you may have seen *60 Minutes* do a real hatchet job on our union last night. The corporate interests that run CBS and the other networks cannot resist the temptation to drag our powerful union through the mud."

That weekend had been a long nightmare for Durham. The day before the "60 Minutes" offering, Billy McCarthy was beaten by more than 2–1 in an election for the presidency of Boston Local 25, which he had headed for thirty-five years.

The loss was unprecedented. No general president had ever lost a race in his home local. "It was a sign of the times," said the victor, George Cashman, a Carey supporter. The Cashman slate swept the election, with McCarthy being destroyed by a 2,894 to 1,158 vote. And Dennis Nagle, a TDUer, was elected as business agent.

The unpredictable McCarthy turned out to be a gracious loser. Cashman said, "He was very cordial. It was a very difficult time for him, and I felt a tremendous amount of compassion. It is not easy to watch a dynasty crumble even if you are responsible."

Alarmingly for the old guard, the Local 25 election wasn't an isolated incident. In the previous two weeks, Carey allies had ousted incumbents from locals in Allentown, Pennsylvania; Knoxville, Tennessee; Hartford, Connecticut; and Los Angeles. The Carey forces were on a roll.

11

The Carey Landslide

The last mail pick-up by Election Officer Michael Holland's staff from the Capitol Heights Post Office was at noon on Tuesday, December 10, 1991. The ballots were carried to the eleventh floor of an office building, in space once occupied by a law firm gone bankrupt, on Connecticut Avenue. There the final sorting, alphabetizing, and breakdown into locals was taking place. This had been going on for weeks, and the final tally of ballots cast when the counting began at 4:00 P.M. that day was 424, 392. Only 28 percent of the Teamsters had voted!

The four hundred men and women Holland had hired would work in two shifts, from 8:00 A.M. to 3:00 P.M. and from 3:00 P.M. to 10:00 P.M. Holland, who had overseen the process with the attention to detail of a field marshal sending an army into battle, set a goal of counting at least 100,000 ballots a day. His plan was to count the ballots from the five area conferences simultaneously, starting with the lowest-numbered local in each area, so that those following the returns would have a North America—wide count with the ability to determine whether a candidate was leading across the board.

As soon as a local's vote was tallied, the results were put in file drawers accessible to the candidates' watchers and the media.

Within a few hours the numbers coming out of those drawers began to make the Durham watchers uneasy. "We started feeling bad at six-thirty or seven," a Durham insider said. "And started really worrying. You know where you expect to do well, and we didn't. Around nine o'clock it became pretty clear it wasn't all over, but things weren't going our way."

Eddie Burke read the results at 8:30 P.M. from the first twenty-three locals counted onto a telephone hotline so that supporters could be updated: Carey: 4,612 (51.9 percent); Durham 2,679 (30.1 percent); and Shea 1,585 (17.8 percent). That added up to only 2 percent of the vote. "Long, long way to go," Burke said wearily.

At 11:30 P.M., Burke reported that Carey was still out front. With sixty locals tallied, Carey had 50.8 percent, Durham 37.6 percent, and Shea 11.4 percent.

Carey was still out front when Burke made his 11:15 A.M. report the next day. With eighty-three locals in, Carey had 52.5 percent of the vote to Durham's 37.2 percent and Shea's 10.1 percent.

That Wednesday afternoon at noontime, Susan Jennik of the AUD told reporters in the pressroom on the eleventh floor of the building where the ballots were counted, "I'd say Carey's got it. Since last night at seven o'clock, he's had an absolute majority, and today his lead is widening. There's been enough of a random count from the locals all over the country to predict the outcome."

Ken Paff happily told a reporter, "I can't see Durham catching up. When our people saw the results from North Carolina, with the locals from Durham's home state going overwhelmingly for Carey, they said, 'We're going to win this thing.' "

Carey was winning by margins of 3–1 and 4–1 in locals with concentrations of his supporters, while Durham was carrying his allies' locals by narrow margins. "Dinky margin" was the way Paff put it. He said, "They needed the local officials to turn out the vote, and they didn't."

Detroit Local 299, the home local of the missing Jimmy Hoffa and the late Frank Fitzsimmons, voted for Carey, as did Roy Williams's Local 41 in Kansas City and McCarthy's Local 25 in Boston. Durham squeaked past Carey in Jackie Presser's Local 507 in Cleveland, 538–514. While Carey won 33 percent of the votes in Durham's home local, he got 97.5 percent in his own Local 804 in New York.

At three o'clock that Wednesday, Burke told reporters, "We're sprouting wings." But he wasn't ready to declare victory. "We're sure as hell not going to come out and proclaim anything with

300,000 votes still out." But he did say, "With what I've seen here, none of our vice presidents have anything to worry about. If Carey wins, they all win. Slate voting prevails!"

Even at that early hour, a key Durham insider said, "It's pretty obvious Carey's going to win."

The insider was at a loss to explain the grass-roots landslide against Durham. The question was Did the local officers try, or did they sit on their hands? "I'd like to think they tried and failed. As in any election, sometimes the perception is the reality. Sometimes when you got it in the bag, there's no need to hustle."

Chris Scott had put together an efficient headquarters operation that kept tabs on the locals and pressed the officers to do the job. The Durham insider said, "It was loose knit to the extent that these are people politically successful on their own and they have a good sense of what they needed to do to get their vote out. There were phone calls, faxes, assignments. Some were told, 'Your local is not turning out. Do something.' We kept a pretty good handle on the votes coming in."

Durham stayed out of sight that day and for the rest of the week.

When Shea arrived Wednesday afternoon, the press chased him down a hallway, asking if he considered Carey the winner. "Hell, no," Shea said.

Doug Mims, vice president of Atlanta Local 728 and a Carey vice presidential candidate, offered his explanation for the sweep in process: "It was just a matter of members wanting a change. Carey had that part of the membership who reads the newspapers and magazines. Fifty percent wanted a change from the old guard to the new. They didn't vote for Carey. They voted against the people in there. That conclusion stems from my visits to the barns. They say I'm going to vote for whoever is not in there."

Mims, a dark-haired fifty-four-year-old with the telltale big hands of a trucker, was a veteran campaigner. He and his associates fought Weldon Mathis and his sons for fourteen years before finally sweeping them out of their local in 1990.

Mims said of Durham's local officer supporters: "You get a local leadership that's been in office twenty or twenty-five or thirty years, they think it beneath them to campaign. Campaigning is hard work. You got a barn in Marietta that changes shifts every three hours, you got to be there those twenty-four hours. It's beneath them to stand out in the rain, sleet, and snow."

Wednesday night, Carey arrived in Washington by train from New York. The big joke among his supporters was that he probably took the subway to the Dupont Plaza rather than spend the campaign's money on a taxi. He had a couple of beers in the bar with Burke and friends from Local 804 before retiring for what promised to be a big day ahead.

Thursday morning, a subdued Chris Scott, standing in a hallway on the eleventh floor of the Connecticut Avenue office building where the count continued, for the first time gave some insight into the bad news the Durham pollsters had been providing in findings from polls that had been kept secret. He said, "Despite the brave front we put up, this does not come as a shock to me. Our poll back in July showed that Carey was likely to win. When the Carey poll came out, we thought that maybe he had stolen a copy of our poll. We had virtually the same numbers as the Carey poll.

"We felt that way because we had Carey at twenty-nine in July. I think we were at twelve and Shea was at fourteen."

Asked the classically sad question What would he have done if he had it to do all over again? Scott said, "If what you were looking at was winning, given the landscape, given the backdrop, the only realistic chance we might have had would have been if we could have reduced the Shea and Durham tickets down to one. Of course there were attempts to do that. It's widely believed the person who kept that from happening was Joe T."

The election would put Carey in office for five years. Scott mused aloud, "The world will be so different in five years. Who knows what it will be like? Maybe Carey will resign in two and a half years. In five years it is conceivable that Carey is so popular that he makes Jimmy Hoffa look like a footnote in history."

THE NEW TEAMSTER UNION

That Thursday afternoon, television and print reporters packed the Zenger Room at the National Press Club for a press conference with Carey.

"I want to welcome all of you to a new Teamster union," Carey said in his opening remarks. "The union that's been won back by its members. The union that's going to work for its members. A union that will not be tolerating corruption.... What our members have said today is good-bye to the Mafia, good-bye to concessionary contracts, it's good-bye to those who have lined their pockets and put the membership in last place."

When Roy Williams was elected at the 1981 convention, and Jackie Presser at the 1986 convention, both kept the press at bay, not willing to face the media at a time when they were facing federal trials. McCarthy did hold a press conference after his selection by the General Executive Board (GEB) in 1989, then snappishly refused to answer most questions.

Carey told the press, "This is a new Teamster union, with new ideas, new directions, and a whole new purpose. . . . The Teamster union will not be sitting in the background; we'll be out leading the charge. . . . Starting today, we will start to build this new Teamster union."

The Hoffa era, with its undercurrents of organized crime and corruption and the resulting constant state of siege to ward off the press and prosecutors, had come to an end. The election of Carey, as he proclaimed, had begun a new order in the Teamsters, rooted in the rank and file who cared enough to vote.

The 28 percent turnout raised the question of the depth of Carey's mandate. Compared to McCarthy, who was elected by nine elderly men behind closed doors, or Presser or Williams, who owed allegiance to the mob and were elected at rubber-stamp conventions, the constituency sending Carey forth was the broadest and deepest in the eighty-eight year history of the union.

Carey gave an indication of things to come by announcing in response to a reporter's question that he would cut the general president's salary from $225,000 to $175,000.

In the final tally, Carey received 188,883 votes (48.48 percent) to Durham's 129,538 (33.24 percent) and Shea's 71,227 (18.28 percent). Holland did not count 29,009 ballots because they were voided or challenged and would not have affected the outcome.

Carey's entire fifteen member slate, including a woman, a black, a Latino, and ten TDU members, was swept into office with him.

Elected general secretary-treasurer was Thomas Sever, fifty-six, president of Local 30 in Jeannette, Pennsylvania.

The vice presidents at large included James Benson, fifty, a rank-and-file member of Local 104 in Phoenix, Arizona; Diana Kilmury, forty-four, a rank-and-file truck driver from Local 155 in Vancouver, British Columbia, and a TDU member; Mario Perrucci, secretary-treasurer of Local 177 in Hillside, New Jersey; John Riojas, thirty-five, a rank-and-file UPS driver from Local 657 in San Antonio, Texas; and C. Sam Theodus, president of Local 407 in Cleveland, Ohio.

Central Conference regional vice presidents elected were all TDU members: Leroy Ellis, rank-and-file truck driver from Local 705 in Chicago; Dennis C. Skelton, rank-and-file truck driver from Local 600 in St. Louis, Missouri; and Bill Urman, secretary-treasurer of Local 792 in Minneapolis, Minnesota.

The two Eastern Conference regional vice presidents voted in were Gene Giacumbo, a TDU member and president of Local 843 in Springfield, New Jersey; and Tom Gilmartin, Jr., president of Local 559 in South Windsor, Connecticut.

The Southern Conference regional vice presidents elected from Carey's slate—both members of TDU—were Aaron Belk, a rank-and-file dockworker from Local 667 in Memphis, Tennessee; and Doug Mims, fifty-four, vice president and business agent of Local 728 in Atlanta, Georgia.

And the two Western Conference regional vice presidents from Carey's slate were also TDUers: Ken Mee, fifty-three, rank-and-file car hauler from Local 287 in San Jose, California; and Thomas M. Shay, forty-three, secretary-treasurer of Local 57 in Eugene, Oregon.

John Morris of Philadelphia, who ran on the Shea slate, was elected a regional vice president for the Eastern Conference, a slot that would have gone to Eugene Bennett of New York Local 272 had he not backed out of the opportunity to run on the Carey slate.

Canadian truck driver Diana Kilmury won the highest tally of any at-large vice president, a victory that placed her second in the order of succession to the presidency should Carey leave office before his term expires.

———

The votes were still being counted that Thursday when Durham issued what appeared to be a conciliatory concession statement. "The members have spoken, and I wish [Carey] well as he takes over the reins of our union. . . . I urge all Teamsters to do what I plan to do as president of Local 391—put the welfare of Teamster families ahead of individual political differences," the statement said.

But instead of accepting the overwhelming election of Carey, who defeated him by about a 3–2 margin, Durham filed an election protest on what had become tired grounds: that Teamsters for a Democratic Union, the Teamsters Rank and File Education and Legal Defense Fund (TRF), and the Association for Union Democracy failed to file financial disclosure forms with Holland, that Carey "failed to properly and timely pay the full cost of using the International union's bulk-rate nonprofit postage permit," that a video by an independent filmmaker was financed by a foundation grant, and that Carey and newly elected vice president Mario Perrucci used union resources in their campaign.

With his usual thoroughness, Holland investigated each allegation, then denied Durham's protest. He ruled: "The election will not be rerun, and the election results will stand."

THE INAUGURATION

The seemingly simple ceremony inaugurating Ron Carey as the first general president of the International Brotherood of Teamsters (IBT) to be elected directly by the members was laden with symbolism.

Three persons held direct roles—Eddie Burke, who represented the grass-roots Carey campaign of the past two years; Pat Pagnanella, secretary-treasurer of Local 804, who represented Carey's roots in decent, representative unionism; and Joyce Mims, who represented the dissident movement that fought the corruption and excesses of the oligarchy and its minions for decades.

The swearing-in ritual took place on February 1, 1992, a pleasant Saturday afternoon, on the steps of the Marble Palace, against a backdrop of banners proclaiming "The New Teamsters." The audience of two thousand was a mix of exuberant rank and filers, Teamster officials, including Walter Shea and R. V. Durham, AFL-CIO President Lane Kirkland, and assorted other labor dignitaries.

Burke, serving as the master of ceremonies, told the crowd,

"We are plowing up a large chunk of history here today," as a prelude to introducing Pagnanella to swear in Carey.

Carey spiced his oath of office with promises that brought cheers from the rank and file, who interrupted him three times: when he pledged to rid the IBT of corruption; when he promised to restore democratic principles to the union; and when he vowed never to forget that it was the members who put him in office. He ended by saying, "It is the members whom I will serve," bringing more cheers and chants of "Carey! Carey! Carey!"

Joyce Mims, the wife of the new Southern Conference International vice president, Doug Mims, introduced Carey. Joyce Mims had worked with her husband and other TDU members in the long and finally successful campaign to oust the Mathis family from control of Atlanta Local 728.

Aside from a promise to immediately sell the IBT jets, the condo in Puerto Rico, and other perks of the hierarchy, Carey laid out an agenda to revitalize the Teamsters and perhaps the American labor movement:

> We have the money, the talent, the technology, and the organization to be the strongest voice for working people in the world, and that is just what this union is going to be.
>
> Now is the test. Our mission is to take the enormous resources of this union and give them new direction and new purpose, to win better contracts, to improve pensions, and to organize new workers, to pass a national health insurance. . . . Today the eyes of the world are upon us. We have stepped into the history books, and the story is ours to write.

After the expected cheering and applause had died down, Carey told the crowd, "This building belongs to you. Come on in."

And they did, in a rush through the front doors, filling the Marble Palace and wandering through it in a scene reminiscent of the crowd surging into the White House after the inauguration of Andrew Jackson, the first American president to come from the ranks of the common man. On that memorable occasion in 1829, people stood on the furniture, craning to see the president. In the Teamsters' building, a woman from the crowd sat in the general president's chair and put her feet up on his desk—to the glee of everyone around her.

Ron Carey's promise to lead the Teamsters into better, prouder times came as the American labor movement's power had waned and the IBT had passed through twenty years without a major triumph to mark its way. A revitalization of Teamsters could mean a revitalization of the labor movement. Whether he would become the charismatic figure, missing from labor's landscape, capable of achieving that monumental task remained to be seen. Carey had demonstrated that through the enchantment of total commitment he could overcome seemingly insurmountable barriers on his way to the presidency of the most powerful union in North America.

As Goethe said,

> *Whatever you can do, or dream you can, begin it.*
> *Boldness has genius, power and magic in it.*
> *Begin it now.*

Epilogue

Ron Carey plunged into the IBT presidency with a verve and energy that thrilled labor activists. Within a few months, Carey's performance provided a resounding *yes* to the question of whether he could successfully leap from the presidency of a medium-sized local in New York to the general presidency of the largest private-sector union in North America.

On assuming office, Carey named Eddie Burke as his special assistant and Rick Gilberg as Teamster General Counsel.

Within days of winning the election, Carey was on the road again campaigning at airports all over the country to persuade eighty-four hundred disgruntled Northwest Airlines flight attendants to stick with the Teamsters instead of switching to another union. By March 12, his assurances that the "new Teamsters" would focus on members' needs paid off, with the flight attendants voting by a 2–1 margin to continue as Teamsters.

In an effort to reverse the trend of a continuously shrinking Teamsters union base—dropping from 2.2 million in the mid-1970s to 1.5 million in 1991—Carey ordered a tenfold increase in the international organizing staff. He kept Vicki Saporta on as international organizing director, expanded the number of organizers to forty, and gave her a budget of $35 million for the next three years. Carey also instituted a policy ending the Teamsters' long and wasteful practice of raiding other unions for members.

Carey brought to office an aversion to concessionary bar-

264

gaining—and he quickly demonstrated his willingness to be both harsh and innovative in countering employer demands for give-backs at the bargaining table.

Within three weeks after he took office, executives from North Penn, a Pennsylvania-based trucking company, confronted Carey at the Marble Palace demanding that he approve a 22 percent wage cut for the firm's three-hundred employees—on top of the 3 percent giveback made the year before. Carey refused. He pointed out that the National Master Freight Agreement—negotiated by his predecessors—provided for maximum wage cuts of 15 percent for troubled companies. He would give no more, despite pleas from members' families. The next day, North Penn folded. Carey said he hated to see three-hundred workers lose their jobs, but he was confident that he had made the right decision. "I am not in favor of concessions. [They are] another way for employers to stick their hands in the employees' pockets."

In March, Carey took charge of the unresolved national car haul contract negotiations, which had been deadlocked for fif-teen months. The sticking point was "double-breasting," a prac-tice in which a parent company has both union and nonunion subsidiaries. The Teamsters complained that their work was be-ing shifted to the less costly nonunion subsidiaries. In response, Carey launched the IBT's first "corporate campaign." Teamsters around the country distributed leaflets every Saturday outside Ryder truck rental outlets as part of the strategy of bringing pressure on the largest company covered by the contract. In another unprecedented move, Carey met with drivers at key locals to bring them up to date on negotiations and to explain what he was trying to do through the corporate campaign. By April 11, the National Automobile Transporters Association had reached an agreement with Carey for a new three-year contract with no concessions, a freeze on double-breasting, and wage hikes.

The elated Teamsters attributed the victory to Carey's corpo-rate campaign—and he vowed to use this technique whenever the union came up against recalcitrant employers.

Carey took new initiatives in the political field as well, by break-ing with the old Teamsters penchant for backing Republican candidates for the White House. He endorsed Democrat Bill Clinton and pledged to spend $4 million on the most intense effort ever by the Teamsters to turn out the membership to vote for the chosen candidate. Carey also assumed a leading role in a campaign to press for labor and environmental protections in the North American Free Trade Agreement.

Along with selling the international's corporate jets for $11 million—using the proceeds for the organizing budget—and dropping his libel suit against R. V. Durham, Carey put together the union's first budget with strict controls on spending.

Carey's first year in office was sullied only by a conflict with U.S. District Court Judge David Edelstein over the rules governing the Independent Review Board. In August, the judge dashed Carey's hopes of reducing the board to a passive role, with the Teamsters policing themselves and in the process hurrying an end to government intervention.

Judge Edelstein approved Frederick Lacey as the Justice Department's representative on the Independent Review Board but told Carey that his chosen representative, Eddie Burke, couldn't serve unless he quit as Carey's special assistant. Over Carey's objections, Judge Edelstein approved the appointment of William H. Webster, former director of the FBI and the Central Intelligence Agency, as the so-called independent member of the board.

Carey will be tested in coming years by how he deals with the raw power the 1989 Consent Decree vested in the Independent Review Board to pursue and punish corrupt or mob-connected Teamsters—whether he wastes his energies fighting the board or pursues his strategy of undermining it by giving it little to do as the Teamsters cleanse themselves.

In his decision on August 25, 1992, affirming Webster's appointment, Judge Edelstein made a telling point: "The IRB will serve as a perpetual agent of reform." Nothing lasts forever, but Carey can expect the Independent Review Board to be watching over the Teamsters until Judge Edelstein passes from the bench. One result of the process could be the evolution of the IBT into a union with a sparkling reputation, whose membership develops a culture in which shady, self-dealing officials are no longer tolerated.

Structure of the International Brotherhood of Teamsters

The Constitution

The document governing the operation of the International Brotherhood of Teamsters (IBT).

The Convention

The IBT holds a convention to which delegates from all local unions are sent every five years to amend the constitution. Up until 1986, all officers were elected by the convention delegates. Beginning in 1991, the delegates continued to elect the International trustees at the convention but were limited to nominating candidates for the other officer positions to run in the secret-ballot, rank-and-file elections to be held later in the same year.

Officers

General president, the chief executive officer.

General secretary-treasurer, the chief financial officer.

Sixteen International vice presidents (changed in 1991 to seventeen International vice presidents: five elected at large, three from the Eastern Conference, three from the Central Conference, two from the Southern Conference, two from the Western Conference, and two from the Canadian Conference).

Three International trustees.

General Executive Board (GEB)

The governing body of the IBT between conferences. The GEB is composed of the general president, general secretary-treasurer, and the International vice presidents.

Five Area Conferences

Eastern, Western, Central, Southern, and Canadian. The conferences coordinate Teamster activities over a broad area comprised of either a number of U.S. states or the entire Canadian nation. The conference director is appointed by the general president and serves as his liaison officer at the conference. The conference chairman, elected by the Policy Committee is the chief executive officer. Delegates to conference conventions elect the members of the Policy Committee, usually seven.

State Conferences

There are ten single or multistate conferences, which provide an additional level of service to their geographic areas. The ten are Arkansas-Oklahoma Conference, Georgia-Florida Conference, Illinois Conference, Indiana Conference, Iowa Conference, Kentucky–West Virginia Conference, Missouri-Kansas Conference, Ohio Conference, Pennsylvania Conference, and Texas Conference.

Joint Councils

There are forty-four Joint Councils, which coordinate the activities of IBT locals in their geographic area. For example, New York Joint Council 16 covers fifty-one locals, with 150,000 members in New York City and Long Island. Delegates from the locals elect the seven-member executive boards, which govern the joint councils. The president is the chief executive officer.

IBT Locals

There are 615 locals, although the number is subject to change as new locals are created and existing locals merge. Each local has seven officers: president, secretary-treasurer, vice president, recording secretary, and three trustees. In some locals the president is the principal officer, and in others the secretary-treasurer is.

The Members

The IBT had 1,560,000 members in 1992.

APPENDIX B

The Defendants in the IBT RICO Suit

United States of America
-v-
International Brotherhood of Teamsters, Chauffeurs, Warehousemen,
  and Helpers of America (AFL-CIO),
The Commission of La Cosa Nostra,
Anthony Salerno aka Fat Tony
Matthew Ianniello aka Matty the Horse
Anthony Provenzano aka Tony Pro
Nunzio Provenzano aka Nunzi Pro
Anthony Corallo aka Tony Ducks
Salvatore Santoro aka Tom Mix
Christopher Furnari, Sr., aka Christie Tick
Frank Manzo
Carmine Persico aka Junior and The Snake
Gennaro Langella aka Gerry Lang
Philip Rastelli aka Rusty
Nicholas Marangello aka Nicky Glasses
Joseph Massino aka Joey Messina
Anthony Ficarotta aka Figgy
Eugene Boffa, Sr.
Francis Sheeran
Milton Rockman aka Maishe
John Tronolone aka Peanuts
Joseph J. Aiuppa aka Joey O'Brien, Joe Doves, Joey Aiuppa
John P. Cerone aka Jackie the Lackie, Jackie Cerone

Joseph Lombardo aka Joey the Clown
Angelo Lapietra aka The Nutcracker
Frank Balistrieri aka Mr. B
Carl Angelo DeLuna aka Toughy
Carl Civella aka Corky
Anthony T. Civella aka Tony Ripe

General Executive Board of the International Brotherhood of Teamsters,
Chauffeurs, Warehousemen, and Helpers of America:
Jackie Presser, General President
Weldon Mathis, General Secretary Treasurer
Joseph Trerotola aka Joe T, First Vice President
Robert Holmes, Sr., Second Vice President
William J. McCarthy, Third Vice President
Joseph W. Morgan, Fourth Vice President
Edward M. Lawson, Fifth Vice President
Arnold Weinmeister, Sixth Vice President
John H. Cleveland, Seventh Vice President
Maurice R. Schurr, Eighth Vice President
Donald Peters, Ninth Vice President
Walter J. Shea, Tenth Vice President
Harold Friedman, Eleventh Vice President
Jack D. Cox, Twelfth Vice President
Don L. West, Thirteenth Vice President
Michael J. Riley, Fourteenth Vice President
Theodore Cozza, Fifteenth Vice President
Daniel Ligurotis, Sixteenth Vice President
and Salvatore Provenzano aka Sammy Pro, former Vice President.

APPENDIX C

A Chronology

August 1903

Founding convention of IBT in Niagara Falls. Cornelius Shea elected first president.

February 26, 1957

The McClellan Committee begins hearings, taking testimony over the next two years from fifteen hundred witnesses, with 270 days of public sessions. Of the fifty-eight volumes of testimony, thirty-four were devoted to the IBT.

1957

James R. Hoffa becomes IBT president (1957–1967).

December 14, 1957

Former IBT president Dave Beck is convicted in Washington State of stealing $1,900 in union funds by pocketing the proceeds of the sale of a union-owned Cadillac.

February 19, 1959

Dave Beck is convicted of evading $240,000 in income taxes from 1950 through 1953 and failing to file returns. He is sentenced to five years in prison and a $60,000 fine.

March 1967

Frank Fitzsimmons replaces Hoffa as IBT president after Hoffa begins his prison term in Lewisburg, Pennsylvania.

1973

Jackie Presser secretly becomes an FBI informant.

July 30, 1975

Jimmy Hoffa disappears and is presumed murdered.

February 1, 1976

U.S. Labor Department sues Central States Pension Fund, naming as defendants Frank Fitzsimmons, Roy Williams, Don Peters, Robert Holmes, and Joe Morgan.

May 1976

The PROD report "Teamster Democracy and Financial Responsibility" is published.

June 5, 1976

Thirty-five people meet in Cleveland to transform TDC into TDU.

June 14, 1976

IBT Convention opens in Las Vegas. Peter Camarata presents PROD's program calling for direct elections. Fitzsimmons tells the reformers to go to hell.

November 3, 1979

PROD and TDU merge.

May 15, 1981

GEB elects Roy Williams as interim President of IBT following Fitzsimmons's death.

August 24, 1981

Cleveland *Plain Dealer* article reveals that Jackie Presser and his father, Bill Presser, were informants for the IRS beginning in 1971 and that Jackie was an informer for the FBI.

March 9, 1982

The Civil RICO complaint is filed against New Jersey Teamsters Local 560, contending that the local was a captive of the Provenzano crime group.

January 20, 1983

Allen Dorfman murdered in parking lot in Lincolnwood, Illinois.

April 21, 1983

Jackie Presser appointed IBT president following Williams's resignation.

October 27 and 28, 1983

Angelo Lonardo provides four FBI agents with the details of how he and Milton Rockman traveled between three cities to lobby for mob support for Roy Williams and then Jackie Presser.

March 1986

President's Commission on Organized Crime issues report: *The Edge: Organized Crime, Business and Labor Unions.*

May 9, 1986

Senate Permanent Subcommittee on Investigations issues a report which provides the first official confirmation that Jackie Presser was an FBI informant.

May 17, 1986

Jackie Presser, fifty-nine, became the fourth IBT president to be indicted over the past thirty years.

June 23, 1986

Federal judge installs a trustee to run Local 560.

November 24, 1986

Genovese Crime Family Case (including Tony Salerno) filed, accusing mob figures of arranging the election of Jackie Presser.

January 1987

The Rastelli Case. The Boss of Colombo Organized Crime Family goes to prison over his control of Teamsters Local 814.

October 24, 1987

AFL-CIO Executive Council votes to readmit IBT, which quit the federation thirty years before.

December 1, 1987

FBI memo "Synopsis: Jackie Presser" is unsealed at a court hearing. The memo says Presser provided information on sixty-nine people in eleven cities and described alleged organized-crime ties of several Teamster vice presidents.

May 4, 1988

Presser takes leave of absence from IBT presidency because of ill health. Weldon Mathis's brief reign begins.

June 28, 1988

U.S. Government files Civil RICO Suit against IBT in U.S. District Court in Manhattan.

July 9, 1988

Jackie Presser dies.

July 15, 1988

GEB meeting: Billy McCarthy elected president in split 9–8 vote, defeating Weldon Mathis.

December 1988

IBT General Counsel James Grady approaches Randy Mastro to open negotiations for a settlement of the RICO case. At the same time, Mathis, West, Lawson, Holmes, Cleveland, and Schurr are negotiating separately with the government for settlements.

January 28, 1989

IBT vice president Robert Holmes of Detroit resigns all IBT positions after fifty-two years as a Teamster.

March 3, 1989

Mathis, West, and Lawson settle.

March 13, 1989

McCarthy and remaining members of the GEB sign the RICO settlement at the UN Plaza Hotel. The settlement provides for the first rank-and-file vote for the IBT's international officers.

May 31, 1989

Judge David Edelstein appoints Frederick Lacey, Charles Carberry, and Michael Holland as administrator, investigations officer, and elections officer, respectively.

September 17, 1989

Ronald Carey, president of New York Teamsters Local 804, announces his candidacy for the presidency. He is the first candidate.

November 1989

TDU endorses Ron Carey for President.

July 10, 1990

Judge Edelstein issues opinion and order requiring Holland to administer as well as supervise all delegate elections.

August 19–24, 1990

The Eastern Conference convention at Hilton Head, South Carolina. Joe T's forces dump McCarthy's ally vice president Frank Hackett from Eastern Conference Policy Committee, electing New York Teamster Barry Feinstein in his place.

October 1990

GEB meeting at which McCarthy removes Joe T as director of the Eastern Conference and announces he is not running for reelection as president. R. V. Durham emerges as the majority bloc's candidate for president.

November 5, 1990

Shea announces he is running for president.

June 24–28, 1991

The IBT Nominating Convention in Orlando, Florida. Three slates emerge, headed by Carey, Durham, and Shea.

October 25, 1991

Joe T's final day in the IBT following his forced resignation from the union and from all Teamster positions, including IBT vice president, chairman of the Eastern Conference, President of New York Joint Council 16, and vice president and trustee of two New York locals.

December 10–13, 1991

Ron Carey and his entire slate are elected.

February 1, 1992

Ron Carey is sworn in as general president of the IBT by Pat Pagnanolla.

Teamsters Charged with Ties to Organized Crime

Court-appointed Investigations Officer Charles Carberry brought charges against 214 Teamsters—including sixty-six related to organized crime—during the three years and four months he operated.

Accused of Being Members of Organized Crime

Anthony Calagna, Sr.
President, Local 295, Jamaica, New York
Barred from IBT.

James V. Cozzo
Executive Coordinator, Local 786, Chicago, Illinois
Barred from IBT.

Liborio (Robert) Crapanzano
President, Local 27, New York, New York
Resigned from IBT.

Pasquale Crapanzano
Secretary-Treasurer, Local 27, New York, New York and vice president, New York Joint Council 16
Resigned from IBT.

William Cutolo
President, Local 861, New York, New York
Barred from IBT.

Joseph Glimco, Sr.
President, Local 777, Chicago, Illinois
Resigned from IBT.

Nicholas Grancio
Vice President, Local 707, Woodside, New York
Resigned from IBT. Murdered in mob war.

Vincent Gugliaro
Vice President, Local 617, Jersey City, New Jersey
Resigned from IBT.

Anthony M. Parrino
Vice President, Local 682, St.
  Louis, Missouri
Resigned from IBT.

Joseph Pecora, Sr.
Secretary-Treasurer, Local 863,
  Mountainside, New Jersey
Resigned from IBT.

Louis Rumore
Vice President, Local 812,
  Scarsdale, New York
Resigned from IBT.

Dominic Senese
President, Local 703, Chicago,
  Illinois
Barred from IBT.

Philip Tortorici
Trustee, Local 531, Yonkers,
  New York
Resigned from IBT.

Anthony M. Zappi
Secretary-Treasurer, Local 854,
  Valley Stream, New York
Barred from IBT.

Accused of Organized Crime Related Charges

Joseph Abbate
President, Local 945, Wayne,
  New Jersey
Pending.

Bernard Adelstein
Secretary-Treasurer, Local 813,
  New York, New York
Barred from IBT.

Victor Alfieri
Vice President, Local 272, New
  York, New York
Barred from IBT.

Ralph J. Alimena
Secretary-Treasurer, Local 707,
  Woodside, New York
Resigned from IBT.

Salvatore Barbato
On-site Steward, Local 282, Lake
  Success, New York
Resigned from IBT.

Thomas Baron
Trustee, Local 531, Yonkers,
  New York
Resigned from office.

Eugene Bennett
Secretary-Treasurer, Local 272,
  New York, New York, and
  Recording Secretary, New
  York Joint Council 16
Barred from IBT.

James Buckley
Recording Secretary, Local 707,
  Woodside, New York
Barred from IBT.

Paul E. Bush
President, Local 506, Auburn,
  New York
Pending.

Anthony Calagna, Jr.
Recording Secretary, Local 295,
  Jamaica, New York
Barred from IBT.

Michael Carbone
Secretary-Treasurer, Local 282,
    Lake Success, New York
Resigned from IBT.

Salvatore Cataldo
Trustee, Local 295, Jamaica,
    New York
Barred from IBT.

George Chiavola
Member, Local 41, Kansas City,
    Missouri, and staffer, Central
    Conference
Barred from IBT.

Joseph Cimino
President, Local 107,
    Philadelphia, Pennsylvania
Barred from IBT.

James L. Coli
Secretary-Treasurer, Local 727,
    Chicago, Illinois
Barred from holding IBT office.

Vincent Cordato
Trustee, Local 707, Woodside,
    New York
Resigned from office.

Theodore R. Cozza
Vice President, IBT
Barred from IBT.

Patrick Crapanzano
President, Local 27, New York,
    New York
Barred from IBT.

Anthony Cuozzo
Vice President, Local 295,
    Jamaica, New York
Barred from IBT.

Louis De Angelis
Vice President, Local 531,
    Yonkers, New York
Resigned from IBT.

Ralph Delsardo
Trustee, Local 295, Jamaica,
    New York
Barred from IBT.

Nick A. Digirlamo
Member, Local 41, Kansas City,
    Missouri
Pending.

Michael DiLeonardo
On-site Steward, Local 282, Lake
    Success, New York
Resigned from IBT.

Frank Fappiano
On-site Steward, Local 282, Lake
    Success, New York
Resigned from IBT.

Richard Heilbrun
Secretary-Treasurer, Local 531,
    Yonkers, New York
Agreed to three-month
    suspension from office.

Murlene Herron
Trustee, Local 777, Chicago,
    Illinois
Resigned from office.

Joseph Kosey
Secretary-Treasurer, Local 777,
    Chicago, Illinois
Barred from IBT.

Louis Lanza
Vice President, Local 27, New
    York, New York
Barred from IBT.

Camillo Lombardozzi
On-site Steward, Local 282, Lake
  Success, New York
Resigned from IBT.

George Lombardozzi
Secretary-Treasurer, Local 918,
  Brooklyn, New York
Barred from the IBT.

James E. McNeil, Jr.
President, Local 707, Woodside,
  New York
Barred from IBT.

Dominick Milano
Trustee, Local 707, Woodside,
  New York
Barred from IBT.

Angelo Misuraca
Vice President, Local 398,
  Rochester, New York
Barred from IBT office or staff
  jobs.

John Moran, Jr.
Trustee, Local 295, Jamaica,
  New York
Barred from IBT.

David Morris
Trustee, Local 707, Woodside,
  New York
Barred from IBT.

Michael J. Morris
Secretary-Treasurer, Local 707,
  Woodside, New York
Barred from IBT.

Joseph Murray
Trustee, Local 777, Chicago,
  Illinois
Resigned from office.

Girolemo (Sonny) Musso
President, Local 641, Secaucus,
  New Jersey
Resigned from IBT.

Charles O'Brien
International Representative,
  IBT.
Barred from IBT.

Andrew Reynolds
Organizer, Local 641, Secaucus,
  New Jersey
Barred from IBT.

Robert W. Rheinhardt
Vice President, Local 295,
  Jamaica, New York
Barred from IBT.

Cirino (Charles) Salerno
President, Local 272, New York,
  New York
Barred from IBT for life.

Frank Salerno
Member, Local 272, New York,
  New York
Pending.

Henry Saltalamachea
Vice President, Local 707,
  Woodside, New York
Resigned from IBT.

Robert Sansone
President, Local 682, St. Louis,
  Missouri
Barred from holding IBT office.

Gene Santora
Business Agent, Local 531,
  Yonkers, New York
Resigned from IBT.

Robert Sasso
President, Local 282, Lake
  Success, New York
Resigned from IBT.

Warren Selvaggi
President, Local 240, Bronx,
  New York
Resigned from IBT.

Joseph Talerico
Business Agent, Local 727,
  Chicago, Illinois
Barred from IBT.

Joseph Trerotola
Vice President, IBT, and
  President, New York Joint
  Council 16.
Resigned from IBT.

John Trivigno
President, Local 398, Rochester,
  New York
Barred from IBT.

Michael Urso-Pernice
Secretary-Treasurer, Local 295,
  Jamaica, New York
Barred from IBT.

NOTE: The above are latest data available as of June 17, 1992.

The 1991 Election Results

CAREY SLATE	DURHAM SLATE	SHEA SLATE	INDEPENDENT
General President			
Ronald Carey 188,883	R. V. Durham 129,538	Walter Shea 71,222	
Secretary-Treasurer			
Tom Sever 188,528	Harold Leu 127,423	Dan Ligurotis 71,735	
Vice President at Large			
Diana Kilmury 187,537	Edward James 130,094	Vickie Saporta 82,373	
Jim Benson 185,819	John Neal 129,975	Jack Cox 75,831	
Sam Theodus 180,258	Edward Lawson 128,215	Dan Darrow 75,584	
Mario Perrucci 179,339	Walt Engelbert 125,761	Barry Feinstein 72,278	
John Riojas 177,524	Erv Walker 122,801	Bill Genoese 69,502	
Vice President, Central Conference			
Leroy Ellis 64,289	William Hogan, Jr. 53,134	Garry Sullivan 23,238	
Bill Urman 63,925	Larry Brennan 52,418		
Dennis Skelton 63,567	Robert Sansone 51,364		

CAREY SLATE	DURHAM SLATE	SHEA SLATE	INDEPENDENT

Vice President, Eastern Conference

CAREY SLATE	DURHAM SLATE	SHEA SLATE	INDEPENDENT
Tom Gilmartin, Jr. 58,223	Frank Hackett 31,516	John P. Morris 43,266	Robert Sasso 10,044
Gene Giacumbo 56,541	Dan Kane 30,885	Frank Carracino 38,968	
	Phil Feaster 28,879	Victor Olivadoti 37,707	

Vice President, Southern Conference

CAREY SLATE	DURHAM SLATE	SHEA SLATE	INDEPENDENT
Doug Mims 16,465	Jerry Cook 9,861		T. C. Stone 7,641
Aaron Belk 16,308	Don West 9,729		W. C. Smith 7,081

Vice President, Western Conference

CAREY SLATE	DURHAM SLATE	SHEA SLATE	INDEPENDENT
Tom Shay 39,021	Chuck Mack 25,921	Nobby Miller 11,306	William Sarver 3,371
Ken Mee 37,930	Mike Riley 25,073	Gene Allison 11,194	

Notes

1. Jim Green, "Camp Solidarity/United Mineworkers Continue Fight for Justice," *New England Labor News & Commentary* (November 1989).

2. Dwayne Yancey, "Thunder in the Coalfields," *Roanoke Times & World News*, April 29, 1990.

3. Dan Moldea, *The Hoffa Wars* (New York and London: Paddington Press Ltd., 1978), p. 112.

4. James Neff, *Mobbed Up* (Boston: Atlantic Monthly Press, 1989), p. 94.

5. Ibid., p. 398.

6. *Business Week,* June 15, 1981.

7. "The Teamsters Keep Trucking," *Newsweek,* June 15, 1981, p. 70.

8. *Washington Post*, April 25, 1986.

9. *Convoy-Dispatch*, August 1987, p. 1; and 1986 Eastern Conference LM-2 (annual financial report), Schedule 14, International Convention Expenses, filed with U.S. Labor Department.

10. The author was present to cover the convention; Joe Conason in *Village Voice,* June 10, 1986; and *Los Angeles Times,* May 21, 1986.

11. Dan La Botz, *Rank and File Rebellion* (London and New York: Verso, 1990) pp. 30–38; and interviews with Steve Kindred in 1991.

12. Kindred interviews in 1976 and 1991.

13. Kindred interview, 1976; TDU press release, November 1975; and TDU pamphlet, 1975.

14. La Botz, *Rebellion,* p. 177; interviews with Arthur Fox, Ken Paff, and Kindred in 1991.

15. Interview with John Sikorski, 1991.

16. Fox and Sikorski interviews.

17. Dan Moldea, *The Hoffa Wars* (New York and London: Paddington Press Ltd., 1978), pp. 410–13; and Fox and Paff interviews.

18. Proceedings of the 1976 IBT Convention, pp. 40–41.

19. Proceedings of the 1981 IBT Convention, p. 48.

20. Proceedings of the 1976 IBT Convention, pp. 92–95.

21. Kindred interview, 1976.

22. Randy Kehrli's team included Organized Crime Section attorneys Peter Sprung and Diane DeForrest; Craig Lawrence, an assistant U.S. Attorney for the District of Columbia; U.S. Labor Department investigator Mike Moroney; and the FBI Liberatus Squad: John Joyce, Stanley Nye, Bill Jenkins, Duncan Wainwright, and Jack Vespery.

23. Interview, Walter Shea, April, 1991.

24. *Business Week,* September 5, 1989, pp. 58–59.

25. Shea interview, April 1991.

26. "$100,000 Club," *Convoy-Dispatch,* August 1989.

27. Statement by Weldon Mathis, March 31, 1989.

28. *Los Angeles Times,* Henry Weinstein and Ronald J. Ostrow, "Teamster Executives Reject Plan to Settle Racketeering Suit," January 29, 1989.

29. Crowe, "2 Teamster VPs Break Ranks," *Newsday,* January 30, 1989.

30. *Union Democracy Review,* June 1989, p. 4.

31. Grady interview, June 1991.

32. Francis W. Hackett interview, October 1991.

33. Shea interview, April 1991.

34. Frederick Lacey, "Report I of the Independent Administrator to U.S. District Court Judge David N. Edelstein, Southern District of New York under the Consent Order in the *United States* v. *International Brotherhood of Teamsters, et. al.,* entered March 14, 1989."

35. Michael J. Goldberg, "Cleaning Labor's House," *Duke Law Journal,* 4:1989, pp. 986–87.

36. James Neff, "Billy McCarthy's Follies," *Boston*, August 1991.

37. On the afternoon of January 7, 1992, the day the ballots were counted in the new Local 707 election, the local's ousted vice president, "Nicky Black" Grancio, was shot to death in the Gravesend section of Brooklyn—another casualty in the Colombo family mob war.

38. "$100,000 Club," *Convoy-Dispatch*, August 1989.

39. Ronald Carey interview, December 13, 1991.

40. Carey interview, January 4, 1991.

41. Carey interview, December 13, 1991.

42. Steven Brill, *The Teamsters*. (New York: Simon & Schuster, 1978), pp. 181–82.

43. William Serrin, *The Nation*, January 8/15, 1990.

44. McGinty interview.

45. Joseph Trerotola interviews on October 10, 1990, and June 22, 1991.)

46. John Morris interview, June 25, 1991.

47. Jack Cox interview, October 8, 1990.

48. The McCarthy majority included McCarthy himself, Mathis, Durham, Cozza, Weinmeister, Vitale, Hackett, Yager, Mitchel Ledet of New Orleans, Mike Riley of Los Angeles, Edward Lawson of California, and Don West of Birmingham.

Along with Joe T, the minority bloc included Shea, Ligurotis, Cox, and Joseph Morgan of Hallandale, Florida.

49. Cox interview, Trerotola interviews, October 9, 1990, and June 22, 1991.

50. "$100,000 Club," *Convoy-Dispatch*, August 1989.

51. R. V. Durham, interview, January 23, 1991.

52. Trerotola interview, October 10, 1991.

53. Shea interview, April 4, 1991.

54. Walter Sheridan, *The Fall and Rise of Jimmy Hoffa*, (New York: Saturday Review Press, 1972), p. 192.

55. Shea interview, February 1991.

56. John Lippert, "Hoffa seeks top Teamster job," *Detroit Free Press*, February 21, 1991.

57. The IBT appealed Lacey's finding. On June 18, 1991, Judge Edelstein upheld Lacey.

58. David Moberg, "Teamster Player," *In These Times*, February 27, 1991.

59. *Boston Herald*, March 11, 1991.

60. Eddie Burke interview; Carey interview.

61. Neil Modie, "End of an Era for Teamsters Leader," *Seattle Post-Intelligencer*, January 31, 1992.

62. Morris interview.

63. Proceedings of the 1981 IBT Convention, p. 457.

64. Chris Scott interview, December 12, 1991.

65. A barn is a Teamster term for a place where trucks are stored. It is a holdover from the days Teamsters drove horses and wagons.

66. Ligurotis statement of November 25, 1991; *Chicago Tribune* stories by John O'Brien on August 24, 1991, and O'Brien and Robert Blau on September 1, 1991.

67. Durham interview, October 16, 1991.

68. Subsequently, Lacey issued a decision barring Sansone from holding office in the IBT.

69. Carey campaign flier "Old Guard Teamsters Have Spent Thousands Trying to Beat Carey!"

Bibliography

Brill, Steven. *The Teamsters*. New York: Simon & Schuster, 1978.

Dobbs, Farrell. *Teamster Politics*. New York: Monad Press, 1975.

Fox, Arthur L. II, and John C. Sikorski. *A PROD Report: Teamster Democracy and Financial Responsibility*. Washington, D.C.: PROD, Inc., 1976.

Franco, Joseph. *Hoffa's Man*. New York: Prentice Hall Press, 1987.

Friedman, Allen, and Ted Schwarz. *Power and Greed: Inside the Teamsters Empire of Corruption*. New York: Franklin Watts, 1989.

Goldberg, Michael J. "Cleaning Labor's House: Institutional Reform Litigation in the Labor Movement," *Duke Law Journal*, 4:1989.

La Botz, Dan. *Rank and File Rebellion*. London and New York: Verso, 1990.

Moldea, Dan. *The Hoffa Wars*. New York and London: Paddington Press Ltd., 1978.

Neff, James. *Mobbed Up*. Boston: Atlantic Monthly Press, 1989.

President's Commission on Organized Crime. *The Edge: Organized Crime, Business and Labor Unions*. Washington, D.C.: U.S. Government Printing Office, 1986.

————. *Organized Crime and Labor-Management Racketeering in the United States*. Chicago, Ill. Hearings: April 22–24, 1985.

Proceedings. Teamsters 21st International Convention, Las Vegas, 1976.

Proceedings. Teamsters 22nd International Convention, Las Vegas, 1981.

Proceedings. Teamsters 23rd International Convention, Las Vegas, 1986.

Proceedings. Teamsters 24th International Convention, Orlando, Fla., 1991.

Robinson, Archie. *George Meany and His Times.* New York: Simon & Schuster, 1981.

Sheridan, Walter. *The Fall and Rise of Jimmy Hoffa.* New York: Saturday Review Press, 1972.

Stewart, James B. *Den of Thieves.* New York: Simon & Schuster, 1991.

U.S. v. International Brotherhood of Teamsters, Chauffeurs, Warehousemen and Helpers of America et al. 88 Civ 4486. U.S. District Court, Southern District of New York.

U.S. Senate, Committee on Labor and Human Resources. *Oversight of the Teamsters' Union, 1983.* Hearing: June 7, 1983.

U.S. Senate, Permanent Subcommittee on Investigations. *Organized Crime: Twenty-five Years After Valachi.* Hearings: April 11, 15, 21, 22, 29, 1988.

———. *Organized Crime and Use of Violence.* Hearings: April 28, 29, 30, and May 1, 1980.

———. *Oversight of Labor Department's Investigation of Teamsters Central States Pension Fund.* Hearings: August 25, 26, and September 29, 30, 1980.

———. *Report: Oversight Inquiry of the Department of Labor's Investigation of the Teamsters Central States Pension Fund.* 1981.

U.S. Senate, Subcommittee on Labor. *Teamsters' Union Central States Pension Fund, 1976.* Hearing: July 1, 1976.

Velie, Lester. *Desparate Bargain: Why Jimmy Hoffa Had to Die.* New York: Reader's Digest Press, 1977.

Windrem, Robert B. *Teamster Pensions: A PROD Analysis of Where the Money Goes.* Washington, D.C.: PROD, Inc., 1978.

Index

ABOUT THE AUTHOR

Kenneth C. Crowe has covered labor for *Newsday* since 1976 and was a member of the investigative team whose work won the 1970 Pulitzer Prize and fifteen other journalism awards. His reportage has ranged across the spectrum of labor, from workers and the workplace to contract negotiations, strikes, union politics, dissident movements, corruption, and the role of organized labor in society. He has covered every major labor conflict of the past fifteen years, including the strikes at Pan Am, Pittston Coal Company, Eastern Airlines, Greyhound, and the New York *Daily News*.

In 1974, Crowe won an Alicia Patterson Foundation fellowship that enabled him to spend a year studying foreign investment in the United States. This research took him to Iran, Kuwait, Saudi Arabia, Paris, London, Amsterdam, Rotterdam, and Düsseldorf, and led to the publication of his first book, *America for Sale*, in 1978.

Crowe's labor reporting has earned him the Front Page Award of the New York Newspaper Guild three times, in 1983, 1984, and 1986. In 1985, the Labor Press Council of Metropolitan New York gave him its Distinguished Labor Communications Award and the New York State Associated Press presented him with a first-place writing award.

Ken Crowe lives in Melville, New York.